JE MAINTIENDRAI

Adrianus Millenaar, Consul General of the Netherlands in his office with Queen Juliana in background

An Unlikely Hero
Adrianus Millenaar
Dutch Farmer Turned Diplomat
In World War II Europe

ADRIANA MILLENAAR BROWN

SHIRES PRESS
4869 Main Street
P.O. Box 2200
Manchester Center, VT 05255
www.northshire.com

AN UNLIKELY HERO
ADRIANUS MILLENAAR
DUTCH FARMER TURNED DIPLOMAT
IN WORLD WAR II EUROPE

ISBN Number: 978-1-60571-290-1
Library of Congress Number: 2015958865

Building Community, One Book at a Time
A family-owned, independent bookstore in
Manchester Ctr., VT, since 1976 and Saratoga Springs, NY since 2013.
We are committed to excellence in bookselling.
The Northshire Bookstore's mission is to serve as a resource for information,
ideas, and entertainment while honoring the needs of customers,
staff, and community.

Printed in the United States of America

DEDICATED TO
MATTHIJS • DIEDERIK • PHILIP • ADRIANUSA • HELENE • EVELINE • AND • LENI • ANDREW •

CONTENTS

Prologue • i

PROLOGUE | BABYLONBROOK

Here is what my father, Adrianus Millenaar, born in 1899 in Noord-Brabant, The Netherlands, wrote as his earliest memory:

I was four years old. I loved Saar. She was my favorite horse on the farm and she was pregnant. But Father was giving her away. I wept. Farmer Roos, five miles down the dyke, was to give her a new home. The day she left I felt desperate. I screamed, grabbed my father's clogs from the threshing floor, ran over the wet tiles past Mother near the hearth, and flung one clog at our big Bible lying

Jaakie, 1906

open on the supper table. The other clog fell out of my little hand. Mother continued stirring the porridge. I heard farmer Roos' horse neighing out front by the cow barn. Tears streamed down my cheeks as I yelled and yelled. Mother walked in her quiet, dignified way to the front of our farmhouse and reached out her slender hand to greet farmer Roos. To me he said, as he walked through the cow barn to the large kitchen and saw the clog lying on the Bible:

"Tell you what, Jaakie. I'll make a deal with you. When the chestnut is in bloom and when Saar has given birth, you will get the little one. It's a deal. I promise."

That long, hot summer, that windy, gray fall, and icy winter when the sugar beets were plentiful, I waited in anticipation. I watched the pink chestnut tree blossom and gradually change into the ordinary green color that blended with the linden and apple trees surrounding our farmyard. I never heard farmer Roos' horse and buggy pull up at the cow barn again, chasing away the chickens. He never came. It was my first deception. I was misled, and I did not know men played tricks on one another. My trust was shaken. For the first time, in that year of 1903, my life seemed to last so long. The day never turned into night. And even when the night came, I lay in the bedstead with my three brothers, and all I could think of was the little foal. It was to be mine. I was going to call it Saar, like its mother, my favorite and dearest. I was going to feed it. The haymaker was saving his best mown grass, and I had chosen the perfect stall for her. I would groom Saartje until she was ready to go to green pastures, where I would lead her and train her into the best racing mare in Brabant. In my mind she was a mare of Pharaoh's chariots.

It was 1968 when my father recorded those memories. At age seventy, he had once more turned to writing for solace. He wrote memories of his youth on the farm for his five children and grandchildren scattered across the globe in Canada, the United States of America, Holland, and his fifth grand child and me, in Nepal, of all places.

It was not the first time that writing had helped him to overcome the pain of losing loved ones to global dislocation, the hallmark of the twentieth century. In the darkest hours of 1943, shortly after Christmas, the unimaginable days, nights, weeks, and months of the years 1943, 1944, and 1945 long ahead, with their fear, anguish, terror and torture, hunger, disease, slave labor, deportation, concentration camps, cattle trains, gas chambers, humiliation, helplessness, and speechlessness. As the horror spiraled downward to a cavern totally measureless to man, my father sat down in agony to write the following lines after Professor Regout, a man he had tried desperately to save, had been executed, along with thirty-two other eminent Dutch men:

> We are not yet lost
> With all the tyranny
> Under which our people go
> We will once be free again.

> We could not stop
> The enemy's brute force.
> The sword was taken from us
> No choice was put before us.

> Deprived of all our strength
> Doomed to patience
> All that remained to us was
> To beseech Him to free us.

That hour would definitely come
For stronger than the sword
The spirit of our heroes,
Their faith in God, stood by us always.

That enemy can go on raging
Lacerate us more and more,
He can quench his thirst on our blood.
He will not get us down.

We have not yet gone lost
In spite of grief and tyranny
The trust that we will once be free again
Will stand by us evermore.

These two passages, one a childhood memory, one a poem, written so many years apart, capture much of the character of the man who was my father. From his earliest life he was deeply sensitive, emotional, appreciative of beauty, trusting in "right." Later he incorporated an unshakable faith in God, an inner strength that prevented him from ever giving up, he would never lose the patience that enabled him to cope as a diplomat with the increasingly delicate situations he had to navigate. He sought to learn more, to self-educate and to learn from others in an unkind, and increasingly dangerous world. Throughout all, he had a formidable sense of duty to his family, his country and his people that would lead him into the darkest of times, and lead him out again.

But my father was far from the heroic ideal. He suffered, had wrenching doubts, underwent abuse at the hands of those who considered themselves his "betters." He was unsophisticated, having been brought up a country boy, and was often unsure and even unsuited in that simple role. He felt himself to be under-educated, he failed at many things, and he was seen as weak. He longed for a better world.

So here is the story of a man and his time, an unlikely hero caught in the maelstrom of World War II; an individual who, against odds and expectations, did what he could to serve in the face of monstrous obstacles in the hell that was Berlin during the war.

CHAPTER 1 | GROWING UP

It was many years before I asked myself what my father was doing in Berlin that he could not have done at home in his sweet Babylonbrook. What had driven him away as a young man from following in his father's steps, breeding good horses, growing the bean crop he had sold year in and year out before the Great Depression, growing sugar beets, the chief staple of a diet nine million Dutch were massively addicted to before World War II? Why had he gone East, not West to Brooklyn—or rather Breukelen—near Midwout and New Utrecht, where his forebears the Voorhees, Couwenhovens and Cortelyouws had found their fortunes and their Marretjes and Adriaantjes?

Still a young man at nearly thirty years of age, he took up a post as an assistant to the agricultural attaché of the Netherlands Embassy in Berlin in 1928. My father had been rejected for a similar post in Paris due to the unfortunate coincidence that the other agricultural specialist was hard of hearing, as was my father. It would not be conducive to picking up agricultural trade news, so vital for the Dutch, whose economy was largely based on the export of its fruits, vegetables, and dairy products to neighboring countries. Germany was Holland's biggest trading partner, and half the Dutch export to its eastern neighbor consisted of agricultural products with transit trade from and for Germany, providing funding for a solid reservoir of foreign exchange. Germany it was.

Thus Adrianus, nicknamed Jaak, left the security and calm of the river land where alluvial soil nourished root and leaf crops, meadowland, champion horses—but not tulips. (They crave sand found behind the dunes in northern Holland.) Had my father had enough of the vandalism going on in his village, never expecting in his cruelest nightmares to witness atrocities so heinous as to defy any God-abiding citizen's imagination?

As a teenager he had been shocked and disgusted as a witness to—as well as a forced accomplice of—the tricks played by school gangs on the riverboat he had to travel in order to attend secondary school. The school was upstream in the busy town of Gorinchem or Gorkum, once an important stronghold. Back then, on a late autumn day, when an apple might have been tossed at a cow or a sheep roaming in the wrong meadow, and when the river was calm for once and still full of river salmon, some bored pupils from the vocational school had brought on board with them an electric transformer. The banisters of the stairs leading to the first class cabin were made of copper rails. They had wired banister to transformer and had cleverly swept the evidence under the red runner underfoot. The boys had often seen the steward of the riverboat, who usually spent his time on the second-class deck, called by first-class passengers. He would jump up, run and leap toward the stairs, grip the copper rods, and slide down onto the main deck to see to their needs. Suspecting no evil on that autumn day, as soon as the bell rang from the first-class deck, the steward made his usual run. He ended up with a concussion. The pupils were banned from the riverboat. They had the choice of giving up vocational school in Gorkum or bicycling half an hour over the narrow, slippery dyke to the ferry and then walking down the northern dyke with the wind howling and cows mooing their disgust at the troupe. As the gang approached the gabled rows of houses of the former fortress of Gorkum first thing each morning, the womenfolk with their empty baskets, clogging their way to the market square to barter beets and cabbages or cod and eel, would scoff and scold them from across the river. The portly women wished to consign them to the devil, but restrained themselves just in time when they spotted the dominee stride solemnly out of the rectory toward his church, which towered squarely over the marketplace. The young hoodlums trod quickly up the steep steps of the vocational school building, doffing their caps with a flourish before pushing them into their knickerbocker trouser pockets.

The same gang had broken into a glass cabinet to steal precious chocolates and candy. Jaak refused to accept any. The scoundrels threatened and intimidated him. He was small for his age, and looked like a momma's boy. Certainly he was the apple of his father's eye, because young Jaak had placed all of his trust, loyalty and good will in this aging, kindhearted man who could read Bible stories so loud and clear. Jaak trembled with Daniel deep down in the den, wrestled with Jacob, and could hear the swishing of the whips on the naked bodies of the slaves building the tower of Babel ever higher, making Jaak feel even smaller than David.

No sooner had the school gang on board the riverboat coerced Jaak into accepting the chocolates than his conscience began to nag. He grew uncomfortable, no longer able to look his mother or father straight in the eye. His lips twitched, his hands fiddled, he felt awkward in his lanky body, but he would certainly not cry the way he had seen his two older brothers do when teased by the farmhands or thrown off a horse. Once he had even tossed the tempting chocolates into the hollow trunk of a knotted willow tree, so haunted was he by the guilt at having been an accomplice to an evil deed. For "Thou shalt not steal" was firmly ingrained in his impressionable, trusting teenage mind.

Even before the banister incident, the vandalism on the riverboat plying the side arm of the river Maas was too much for Jaak. It was not only the prank of nailing an old peasant woman into a bathroom just before the riverboat landed at its final destination early one breezy morning. The poor woman had to wait until dusk before passengers re-embarked for their return voyage from the cattle market and heard her screaming and banging from behind the clapboard toilet door. Nor was it the ground beetles that were let loose in the first class cabin when Jaak's mother had a lady friend from Amsterdam visit. Both had looked forward to shopping in Gorkum, perhaps to pick up a curio or even an old Bible from Synod times, the State Bible every Dutch Protestant household was proud to possess. The lady friend gasped on seeing the creatures teeming over the cabin floor. Jaak's mother knew how harmless they were, but when these critters crept under the lady's long dress and up her legs, the woman fainted. Jaak's mother, with the help of the steward, walked her to the nearest ferry from where they phoned the postmaster of Babylonbrook to send the grocer's son to the homestead to have horse and buggy ready when the ferry landed at Woudrichem, across from Gorkum. It was the first and last visit to the Millenaar farm from this lady of Amsterdam. And why should a fine lady with a dainty waist, muslin summer dress, holding her parasol nonchalantly to cover her pretty face, have paid another visit to the soggy, gloomy mudflats of a province like Brabant, a long day's journey crossing at least ten rivers mostly by ferry and unwieldy rowboats.

Was she haughty?

Perhaps the lady, in her fright, had not been haughty, but rather wise. She might never have coped with the nasty trick played on the old gentleman farmer from the hinterlands. This old man, with a purple stump of a nose, always wearing a tattered vest over his black suit jacket and a frayed top hat on his weather-beaten face, and with mud on his clogs, was supported by several peasant hands as he staggered on the gangplank to board the big riverboat. The big boat headed for Rotterdam, where the weekly cattle market was held. Once on board the old gentleman farmer spent most of his time in the urinal emptying the gallons of beer he had drunk all night long in the river café because he had kept missing the last boat.

It was sunrise and it was icy cold as it can only be in Brabant. Brabant, adjacent to the fields of Flanders, land of dukes and countesses, fields of poppies where soldiers fell during the Spanish Inquisition and during World War I, in spite of promises by kings, by presidents, by gentlemen's agreements, to keep these nether lands neutral.

The big riverboat, the sturdy one with first-class, second-class and third class decks for all the cattle to be bartered, was the only ferry boat that went to Gorkum and on to Rotterdam on Tuesdays. This boat could easily withstand the erratic cross currents from the North Sea clashing up against the ever-increasing velocity of the broad estuaries of the Rhine and Maas rivers.

Jaak, still young and shy, was nervously twitching his lips because he hated school and could not hear half of what his teachers taught and because he dreaded the big riverboat more than the little one. Everything was larger and meaner on this boat. He felt a stranger, lost and alone in a crowd of well-weathered males shuffling around on the icy deck in their large clogs. At times Jaak would hear a loud clap: farmers already making an advance bid in a language Jaak could hardly understand. These Brabanders, let loose from their homely wives, spoke with an exaggerated pitch and rhythm, gurgling their soft guttural sounds far longer than Jaak was accustomed to, and therefore could not comprehend. Deals were made by two farmers slapping right hand to right hand with the force of a north wind.

He never knew what the school gang had in mind, or who would be their next target. On this icy winter's morning, when Jaak was still only thirteen, one of the older gang members, a particularly muscular fellow with a squint, ordered Jaak to post himself in the urinal on the main deck near the gangplank. The scoundrel himself was to crouch and hide behind the urinal with a broomstick. As soon as the old gentleman farmer fumbled around to get out his *manneke pis*, the miscreant would pass the broomstick to Jaak. Jaak was to shove it through the old man's legs and maneuver the rounded smooth end of the stick toward the groping hands of the poor old farmer. To Jaak's utter amazement, the stuporous man took hold of the broomstick, held on to the stump like grim death and unloaded his supply of foamy liquid, burping like a bullfrog.

When the boat laid anchor, a patch of ice had formed near the gangplank. It had trickled in a crooked line from the urinal down the sloping side of the riverboat to gather into a puddle of ice where the passengers were disembarking. Jaak and his accomplice skidded and fell. They were the last to disembark.

Jaak's bucket of troubles overflowed when he was coerced into putting his signature under bills for purchases he was ordered to make. The bored village ruffians forced him to enter a music store, buy a mouth harmonica and have the amount of five guilders (approximately one dollar) charged to his father's account. He knew the gang would beat the living daylights out of him had he refused, and so Jaak did what he was told.

Shortly after this incident the same gang appointed him to step into the hardware store just below the dyke and buy two hundred chicken rings, which identify the fowl belonging to a particular farm or owner, under the pretext his father needed them. The shopkeeper helped him diligently, made note of name and address, which was all too well known to the store owner as belonging to an honest and notable member of the Babylonbrook community, and said he would send the bill to Jaak's father—an alderman of Babylonbrook, a deacon of the Reformed Church and an eminent member of the North Brabant Christian Farmer's Association established three years before Jaak was born.

It was after this performance that Jaak broke down. Back at home, he could not stop crying. He had no control over the anguished feelings he had bottled up for two long years as he plied the river in rain and sunshine with the mean gang hovering over him and coercing the vulnerable and shy young Jaak into executing their lowly tricks. He must have been an easy victim for the big, bored boys who had little or no fear of the moral lessons and plots in Bible stories. After all, the majority of Brabanders were Roman Catholic, and the Millenaars were Protestant. It is said they had fled religious persecution in France under Louis XIV and had settled as Huguenots in northwestern Brabant between the rivers, where the Burgundian dukes might leave them alone since they had bigger fish to fry in the neighboring provinces of Holland, Gelderland, and Flanders.

CHAPTER 2 | ANTONIA ADRIANA

Most of the bullies were Roman Catholics for whom Bible stories, liturgy, sermons, and often hymns were all in Latin, making it difficult if not impossible for the restless teenagers to understand. Jaak, however, reveled in the sonorous voice of his father, who read the agonizing story of Job or the valiant tale of David and Goliath in Dutch. And when he heard his mother's voice, his mood positively soared. She mesmerized him. He found ecstasy in her readings. After all, her favorite pastime was putting words to rhyme. She disliked farm chores; for that she had maids. They mopped, swept,

My grandmother Antonia Adriana, 2ⁿᵈ left Jaak

and polished, baked, canned, and pickled morning till evening. On a Sunday at mealtime after the long church sermon or whenever his father was sore or tired from worry about his horses or his sprawling acres of land, he would hand his wife the heavy copper-edged State Bible. In her soft voice she would immerse herself in the Song of Songs, lingering melodiously over the multitude of short and long sounds so plentiful in the Dutch language. Jaak could hear his mother's passion ring out over the long supper table where all his brothers and sisters sat demurely amongst the maids and the live-in farmhands. Softly she would begin, "Let him kiss me with the kisses of his mouth"

The Brabant dialect with its easy flowing consonants, the exotic names of flowers, animals, and mysterious place names always put Jaak in a pleasant, tingling mood. He had even felt his first arousal at the passage, "By night on my bed I sought ... the smell of thine ointments ... Thy lips ..."

Yet he kept quiet about the strange swelling that occurred during these rare erotic biblical readings lest his brothers mock him, making him blush all the way to his big distended ears. For he felt shameful and embarrassed at this new condition and did not know where to turn for advice. His father was too preoccupied breeding new foals and figuring out which fields would lie fallow. Moreover, fighting was in full swing in neighboring Flanders. Brabanders were worried about the spillover into their territory in spite of the Netherland's policy of neutrality in this Great War.

Sixty or more soldiers were billeted in barns, sheds and even in haystacks around the farmstead. Jaak, home after a first apprenticeship, anxiously avoided these uniformed men who would hail him and make obscene gestures. He was flustered whenever he had to pass from the stately farmhouse to a chicken coop to feed the fowl or walk to a field to pick princess beans. Even in the coldest weather some of these men unbuttoned their pants as soon as they spotted reticent young Jaak. He was only fifteen, sixteen, and seventeen, blond and blue-eyed and briefly home in-between apprenticeships, when the horrific trench war took place, the war that killed 8,700,000. He heard vague mention of poison gas, the introduction of tanks, rat infested trenches, miles and miles of concertina—the barbed wire that was to give protection but had to be cut by petty orderlies who crawled through machine-gun fire to reach it before any advance could be made. Those billeted soldiers who,"...tripped by clutching snare of snags and tangles..."

The harassment he underwent from these frustrated, trench-locked, disheveled, neurasthenic males confused him sexually and inhibited him later after he had met and married. His wife could not understand after one year of marriage, less so after two, why this stranger she loved so was impotent and dysfunctional in the prime of his manly prowess. So she read Freud. In her *Schmerz* (pain) she read Inhibitions, Symptoms, Anxiety: Repression, about the Id, anything.

There was another season when Jaak descended from relative bliss to a vale of tears. Usually this came in the fall just before he had to leave for another apprenticeship, when the apples fell and scared cows away from the orchard. He valiantly tried to hide this somber mood from his siblings at mealtimes when his father handed the Bible to his mother. She would turn the big folios of the book of Ruth. Her voice quavered, she would begin to stammer. Jaak saw how she blinked away a tear. He was puzzled and confused until he himself married a foreigner—my German mother—who was no Moabitish damsel but one from Cologne in the Rhineland and a Roman Catholic—not a redeeming feature for the Protestant-Huguenot clan Jaak descended from.

It was then that he learned that his own dear mother, Antonia Adriana, had come from across the river, from the land of Herwijnen in Gelderland to marry Willem Millenaar from Brabant. Antonia Adriana and Willem Millenaar had met as youngsters at the day-long funeral of an old uncle who had moved up river, halfway between Babylonbrook and Herwijnen, by the river in the fortress village called Woudrichem. Woudrichem on the river Waal across from the city of Gorinchem, where Jaak had failed school and had become a dropout, harassed by the gang of vandals.

Antonia Adriana van Herwijnen took Willem Adriaan Millenaar as her husband in 1890. After their first encounter at the uncle's funeral, they attended every family wedding, christening and funeral, and always sought each other's company as soon as the ceremonies were over and the merriment of a fiddle set in. They ignored toasting glasses, yapping spaniels, the dance over eggs, and laughing matrons with their broad-brimmed gentlemen farmers; they had eyes only for each other. Both were tall and slender, with graceful features despite pronounced noses. What attracted them most to each other was a modesty and a certain reticence that stemmed from a quiet understanding that warm affection and love really meant loyalty and trust, not unlike the trust each gave to their favorite horse. Nine months after the wedding she had begotten a son. But this son came into the world fatherless. Alone. A half-orphan. Her Willem had died unexpectedly. "... And she was left..."

Willem, returning late one night from playing billiards at a tavern, had landed horse, buggy, and himself in a ditch. A dark, windy night was certainly no time for anyone to be up and about on a narrow bend of the cobbled dyke. But Willem, celebrating the sale of a champion horse with beer and a dazzling high score in billiards, undoubtedly mistook a muddy ditch for a foggy bank and could not scramble out from under the old mare yoked to the buggy. Willem Millenaar drowned in a billabong of Brabant, a dead arm of the Maas, in 1891.

Antonia Adriana, a forgiving and pious woman, mourned her husband for what seemed to Jaak all her life, the way she silently wept whenever she came to the verse,"... and in the broad ways I will seek him whom my soul loveth ..."

After this tragic but not uncommon death in those boggy hollow lands full of crooked waterways, Antonia Adriana's family urged her to come back home. It had been a love marriage, love at first sight. The flutter of it. The tingle. Those butterflies that stir inside one so intimately and fleetingly.

Antonia Adriana had been brought up by aunts, two spinster sisters of her mother. Her parents had died of tuberculosis, which reigned so cruelly in the 1860s in the southern provinces of the Netherlands and had decimated the population. The aunts from Herwijnen pleaded with their niece to cross the two rivers and come north so they could express their motherly feelings for the baby of their dear orphaned and newly widowed niece, but grief and melancholia kept Antonia Adriana immobilized. She decided to stay in the land of her husband's kin, not leave the side of her mother-in-law where she wanted to raise her little fatherless baby, Willem junior, and where she was consoled by her mother-in-law's people.

It so happened that Willem Millenaar had a younger brother, Gilbert. Gradually, Gilbert found favor in the darkly clad, grief-ridden Antonia Adriana. In Biblical fashion she consented to the shy but insistent overtures of brother Gilbert. So one fall, after the farmhands had gleaned and gathered after the reapers among the princess beans and sugar beet heaps, Gilbert took Antonia Adriana to be his wife. She bore him four sons and two daughters, the third son being my father Adrianus, (Jaak for short) named after her father Adrianus van Herwijnen in customary patronymic Dutch fashion.

CHAPTER 3 | APPRENTICESHIP

In 1913, when Holland celebrated a centennial and commemorated its liberation from the French, Jaak's parents had reached their sixtieth year. Jaak, age fourteen, had dropped out of school. He had had a crisis of confidence. A nervous breakdown. The soft down that was sprouting on his cheeks, his chest and in hidden places was embarrassing to him. He had not been prepared for these changes. His mother had left it up to Jaak's two older sisters and two older brothers to inform, educate, and enlighten him. For in short succession at the turn of the twentieth century, two more brothers were born. Antonia Adriana had fervently hoped that after her fourth child and after her fortieth birthday she could devote her time to the poetry in the Bible. Instead, after Willem Hendricus Adrianus, Davina Adriana, Artje Adriana, Adriaan, and my father Adrianus were born, before 1900, she had a Dirk and a Gilbert to nurse for a few more years. So by the time Jaak reached puberty and Antonia Adriana had gained what she thought was the age of wisdom and reason at age sixty, she had left more and more of the farm work to the maids and a faithful farmhand. The upbringing of her three youngest adolescent sons was left to her dutiful and trustworthy daughters.

How shocked and troubled mother Antonia Adriana must have been when her favorite son, downy young Jaak, collapsed and could not stop crying after the incident of the two hundred chicken rings he was bullied into buying. And the terrible day he had fallen from the loft of a hay barn onto a stone and lay unconscious for hours. Once he regained his senses he was still dizzy for a week. But eventually, as the dizziness disappeared, it was time to move on, though the accident had worsened his already bad hearing.

What to do with Jaak the dropout? If he answers the exam question: "When did William of Orange die?" with, "I didn't know he had died," or, "Where are the villages of New Utrecht and New Amersfoort?" with "I didn't know there were any new ones." And if he could not stop crying about the two hundred chicken rings, then it was time for Gilbert and Antonia Adriana to deal with the dominee, a schouten or selectman, or even the burgomaster. It was high time for Jaak to learn the hard way: hands on. Time to serve a master. A master could instruct, show Jaak by repetition and patience a craft, a trade, a skill. As long as he would learn a skill, well, then he could hold a job. An indenture was drawn up: all parties agreed, and floriculture was to be Jaak's destiny. Tulips, hyacinths, daffodils. Fields and fields of reds, whites, and blues. Holland's bridge to the future. Voyagers would come from afar to marvel at Holland's floricultural miracle growth. Bulbs could be exported.

"Imagine beds of emperors, Queen Elizabeths, and Woodrow Wilsons in every American garden. Imagine Jaak the exporter, the director," Antonia Adriana said to Gilbert, hoping fully their son would succeed at the florist's, Summer Joy. It was in the city of Nijmegen, an eminent Roman settlement with one of the most important ports on the inland waterway between Rotterdam and the industrial Ruhr of Germany. Nijmegen in the province of Gelderland, Antonia's province at the east end of Gelderland near Germany. Nijmegen where the allied airborne troops later wrested occupied Netherlands in September 1944 from the Nazi terror. Nijmegen where the Rhine had been renamed the Waal, the river Antonia Adriana had grown up by, across from the banks of the Maas. The German Rhine and the French Maas coming together in Holland, coming together in a treaty of Maastricht. Nijmegen so near Arnhem, just eleven kilometers north. In the city of Arnhem on the Lower Rhine, these same allied troops would fail and a "hunger winter" would set in, the worst winter, the worst famine. . .

At Summer's Joy, so far away from home, it was not the father, W.F. van Ingen, but his son, Dirk van Ingen, who waved the sceptre and ordered Jaak to kill the worms devouring the roots of the violet crop. It was a cold and filthy job, outdoors in wind, rain, sleet, and deep mud. Jaak was homesick, wrote daily letters imploring his father to allow him to return home.

Gilbert and Antonia Adriana answered in haste to their unaccommodating, melancholic son, "Read Job, spell out and memorize 'Gird up thy loins now like a man.'"

Poor Jaak was even more confused. Visibly doleful, he was finally transferred indoors to the hothouses where he had to bite his tongue and harden his hands, ignoring the rose thorns by concentrating on pruning. Slowly, painfully, calluses grew on his fingers. His male cohorts started to consider him an equal when he became an expert in grafting, for he was patient and meticulous while gently inserting a tender young rose shoot into the slit of a sturdier and older stem. But during his first winter away from home, mean spirit and arrogance again reared its head. This time it was not the riverboat ruffians, whose attitude had been beyond his comprehension. This time it was Dirk van Ingen, the son of his boss. Dirk who snubbed all those around him, even his own father to whom he showed no respect by putting him down as an inferior, worthless old ignoramus.

It did not take Jaak long to realize he must not let defeat get the better of him this time. Moreover, he had at least one ally in old man Van Ingen himself, and Jaak would show him where his loyalty lay. Once he completed the long, unbearable apprenticeship, Jaak could only imagine the satisfaction of seeing the joy in W.F. van Ingen senior's eyes, and the fury in Dirk van Ingen junior's flushed face, when the big roadside bed on a crisp spring morning popped out in grand capital letters delicately green against the rich dark river soil, W.F. VAN INGEN. Contrary to Dirk's clear instructions at the end of autumn, Jaak had taken his revenge, naming only the gentle, evenhanded proprietor, Van Ingen senior, the well-known florist in Nijmegen.

During his second apprenticeship in a town south west of Amsterdam, Aalsmeer, where now stands the biggest flower auction hall of all of Europe, Jaak would learn to forget the rose pricks inflicted on his filial soul at the Van Ingen's, and he would enter a terrible secret learned from the delicately hued lilacs.

All summer, young lilac shrubs stand outdoors looking bare. In autumn they are transferred indoors to hothouses, where they are fed with manure collected from the night soil of the cities around Aalsmeer, mainly Amsterdam. This night soil is transported by barges to the surrounding floriculturalists and then carried in buckets to the hothouses to be spread around the young lilac trunks. When Jaak was first asked to help, he refused.

"Come, come," his boss had said, "don't be so squeamish. As a good floriculturalist you first have to taste the night soil to make sure it isn't diluted with water."

To put force to his words and to convince Jaak he was not joking, his boss stuck a finger in the bucket, then licked it. Jaak, utterly disgusted, said: "Now, I'm certainly not going to do this work, even if the success of the lilacs depends on it."

Later that same autumn evening, after supper and after the Bible reading, Jaak's boss must have taken pity on his mopish apprentice and told him he had indeed put his finger in the bucket of night soil, but had licked off a different one.

A few apprenticeships later, when Jaak tried to improve the cultivation of vegetables on his father's farm, he applied the same method to the unwilling farmhands whose chore it was to spread night soil around growing seedlings.

CHAPTER 4 | GRAPES

During his last apprenticeship in the Westland, a dune-filled stretch located between The Hague and the North Sea, and before he went back home to distant Babylonbrook to apply his newly acquired knowledge of horticulture to his father's farm, and before he was to sail halfway around the world all the way to South Africa, and long before World War II, my father had learned to prune, thin out, air, compost, and protect from too much sun the Alicante and Frankenthaler grape vines cultivated in Westland hothouses. The grapes were ripening, Jaak and his master's son, Hugo, were both seventeen, and the girls in the Westland looked pretty with their flowery cotton dresses billowing out from their bicycles.

Driven by biological yearning for the fair sex, Jaak and Hugo mustered the courage to approach two blue-eyed wenches, a baker's daughter and her friend, and invited them to feast on grapes.

Before the hothouse was to be locked up, Jaak and Hugo had secreted some ripe clusters of grapes near two mats they had spread out for the evening feast after their planned bike trip through the dunes to whet the appetites of the pretty girls. The one Jaak hoped to hold hands with was the girl with the straw hat.

Her smile sparkled as if a mermaid had risen from the North Sea and softly brushed his downy cheek. Atop a dune, in the breeze, and when it was still a long, long time from May to September, the two apprentice lads nestled themselves in a grassy hollow as close as they dared to their damsels.

Ah, how sweet the fragrance of a few late-blossoming rose hips - a perfume Jaak had never known up until that moment on top of a gently sloping dune still warm from the setting sun. He could not take his eyes off the deeply cut cotton dress, underneath which the soft breathing bosom harmonized with the waves rolling onto the glistening sand of the shore. Jaak was dizzy with delight.

At sunset in the Westland, Jaak and Hugo cycled their girls back to the hothouse, Jaak putting his arm around the girl with the straw hat, pedaling twice as hard so she could freewheel her way up and down the dunes. A nightingale sang, and the sweet perfume of rose hips hung in the evening air. The young men had to grope around for the two mats they had spread out in the alleyway between the rows of vines. After the girls had eaten the heavenly fruit, they sang in unison, "Ambrosia, nectar. Time to go home."

And sure enough, to Jaak's surprise, the girls brushed off their flowery cotton dresses. The baker's girl's friend straightened her straw hat. The two walked back to the glass door through the narrow path, not stumbling once in the pitch-black hothouse. Jaak and Hugo scrambled after the girls, hands filled with clusters of grapes, and shouted, "Here, take these, take these grapes home. Tomorrow night, same time, same place!"

"No. We've had enough. And we don't have pockets to put them in."

The young men quickly and boldly stuffed thick bunches of the crimson grapes into the low-cut openings of their damsel's cotton dresses. Then simultaneously, as if by prior agreement, before the girls had a chance to grab their bicycles standing next to the glass door outside the hothouse, Jaak and Hugo pulled the girls into their arms, held them tightly, kissed them tongue and all, embraced them with a force so arduous, so tempestuous that they cleaved to the bosoms of the pretty girls as if they dreaded a wrathful God would arise from the crest of a high-rolling wave to swoop them up, stake them on his three-forked trident, only to plunge them down onto the murky sea floor, where the two sinners would have to genuflect to atone for their sins of the flesh through eternity.

The girls never again looked at Jaak and Hugo. The Westland village was a hamlet in 1916 and 1917. Workers, farmers, wives, children on clogs, the greengrocer, the butcher and baker, apprentices, and seasonal hands all knew each other. When passing in wind, rain, cloudy Ruysdael skies, or in sunshine; on bicycle, on foot, in horse and buggy, or on a gnarled old walking stick, all stealthily looked each other up and down. Each knew each other's clothes, habits, voices as they nodded in acknowledging each other with a peremptory, *"Goededag."* Those who did not attend the Protestant Sunday morning church service were prayed for to be forgiven for hanging out too long in the local taverns, playing cards, smoking pipes, drinking home brewed-beer, telling jokes or bragging how they had dared squeeze a girl on a hot summer's night so that the cluster of grapes adorning her bosom had forever sent the once clean and starched cotton dress to the mending basket.

ACHTERSTRAAT ANDEL (N. B.)

Village Street, Andel, Noord Brabant where Jaak was born
(Babylonbrook Village is nearby)

CHAPTER 5 | EMIGRANT

The Great War had been raging in Holland's
neighboring countries for two full years. Soldiers
had been living in trenches with rats, shells, bombs,
lice, gas masks, mud, sleet, explosions. They would
advance a few feet, retreat a few feet. Detonations,
concertina, blue gas, rain, muck, boredom, fright, so
many unmentionable, unimaginable diseases—as well
as human longing—dwelt in the fields of Flanders. But
Jaak gained a solid high ground. Since the Netherlands
had remained neutral during the Great War, a time
when neutrality was still respected, the lowlands had
been unaffected by the devastation and had become
Germany's number one food basket.

Jaak being the restless and still homesick soul that he
was, after several apprenticeships and disappointments,
had persuaded his father he could just as easily grow
tulips and carrots on the homestead back in Brabant.
Moreover, he could make big profits at the auction hall
five kilometers up river in Woudrichem.

After the sandy soil of the Westland dunes,
ground fine and loose by a capricious North Sea since
Pleistocene times, the loamy clods of the Brabant River
soil in which Jaak planted his rows of tulips proved only
a rich playground for rats that ripped up the tender

skins of the tulip bulbs. Fortunately, Jaak had seen in the Westland how every inch of soil was utilized and so, in between tulip beds, he had sown carrot seed. That spring and summer of 1917, his carrots brought ten times the price they had delivered before the Great War. How proud mother Antonia and father Gilbert were of their diligent son! Never mind the fact that he was selling out to the enemy at the auction hall where barges shipped produce up the Rhine in spite of Netherland's neutrality. The majority of six million Netherlanders still hoped for British and French victory.

During the spring and summer of 1918, Jaak followed his father's advice on where best to sow and plant seeds and pods for the cold-soil vegetables. He grew a bumper crop that yielded a small fortune at the auction hall of Woudrichem, where barges eagerly loaded the good harvest for the emaciated soldiers in neighboring Germany. They were fighting a losing battle in the trenches of No Man's Land in Belgium in between the rivers where mud, clay, and clods of loam plunged neurasthenic soldiers deeper into the slime created by monarchical talking heads bogged down in terminology and attitudes of honor and hubris. Greater glory for what? The Kaiser?

Thus young Jaak was home to cultivate his father's acres and "nine rows of beans," and celebrate his Queen's birthday at the end of August, at the beginning of a good harvest, by showing off his father's horses at a nearby village fair in the hope of catching the eye of a pretty girl from Brabant, Gelderland, or even Flanders. No matter, as long as she was a Protestant and could sing *Grote God Wij loven U* (Great God we praise You) in good old Dutch, and not Latin.

The tilting competition whereby horse and rider showed their metal was the highlight of the fair, apart from the feast after dark when Chinese lanterns strung from plantain tree to plantain tree would light the village square just enough so intoxicated couples could swing their dancing clogs with an extra swish on the polished old cobblestones, sending sparks up into the happy night sky. The fiddler's tune would ring joyfully to honor the young queen, Wilhelmina, her daughter Juliana, and queen mother, Emma—that proud Netherlandish matriarchal kingdom.

That day Jaak was full of optimism and pride at the profit he had presented to his parents in gratitude for their having stuck with him through thick and thin. After all, he realized how much pain he had caused them by dropping out of school and getting homesick and weary at his various apprenticeships. He was not plagued by nervous twitches that late summer's day, though his hearing was not getting any better after the low trick that had led to Jaak's being chased up a hundred-foot hayloft ladder by one of the riverboat ruffians. He sat cowering and shivering until, trying to descend, he fell and suffered a serious loss of hearing. Even so, Jaak was high-hearted when he stepped into the stable a few hundred yards beyond the village square at the edge of the meadow where the tilting of the ring was set up. He passed the hitched-up horses in their stalls and unbolted the door of an enclosed stall in the good hope of finding his mare, Tegenwind. She was a thoroughbred that had brought forth three prize-winning trotters, one of whom was the famous Champi, winner of forty first and second prizes in various competitions. Jaak had hardly opened the heavy, rough-hewn door when a bridled horse slipped by him from behind and lunged into the stall, its hoofs crashing the door wide open. The horse's flesh trembled, its nostrils quivered as it reared on its hind legs to attack the unsuspecting horse inside the enclosed stall. The intruder was the Hackney-stallion Emigrant, and the horse inside the locked door was the young Oldenburg stallion, Custos, from the Association for the Advancement of Horse Breeding in Brabant. Jaak somehow dodged the now fighting stallions and ran to his older brother, Adriaan, who immediately turned away from the village fair and bolted for the stable, where he witnessed sparks flying, neighing, fuming, blood streaming from horseflesh, and hoofs clashing and smashing into steaming underbellies of once noble creatures now fighting to kill.

Brother Adriaan succeeded in grabbing hold of the bridle Emigrant was still wearing, but could not pull him away. Instead, with a jolt he was flung into the stall by the wild animal. Jaak stood helpless. He ran, this time faster than the horned devil himself. Leaping through the high grass of the meadow back to the feasting villagers in the square, he found his cousin and several other men. He yelled like a siren gone berserk, "Adriaan's dead. The stallions are killing each other. Hurry!"

Out-of-breath Jaak, his cousin David, and a handful of other men ran through the meadow to the stable. They stopped dead, electrified, as if a lightning rod had struck right through their worsted woolen knickerbockers. They blinked and stared at the continuing scene of the battling steeds, worse than Donar ricocheting thunderbolts. No trace of brother Adriaan. Jaak felt it in his gut: Adriaan had been crushed, pulverized. Brother Adriaan—the expert at training horses, the first and fastest at carting wheelbarrows heaped with potatoes through mud, the winner at catching the biggest river salmon in the Maas, the secret love of the Brabant girls. Jaak's cousin David tried in vain to hook the teeth of a rake onto the bridle of Emigrant.

Then, all of a sudden, a miracle, an apparition: brother Adriaan appeared from nowhere. Jaak and the men were speechless. Which guardian angel had been responsible for this wonder? Later, Adriaan told them he had managed to climb onto the hayrack, succeeded in breaking a few splints from it, and crawled through to save himself. And finally, it was brother Adriaan who caught the bridle onto the rake and was able to pull Emigrant out of the stall. By that time the stallions had come to an impasse. Their panting had slowed. No longer could they rear high enough to come crashing down into each other's flesh. Froth dripped from open wounds. Blood poured from gashes onto a petrified mud floor. The straw, soaked red and rigid with blood, lay swept against the rough-hewn walls and corners of the stall- turned-battlefield. The flesh of these once beautiful, glistening creatures was torn open like the fields of Flanders, poppy-red with fresh blood. Emigrant was in better shape than Custos, whose wounds made the men fear for his life.

Had Jaak chosen his own interests over his concern for Emigrant and Custos, he would have gone with flying colors through the tilting of rings to the prize stand. He would have left the stallions to fight the battle for themselves. He would have chosen another horse. Instead, the whole board of the Brabant Stallions

Association for the Advancement of Horse Breeding was called away from the feasting villagers to assemble in the parlor of Jaak's uncle.

The sire stallion, Custos, was insured for 60,000 guilders, an enormous sum in 1918. The chairman of the association, another cousin of Jaak's father, immediately suggested calling the vet to advise him that he write a statement declaring the stallion Custos unfit for breeding, and that he should be euthanized. Many members agreed to the first part of the proposal, yet raised objections of conscience to the latter. Ever since the extraordinarily high insurance cost of Custos, the price of stud horses had decreased considerably, and it seemed that the members suspected the chairman of pulling off a big one under their very eyes. While the members of the Association for the Advancement of the Horse Breeding Race bickered back and forth, the vet arrived, and after close examination, diagnosed Emigrant out of danger and Custos, though a wreck, not severe enough a case to merit the death sentence. Bickering continued, sometimes breaking out in violent—God fearing—expletive language.

The chairman refused to abide by the vet's prescription that the sire Custos be sent to the veterinarian school in Utrecht five river crossings away—to be treated until rehabilitated. More fuming was followed by another round of pewter tankards full of frothy home-brewed beer. The vet, clearheaded like a doctor Tulp, calmly analyzing the anatomy lesson, stuck to his guns and refused to mete out the death sentence for the mangled Custos.

Jaak missed showing off his expertise at controlled cantering on his steed, reins held low but tight on approaching the tilted ring, loosening the reins with his left hand just in time to stick the spear held high in his right through the two-inch hole hanging from an apple bough. He missed the pretty girls laughing in the meadow, cheering him on as if a jostling knight had galloped by for their sake. But that night, the knowledge of the two horses having survived made him swing his clogged heels up to the sky as he twirled one girl after another under the fading lantern lights hanging in the village square on the Queen's Birthday. And until the stallion Emigrant had recovered completely, Jaak avoided his uncle's farm and wrath at the duel he had inadvertently helped to start, and at the insurance bid his uncle had missed out on. Jaak made a big detour through rough terrain with autumn winds whipping his cheeks when visiting cousin David, who lived on the southern end of the Maas River where the pretty girls had come from. Those cheering girls had not been cousins or relatives, not even distant ones, and they did not at all seem standoffish, but Jaak still could not find a sweetheart among them.

CHAPTER 6 | SOUTH AFRICA

In March of 1925, Jaak, barely twenty-six years of age, left for Number 7 Pickering Street, Durban, Natal, South Africa. From the security of Babylonbrook, Brabant, from the warmth and familiarity of his mother tongue and Brabant's customs, he left willingly and fully *compos mentis* for the home of a distant aged cousin who lived one dark continent and a treacherous ocean away beyond the Cape of Good Hope in the land of the *hel're lug* (the clear sky).

Jaak 1925 before boarding for South Africa

Young Jaak set sail on the Meliskerk from the port of Rotterdam to seek the satisfaction he could not find in the economically and agriculturally depressed Netherlands. He yearned to find a grip on his muddled soul, to reassure his rapidly aging parents he could make a living. Above all, he longed to promise his shaky inner self that he would be able to secure a permanent peace in both job and health. Health in the sense of putting his flashing hypothalamus at ease by targeting his arrow at a one-and-only sweetheart, an act he had failed to accomplish thus far.

Nor had the three years' experience as secretary to the manager (his cousin David van der Schans) of the local village municipality rendered him a permanent position. Yet, it was during this administrative apprenticeship that Jaak was given the foundation for the career he was inadvertently catapulted into after World War II. As young as he was, a germ of ambition had been planted in his troubled brain. He had seen enough champion horses on the homestead to know that once a Cicero starts a race he'd better stick to the course and get to the finish, winner or no. Moreover, had not the daily readings in the Bible and the weekly memorization of the psalms taught him to keep the faith in spite of adversity?

Therefore, when six administrations were annexed into one greater municipality, and Jaak pasted rejection slip after rejection slip on his outhouse clapboards as he applied for town and village clerkships elsewhere in Brabant, he dug his heels deeper into the track so as to gain more traction for the next stretch. Meanwhile, he had learned how to deal with more problems afflicting humans than could be imagined, since in a rural municipality there were no academically trained experts as there would be in cities and large townships. The town clerk and his assistant secretary—Jaak—had to rely on their own gumption cum farmer's instincts to handle anything from contested land claims to intestate wills, from pig pests to serious marital dalliances. Even so, Jaak had become superfluous, lost the small job he had, and commenced being a real pain to upright Antonia and aging Gilbert.

The next stretch gave no relief either. Jaak was starting to come apart as he approached the thin line of failure syndrome. He found it hard to rationalize the closure of an eminent bank in the town of Zaltbommel, ten kilometers due east from his farm on the left bank of the river Waal. For one year and a half, through the intermediary of another uncle, he joined this middling bank in the heart of a fortified town, proud of its Hanseatic League membership. Here Jaak learned the art of banking, and was made responsible for checking, balancing, and accounting the books for four entrepreneurs: a grain dealer, an owner of a brick factory, a proprietor of a crate factory, and a grocer, all quite unaccommodating directors and leery of a nosy outsider. To improve his scant knowledge of economics and finances he took a course in bookkeeping and studiously read trade and agricultural journals as well as the regional newspaper. Thus he wanted to demonstrate his willingness to learn to his employer, who, after all, belonged to the notables of a town of standing, a town with city rights and therefore so much more sophisticated than the village hierarchy to which Jaak had been accustomed.

Certainly Jaak was dependable, diligent, eager, and tireless in spite of the long bike ride it took him to get to work. If a storm raged or if the rain on the ten-kilometer-long dyke turned into a torrential downpour, waterlogging his tires and forcing him to push his bike over the cobbled dyke road, the journey to his latest apprenticeship would take well over an hour one way.

Returning home in a nor'wester on the unprotected dyke in cold and howling winter months, when at five or six o'clock the oil lamps lit the supper tables of the farmsteads tucked against the high leaning walls of the dyke, the same journey might take Jaak twice as long. As he rode or walked his steel steed to and from work in inclement weather or under a beating sun, he barely noticed the lowing of cows, the bleating of sheep or the lonely bell of a barge chugging upriver to Germany and Switzerland, or seeking its home port in Herwijnen, Woudrichem, Gorinchem or Rotterdam— the port and world harbor transporting seafarers and adventurers outward bound to horrors and delights.

On these arduous commutes, his thoughts turned sinfully and fleetingly to two beauties of the fair sex employed as assistant bookkeepers in the middling bank. But they were the daughters of prominent burghers of Zaltbommel. A colleague of Jaak's, who had been a former "coolie driver" in the Indies, sneered, "Ha, if you land one of them I'll give you my golden cigarette holder and my golden cigarette case, even my whip."

Jaak knew this dandy, the first he had encountered, would not forfeit one penny since he spent his salary on perfumes, boutonnieres, alligator-hide galoshes. But before one of the beauties had a chance to cozy up in earnest to hard-working Jaak, the bank became insolvent. A nationwide malaise could not be easily teased into a bullish market. On his monthly audits, Jaak, to his dismay, discovered he had to mark all four balance sheets in the red: grocer, grain dealer, bricklayer, and crate manufacturer. He became despondent. He became more deaf. That is to say, he now pretended his hearing was worse than it was. And it was worse because he no longer strained to hear what his parents, his relatives, or his older siblings urgently advised him. He turned inward, slept too long, skipped church, and didn't even go riding on his favorite horse.

One day, on the cold January morning of his twenty-sixth birthday, in his despondency, in his silent desperation and grief, his mother Antonia shook him awake and commanded, "You're going to Africa to cousin Betje's. You're going."

In an elaborate exchange of letters, her favorite cousin Betje had beseeched Antonia to send one of her five sons to come and accompany old Betje back to Brabant. She wanted to sell her "Pinkerton" house, sell her late husband's shares in his Rickshaw business and give part of the profit to the plucky nephew who would risk a plunge, perhaps a sea change, into the dark continent of Africa. Africa, where cousin Betje had fled in 1875, in the hope she could change her dissolute husband's ways.

Her marriage had been arranged, joining the wealth of Brabant's flourishing grain traders. But her youth, her innocence, her femininity, her trust had been wiped out swiftly when local gossip verified the miserable fact that, alas, her groom was a ne'er-do-well who had been leading the life of a grand seigneur in the capital city of Amsterdam, blowing away his riches on six horses, a carriage, dubious women, and *genever* (gin), that ambrosia of grain which dealt so many an earthling the toxic blow. Poor cousin Betje, try as she might to control her womanizing, alcoholic husband, had to buckle under and submit to a higher power. Even the move to South Africa to avoid the evil tongues, the embarrassment done to her rich, grain-trading relatives, and the shame inflicted upon her family's upright reputation, had resulted in a fiasco. Cousin Betje's husband was beyond help. He disappeared—no one knew where—and she, on her own good faith, made her way by oxen cart as a housekeeper, a dressmaker, and a governess through the Cape Province, through Orange Free State north of Basutoland to Natal, where at long last she found happiness with a kindly, well-read, intelligent Captain Thompson, owner and shareholder of a Rickshaw Company in Durban, living on Pickering Street, Number 7.

Jaak grasped at this straw.

A multitude of young men did not inherit land, were not in line as the first - or second-born sons of farming families meant to continue the age-long custom of receiving the dominion of his forefathers' acres, did not walk in their father's footsteps as village notables or as city burghers with degrees and titles, did not develop a natural ability to follow suit as *schepens* or *schoutens*, did not have the bravado to promote themselves as captain of a Bonte Koe, did not have the luck to receive a directorship of a West Wind Spice & Grain Company. And Jaak, one of these unfortunate young males, one day found himself literally at sea, adrift in a thick fog in the middle of the Atlantic Ocean.

After seven days of rough sailing in the tiny freighter with its cargo of luxury goods, Bibles, Makkum pottery, clogs, leather shoes, and linens for tropical wear, the little steamer, Meliskerk, weighed anchor for stretches lasting twenty-four hours and more. The fog was so thick and persistent it was the like of which Jaak had never experienced on his journeys along the dykes, even in the bitter dark winter months. These mist banks out on an eerie, still ocean, worse than the melancholia in his Brabant bedstead, merged with the dull gray waters surrounding him. After seven days sailing for twenty-four indistinguishable hours a day, the watery potato and carrot meals began to taste like the foul fish he smelled in his bunk next to the hold, where the ship's food was stowed. No wonder the three other passengers on board, two loudmouthed, red-faced, thick-necked Germans and one tight-lipped emaciated one, took to their flasks, swearing as their bids were out-trumped and their full houses left incomplete due to their double vision. Jaak turned a deaf ear to the fisticuffs this godless trio of males engaged in, for they reminded him of the riverboat ruffians who had inflicted their twisted psyches on those around them.

But it was not so much disgust as it was pity that afflicted Jaak during these interminable hours of gray walls of mist. It filled him up and made him choke on the recurring thought of that fateful day he had left home. Pity for the card-playing drunkards. Self pity at his dreary lot. Self-pity: the worst of pities, dangerous as it draws one deeper into murky melancholia.

Had he taken the wrong step?

Why help an elderly aunt at the other end of the world?

Why risk his life in the middle of the hell of a God-forsaken ocean?

Perpetual fog. The silent gray mist encompassed him hour after hour. Even the foghorn was out of his ear's reach. He could not imagine palm trees swaying on an esplanade in a mild tropical breeze. He had no idea what bougainvillea was, or coconuts, banana trees, almond blossoms, the flame tree, or the palm tree—that protective, gracious tree providing shade and welcome to overheated, weary travelers.

He despaired, felt deserted, and found no solace even in helping the captain with his logbook entries. The folly of this voyage to nowhere gnawed at him incessantly. Over and over again his brain ground his thoughts as a pestle crushes the seed in a mortar to pulp. Neither mother Antonia nor father Gilbert had ever opened an encyclopedia for Jaak to study the history, vegetation, or economy of the Union of South Africa—nor had it occurred to them to look up the definition of loneliness. All Jaak knew was that he was embarking on an "adventure," that he was to assist his aunt who had promised to remunerate a courageous nephew with a handsome inheritance. And all Antonia and Gilbert had ever read to him were the stories of Daniel in the den, David slinging a shot at Goliath, and on gloomy, windy nights Jonah and Job would be dished up to the Millenaar clan as the farmhands nodded their weary heads over skimpy plates.

Seasickness was not his trouble. On the contrary, it never plagued him. It was the doldrums. But after he had suffered the doldrums in diurnal mist, in nocturnal dread, in fear of another failure, the sun appeared. From then on, the sun came up every day. Jaak rubbed his eyes as he stepped on deck, staring out at a glittering clear sea with not a cloud reflected on its smooth surface. He leaned his elbows over the railing and gazed out into a blue sky with the eye of the day warming his back, a gentle breeze stroking his still downy cheeks. His woolen suit suddenly felt scratchy, but his astonishment and excitement at the clear sky, the balmy air, the captain's singing, the mates whistling as the Meliskerk chugged closer to the Cape of Good Hope, blotted out any discomfort, any staleness of the three-week-old sprouting potatoes and mildewed beets. His mood lifted, he cheered, he ignored the Germans' cursing the sun for burning their skin and necks. The entries in the logbook the captain dictated to Jaak were now shorter as they sailed over the equator. But Jaak's handwriting—always steady even as the ship heaved and rolled as it had off the coast of France and Spain— was now more graceful, with many a flourish. It was his real forté. In school, penmanship had won him first prizes. He had loved the silence of writing, just the paper and himself.

Now he could not wait to leave the captain's cabin, stand out on deck in the bright sunshine. Day in and day out, the light lifted his spirits. He could even hear waves lapping against the hull of the Meliskerk, and occasionally the squawk of a tern tweaked the silence of his ears. The taste of salty ocean water made him thirsty—for what, he was not quite sure.

He mused on the riverboat ruffians in his past. They had been unmannered, sleazy, and full of lowly tricks, but he took them for granted, like wormy carrots tossed aside for pig fodder. He was certain that the vandals who had plagued him on his way to and from school would sooner or later have to do penance. They would be forced into permanent menial labor or serve in houses of correction. His three fellow-passengers on board the Meliskerk seemed to him made of the same cloth. He could not quite make out the German language save words and phrases here and there, so communicating with them was impossible. But it was mostly because they played cards, fought over cards, lost at cards, drank, and slept past noon. They had shunned Jaak, who was not aware that the law-abiding scribe to the ship's captain and the servant of God singing His praises had piqued their pride for the three long weeks on board the cramped vessel.

Land was sighted. Mountains rose up from the coastal plain. These were not like walls of mist, nor like the leviathan of a sea monster. Jaak's wonderment knocked his knees together like the shaky reeds in the Maas River. He would have genuflected except that he had been taught that only the Roman Catholics—those idolaters of incense, hail Marys, and incomprehensible Latin—engaged in that strange custom. He ran to port side of the bow, clasped his hands fast around the hot iron railing, swung his torso over the rail in jubilation, locking his knees tight like ramrods. He prayed to God, thanking Him for a safe landing, beseeching him for good fortune. But, that very second, without warning, as Jaak swayed gently back and forth, praying and staring out at port side approaching the landmass of Luderitzbocht off the Southwest African coast along the Namibian desert, a thunderbolt struck him. With one long shriek he swiveled on his heels, galloped over the deck, slithered down the ropes of the stairs to the hold and bolted into his cabin, knees buckling as he flung himself onto his bunk bed. He blacked out, fainted, broke down, swooned in fright like only dainty muslin-dressed ladies do.

Whatever awoke him, whether it was the sudden stillness of the ship's engine coming to a halt and stopping the reverberations in his ears, or whether it was the fright at what he had seen, he dug his deathly pale face deeper into the pillow of his bunk bed, ripped the coarse under sheet up from the straw mattress and buried his head in it.

"The devil, it's the devil," he shouted. He gasped for air from under the crumpled, sweat- drenched sheet. He beseeched God not to forsake him.

He had come face to face with a black man. A man as black, as grimy, as sweaty, as wicked and iniquitous as the devil himself.

Nowhere in Brabant, nowhere in Gelderland during his apprenticeship at Summer's Joy, nor in the Westland in the province of South Holland had he ever come across a black, glistening face like the one that had topped the ladder thrown out at port side when the Meliskerk anchored at Luderitzbocht. He had seen black pots burnt on a stove, black ravens chasing songbirds away, and Emigrant had been a fierce, shiny black stallion. A black man—as black as the horned devil himself—he had never seen, never imagined, never heard of, never dreamt about. No one had prepared him for a black man. He had never heard of Rembrandt Harmszen van Rijn, who had painted a black man—two of them. Jaak was in shock. Fear crawled under his white skin. He hid, isolated and separated himself from this Caliban, felt an ocean and a continent removed, apart.

But by the time the port of East London was reached, Jaak had become less frightened of the black thick-lipped Hottentot faces that continued to appear. He had noticed their tongues were pink, their palms were pink, the soles of their feet were pink, their teeth glistened white like new-fallen snow on the dyke along the Maas, so far away in Brabant. As he watched these *kaffers*, as the Captain called them, clamber up the rope ladder to supply the Meliskerk with fresh water, strange rice kernels, odd beans, and bottles of a reddish kind of sweet juice he had never tasted before, he pondered the glossy blackness of these beings.

"How beautiful they are, how supple and limber their bodies, how careful their agile fingers stack sacks and bottles and kegs in the right order, how sweet their melodies as they hum and go about their work, cheerfully replenishing an empty tired vessel. And inside they are like us: pink and white and bloody. It is only from the outside that their skin is dark, because it has been blackened by a blazing sun. And the blackness they are made of would protect them from prowling lions and hungry hyenas, which would steal around the *kraal*, as the ship's captain had said. So, I don't have to worry. And their souls? Their souls cannot be as sinful as ours. That's impossible. I'll bet their souls are clean, cleaner than those of the damned riverboat rogues, and certainly cleaner than mine, my dark soul that keeps surrendering to gloom, to sloth, often to gluttony, and in the dark night to lasciviousness. Oh, dear God, protect me from evil, evil thoughts, sinful deeds." Jaak said to himself.

Once Jaak was settled at his cousin Betje's, she proceeded to declare her intentions for the future. Promised she would sign her will with Jaak as chief inheritor and executor; was determined to book her passage back to the homeland tomorrow. She guaranteed Jaak she would put her bungalow, shaded with precious fruit trees like the mango, the rose apple, the apricot and coconut, on the market any day. She said, "I will definitely sell my stock in my husband's Rickshaw Company by May. I really will."

She gave Jaak spending money, had a young colleague of her husband's show Jaak around a whaling station. It was here that Jaak showed his new confidence as he stood for a photograph flanked by eight blacks with short-cropped black curly hair, in disheveled shirts and shorts, their lower lips thickly protruding from under their tight upper lips. Pale Jaak was still dressed in his gray woolen suit, a Borsolino hat, and a tie. His companion sported a white tropical suit with matching white shoes. Both men stand straight and smiling as they each hold a long slender stick in their hands—to lean on it seems. Eight black *kaffers* stare quizzically out at the cameraman, even though the middle man, the oldest one, holds an accordion in his hands, stretching the notes as he poses on the platform in front of the corrugated one-story elongated building for cutting and slicing and boiling whale blubber into profitable goods.

Jack 1ˢᵗ left, Durban South Africa

One more time we see Jaak standing, stick in hand, at the edge of a group of two- dozen young blacks. In back of him, turned away from the group, stands a tall black wearing a hat, neat trousers and shirt, also resting, it seems, both hands on a stick. One young boy, sitting with legs sprawled in the middle of a dozen pitch-black-faced fellows with caps and *topis* on, guards a crooked stick between his legs as he smiles roguishly at the camera. Jaak, in his dark suit and tie, gazes, perhaps with uncertainty, at the camera, telling himself he must smile, must feel at ease for the sake of his folks at home. He will send this photograph to Babylonbrook, this photo with the trees and shrubs full of leaves, with small bungalows alongside the narrow, dusty road on the bluff. It is the Umbogintwini Road, the coastal road leading north to Zululand and south as far as Port Edward, where the Mtamvuna River cuts its way down from the high peaks of Basutoland, where the Drakensberg chain looks out onto the Pacific Ocean near Fossil Head. He must show mother Antonia and father Gilbert that he can cope in the strangest of circumstances. Even though he stands apart, he is seemingly in command of his mixed feelings in a land where blacks outnumber the whites in who knows what ratio.

It took Jaak a full year to find his comfort zone in the land of the *hel're lug*, (clear sky) before he discarded his dark woolen suit and dressed in a light tropical one, before he entrusted Thabita, the black kitchen help, with a sigh, acknowledging, "Life is boring, always summer. Mrs. Betje Thompson not wants to return, not wants to sell Pickering house."

Cousin Betje's indecision, coupled with Jaak's boredom, drove him to take a job at a bank. There he found friends, outings in rowboats exploring jungled riverlands in Amanzintoti, picnics on the Durban Bluff, swimming on the Isipingo Beach, moonlight parties beyond the Esplanade with Thabita's baskets filled with tender young hens, accompanied by bottles of *chiripico*, that bittersweet juice that made Jaak dizzy after a second irresistible gulp.

It was the gay twenties. There were eight partygoers. Always an eightsome, four and four dressed for the occasion: heavy woolen swimsuits, clinging trunks covering taut thighs and slender chests. Under the women's broad-brimmed hats you could hardly make out the bangs of three brunettes and the curly bobby cut that Margarida wore. Margarida, the ever-smiling, sweet blonde gently leaning towards Jaak. Her muslin dress with a belt or a ribbon way below her trim waistline to mark her slender hips, one heel of her shoe sunk into the beach sand or slipping off a rocky boulder while the other foot is swung to the side from the knee in the dancing pose of the Charleston. The male consorts touch a lady's arm here, stroke a hip there, rest a hand on a shoulder in blazing sunshine. It was these outings, these picnics, these moonlight parties that made Jaak forget about returning to Babylonbrook, any annoyance at cousin Betje's procrastination, any queasiness at living in permanent summertime on the darkest populated continent. He learned English fast, sang the tunes of Gershwin heartily, acquired a taste for *chiripico*, and for surfing the salty waves of the Pacific.

Then cousin Betje died, of an asthma attack. She died intestate. Her lawyer assured Jaak he was to inherit her fortune, but Jaak's Protestant upbringing led him to refuse any inheritance, pointing out that Betje had brothers and sisters in the homeland. Thabita wailed for days at her mistress' death. Jaak, who had just won a prize for a contest he had entered at the bank, was denied the prize. He was overwhelmed by Betje's death. He was crushed at losing that prize. The jury for the contest at the bank was reluctant to favor a recent Dutch immigrant over an Afrikaner Boer immigrant. He became apathetic. News from Babylonbrook was not good. Severe malaise held all of the Netherlands in an economic stranglehold. Father Gilbert was ailing, forgetful, and quite confused, mixing up names. In one blow, the unexpected death of cousin Betje who had spoiled him as only a mother of an only son can do, nullified Jaak's existence in South Africa. He fell into a catatonic spell. For days he missed work, lay in bed not eating, hardly drinking, oblivious to his friends' entreaties to moonlight parties, deaf to the kakadoo's parroting the parakeet perched in the mango tree outside his screened window. Finally, Thabita's son Dave appeared. Dave, who had come down from the *kraal*. Young, limber, soft-spoken Dave, black, beautiful and erect as the *tulipe noire* Jaak had seen bloom in the Westland sands. Dave appeared with his accordion and played night and day, day and night, "Way down upon the Swanee River. . ."

7 Pickering Street
Durban

Dave played the Swanee song for two long days, two long nights. On the third day Dave's strumming abruptly stopped as Betje's lawyer arrived and addressed Jaak briskly, "A telegram from Betje's brother requests you to stay until the sale of her estate is regulated. You're to be the main inheritor."

Jaak agonized the whole month of December, 1927. Should or shouldn't he stay?

Should or shouldn't he accept the inheritance? Should or shouldn't he go steady with Margarida, whose smile captivated him but whose buckteeth bothered him, and whose sharp-snouted bushy-tailed red-furred fox collar hugging her neck in the heat of December stumped him.

"Jack," she had whispered, "Jack, tonight it's Isipingo Beach, do come, come on Jack, we're bringing my phonograph and *chiripico*, you must come."

By that time, after two years in Durban, Jaak had changed to "Jack," smoother on the tongue for the Afrikaner of British descent, easier for the Zulu man to say "Master Jack," sweeter for Thabita to pronounce, "Masser Jackie?"

In his foggy memory, washed out by the shock of the death of someone he had grown so close to, came to cherish and love like a mother, he vaguely remembered he had promised neighbors of his folks at home in Brabant to visit their relatives near Johannesburg before returning home, if he ever decided to do so.

Unlike cousin Betje, whose intestate will had left him with a big headache, and unlike farmer Roos who so long ago had reneged on his word to give Jaakie that little foal, Jack kept his promise. While the lawyer sorted out the mess of Betje's estate, Jack journeyed north by railway and was happily surprised at the thriving granary mill Oubaas Ambrosius had set up with his sons. Jack's surprise grew to outlandish proportion when son Meeuwis Ambrosius declared, "I've just bought a claim in a newly opened diamond field up north near the Limpopo. *Kom, kom mee..* I'll give you a diamond if you join me."

To mother Ambrosius' dismay, Jack never even so much as blinked at her three marriageable daughters.

Instead, he let curiosity at the vaingloriousness of sighting a sparkling diamond get the better of him. He had already decided he would renounce the money he was to inherit should cousin Betje's estate ever be settled. He'd feel guilty at craving the Mammon, would hand it over to her siblings. But a brilliant—to find, to hold, and to keep a brilliant! And, who knows when it was to happen, but happen it would, he would pierce a heart. For he firmly believed that one day, somewhere in-between the Umbogintwini Road and Babylonbrook, he would at long last find her, his beloved. He was sure of it.

When Jack set out to the diamond field with Meeuwis Ambrosius, his expectations were high. Like many a young man, he felt he had already undergone the worst possible experiences in his twenty-eight-year-old life. He had been cheated as a child, he had been mistreated by bullies, he had failed at cultivating tulips, he had been given the sack at the municipality and the bank, he had gone out of his mind when a black man climbed up the rope ladder of the Meliskerk and stared him in the face with big white teeth, grinning. He had thrown a catatonic fit at death itself.

The spectacle at the diamond field was worse. It was like that "which Habakkuk the prophet did see." "... Spoiling and violence" were before him. "Strife and contention, ... " "Creeping things, that have no ruler over them." Jack was deeply shocked, ready to give up, take the train, sail back home. Try tulips again, carrots, whichever. Yet, somewhere in his left lobe a brilliant sparkled; besides he'd promised Meeuwis he'd come.

What he saw was pure horror. Alongside dusty wagon trails he saw a myriad of erratic ruts ending in heaps of broken pieces of collapsed carts, ruts filled and strewn with diseased, dead oxen, corpses with flesh quivering under the heat of a blazing sun. Skulls. Vultures gnawing, ripping bloody flesh. Vultures circling, swooping up and down in the stench of rotting air. Jack plugged his ears with his trembling fingers but he could not drown out the squawking of these bloodthirsty birds of prey.

The poor Boers, whose farms just would not flourish, whose pennies were too few for cost-effective investment, whose wives silently cursed another pregnancy—these poor farming people had sold the little they owned in the hopes of striking, if not a glittering diamond, at least a Krugerrand by sifting out one semi-precious stone in the remote newly opened mining field where the Limpopo forms a gray greasy borderline between British and Dutch colonial territory.

Conditions for participation had been set by Paul Krueger. What poor Jack witnessed was even worse than "the day that shall burn as an oven." On arrival, one day before the run, Meeuwis had deftly organized a few *kaffers* to set up a shack out of planks long enough to place two stretchers and high enough so they could pull on a spare pair of pants for the fortnight they had expected to spend.

Hundreds of fortune seekers who had survived the trek to this outpost and who had bought one or two claims had pitched low canvas tents as close to the half-kilometer-square mining field as was allowed. Representatives from rich companies and the more fortunate had shacks, sheds, and huts erected out of galvanized iron. The open *veld* had changed overnight into a city of stores, saloons, movie shacks, bordellos, and ramshackle whores' cabins. There was noise, the smoke of burning charcoal, the stench of sweat, grease, cheap cigars and beer, rowdy voices, the hammering and clattering of galvanized iron sheeting, the lowing of weary oxen, the whispers of white emaciated whores and black lascivious prostitutes shamelessly urging, "Six pence, six pence only."

This cacophony drove Jack and Meeuwis off their stretchers into the shack of a "saloon." The relief they were looking for turned into a hell only Breughel could have painted, except that the sharp-beaked birds were shiny pistols cocked by gaunt men only too happy to plug a neighbor if he dared so much as give a blink at his swarthy dame. Thick smoke hung over the "café" from belching men gulping down warm beer, swearing at a bad hand dealt, slapping a card down in a temper. Bony fingers clutched pistol butts. A shot in the air, a shot through the corrugated galvanized thin iron wall made Jack nauseous. He bolted to the loose-hinged plank door opening, holding onto his vomit until he doubled up under the canopy of a neutral night sky. Meeuwis jumped up after his companion. He stumbled over legs and boots stretched out to trip him. "The sissies," he heard. Then jeering, belching, spitting, swearing.

At daybreak, the run began for a one-point-seven square meter piece of soil packed with stones of all sizes on the Wentworth scale at one pound a claim. Each buyer had four sticks. Thousands of speculators had assembled at the starting line patrolled by mounted police. These mounted policemen had combed the one-half-square kilometer field before dawn to make sure that no man had reserved a parcel of land for himself, his boss, or his company. Culprits were dragged before the thousands waiting impatiently at the starting line who were spitting and banging their four marker sticks in the heat of the morning air, hissing at the cheaters. Fistfights broke out before the run. Shots were fired during the run.

Jack had stayed in the rear, at a safe distance from the mayhem. Once the hordes of fortune seekers had made their run, he ventured forth to learn how the earth was mixed with Limpopo water to the consistency of porridge and put into a kind of a washing machine forced through a two-foot-wide opening onto an assembly line of the jute strip. With an iron scraping device, *kaffers* supervised by the claimants, or the poor Boer claimant himself, would sift through the mass of earth, stones, and rocks meticulously, hoping for, expecting, the miraculous. The black *kaffer* women carried the buckets of water on their heads to near the "washing machine," while the men dug their spades deeper and deeper into the hole. Only the companies had lined up enough *kaffers* to shovel dirt for the sum of one pound a day, with a foreman earning more to drive his team on. These company claims were marked off by cables, and the deeper the mineshaft the longer the ropes with lead tied to them to reach down the shaft as far as fifty meters deep. Jack saw how some of the blacks swung these ropes on purpose over to a neighbor's parcel and would thus shovel a heap of dirt into his area. With the foreknowledge of his boss, he knew an extra reward was awaiting him. Cheating was rampant but usually soon discovered, and fights broke out again. After a few days Jack adjusted to the brawls, but he could never get used to bloody fights or fights that knocked out poor farmers, or the sight of limp bodies being dragged to the "city" slung over a comrade's shoulder or just kicked into a pit.

Fortunately, Meeuwis had bought only one claim and was not interested in bargaining over the neutral triangles around his four staked-out sticks. He and Jack made do with a few sheets of mica. Plain mica.

In one sense, the two young adventurers had luck on their side. They had come out of this rough mining field unscathed. Not even the loose women, persistent and obtrusive, had managed to penetrate their shack, let alone arouse their libido, which, with each day's heated search and fights for the elusive brilliant, was dulled until the twelfth day, when Jack and Meeuwis left, disappointed but not embittered.

Little did Jack know that, in his lifetime, he was to see worse. Much worse. Not for a dozen days, but for a dozen years. For thirteen years, every day, he would be a witness to worse.

CHAPTER 7 | BERLIN – RAUCHSTRASSE

In small Dutch villages, everyone knew everyone. Anyone who owned large landholdings, along with champion horses, always knew where to turn for favors. Mother Antonia had been forced to take the reins in hand since Gilbert's brain had tumbled into odd dysfunctional lapses. She began to nudge an upwardly mobile village acquaintance to keep her posted on employment chances for her son, soon to return from Africa.

*Jacq Millenaar,
Berlin 1929*

At last disembarked from his fling out on the great seas, and his feet planted again on the alluvial clay clods of the homestead in Babylonbrook, Jack's muddled feelings lifted. Even though times were austere, with unemployment high and crops unreliable, he listened with anticipation when mother Antonia, on a sober Christmas morning after a long admonitory sermon in a chilly church, announced, "Jaak, remember schoolteacher De Jong Saakes? Well, he took father's advice to heart, went on to night school, and got his diploma in agriculture. We gave him a plot of land by the south meadow for his experiments. Now he's in The Hague at the Ministry of Agriculture, and he said you should write to him regarding possible job openings."

Sure enough, an agricultural assistant was needed at the Paris legation. Jack had learned some French from the Belgian soldiers who had been billeted on the farm over a dozen years earlier, when the war had been at its worst in Flanders on the Somme, and neutral Holland provided refuge and food to neighboring troops. *La ville lumière.* He was thrilled. *Une Parisienne.* That's what he was looking for. He knew about *les fleurs*, not yet *Les Fleurs du Mal.* His dream, however, was short lived.

It would be Berlin, not Paris. Jaak would be assistant to the agricultural consultant at the Royal Netherlands Legation in Berlin, Germany. Though he was eager to move on, to find security somewhere, to earn a decent income to share with his mother Antonia, whose burden had made her thin and reddened her big-boned hands, he hadn't wanted Berlin.

Jack mumbled in horror, "A German wife! *Hausfrau,* a *Berliner Maedel?*" His chagrin at the Paris rejection struck hard. The excuse had been that an agricultural attaché as well as an assistant with a hearing handicap was unadvisable. Sorry. He was deeply hurt, but kept the defeat to himself. In silence he suffered, and in the night with the western winds howling, he sought distraction from his anxiety and fear of the future by thinking of Margarida and the picnics beyond the Esplanade. But thoughts of work, of income, of stability interfered and depressed his spirits. He'd resort to humming a beloved tune or turn to reading Job, always glancing at the High Song, thus bracing himself against permanent gloom.

So within a span of barely three months, Jaak would journey, with mixed feelings, from Durban to Babylonbrook, his home, and on to the cosmopolitan capital city of Germany. Jack would land in Berlin, a metropolis with over four million inhabitants. Berlin, the third largest city in the world after New York and Greater London.

He gradually overcame the disappointment over gay Paris, and though he did not exactly jump at the déclassé opportunity offered to him, he accepted it with flair, simulating *joie de vivre* as he sang the verse he had betted on reciting at the Ministry if, by a miracle, he was accepted for the job. He had won his bet. He had to sing. He shook in his shoes. But he noticed that if he pretended, if he showed bravado, he could actually suppress his shyness, nervousness, and the twitches that had recurred since his arrival from Durban. He sang boldly:

Du bist verrueckt mein Kind
You're crazy old kiddo

Du musst nach Berlin
To Berlin you ought'a go

Wo die Verrueckten sind,
Where the zombies hang out

Dort gehoerst Du hin.
That's where you ought'a roam about.

Poor Jack. He had no idea, when he took the day-long train journey in a third-class wooden coupé on a cold February morning in 1928, that he was riding through a country the majority of whose men had been brought up short by the defeat of their beloved Reich. Or that these same males were disgusted and incredulous at the treatment of the invincible Germans at Versailles when on November 11, 1919, the French decimated their land, their army, their economy, and their unyielding, unaccommodating pride. Even my German grandfather from Cologne had put all his trust and the wealth from all the golden buttons he peddled up and down the Rhine for the lingerie-cum-hosiery company, Heinemann & Co., in Wilhelm II, King of Prussia, Kaiser of Greater Germany. And then, when the Kaiser fled to Holland and made Apeldoorn in Gelderland his home, the dual defeat had utterly toppled my grandfather's pride.

After Jack's long train journey came to an abrupt halt at the Bahnhof Zoo, he was told he had to report to Mr. Albert Joustra at the Netherlands Legation in the Rauchstrasse, district Tiergarten (Garden of Beasts), on February 10, 1928, promptly at nine o'clock.

For one long excruciating year, with diligence, with gratitude and with enthusiasm that was always accompanied by a nervous trepidation unalleviated even on lonely weekends, Jack buried himself in his work. At the Legation, on the second floor of a massive neoclassical, nouveau riche villa on a quiet street in the *Diplomatenviertel* (diplomats district), he zeroed in on his most important mission: getting to know the agricultural markets. How and where would supplies from the Netherlands meet the increasingly rapacious demands of Germany? In the four years past, before Jack's arrival and after the currency reform in 1923, when inflation had reached its climax and suitcases were being carried all over Berlin filled with trillions of Reichsmark, Germany had experienced a frenzy of building, expansion, illegal re-arming, training schools, trafficking, film-making, theatre-production, cabaret-dancing, mud-wrestling, six-day bicycling, waltzing and bee-bopping of the highbrow and the low, the lush and lascivious, the transvestites and the Mackie Messers in one brief Weimar Republican fling.

Jack's main goal was to hang on to his job. To do so he had to learn German fast, speed up his grasp of professional journals, the Dutch as well as the verbose, unintelligible German publications. He would highlight pertinent information for his well-read and eminently published boss, Doctor Joustra.

During Jack's first spring, his first sultry summer, and even the drizzly dreary Berlin autumn and cold winter, he trudged six days a week, after long office hours, back to the fifth-floor, overstuffed, high-ceilinged, and cigarette-tarnished room he had negotiated for fifty Reichsmark, with utilities extra and visitors excluded. His spinster landlady, with her medical-student brother, did include shining the two pairs of leather shoes he had been admonished to leave outside his door in the dark, narrow corridor.

His first year was torture. Deep into the night after a meal (for which he paid extra) of bad potatoes, limp vegetables, a strip of gristly meat followed by yellow or chocolate-colored pudding, he sagged into a worn upholstered armchair with a stack of periodicals, two heavy dictionaries, a rumpled encyclopedia, newspapers, and—only on Saturday nights—one bottle of Berliner Kindl beer.

Only after several years had Jack found a certain comfort level beyond his daily walk to and from the Legation. He explored—not in a luxurious, costly *charabanc*, but in a double-decker omnibus and a trolley—the outskirts of the city filled with thousands of lusty Berliners weary of asphalt, noise, and the rumble and bumble of traffic. They were hungry for sandy beaches, lukewarm lake water, shaded woods, beer gardens, terraces with jazz bands and voluptuous Marlenes. When he had familiarized himself with the strangely cosmopolitan glitter, his knowledgeable boss confided in him: "You know, Wolff said to me soon after you arrived, 'Man, what kettle of fish of an assistant did you get now. He doesn't know his right hand from his left.'"

Dr. Albert Joustra, humane and noble in character, who had suffered the death of a six-year-old daughter after a long illness, himself frail with worry, had shown patience and kindness toward his young assistant, Jack. Joustra's response to Wolff, the Consul General and head of its commerce department at the Legation was, "Give him a chance; he cultivated the best beans in Brabant, knows a peach from an apricot, and is up on this new tomato business."

Consul-General Wolff, who had come as a civil servant from the Dutch East Indies, a diamond in the rough, a lonely, authoritarian, confirmed bachelor, gradually warmed up to the young, diligent, fast-learning assistant. For over six years, until my father was married, Dr. Wolff invited Jack out to the Hofjaeger, where Jack would unwrap his sourdough sandwiches

and watch Wolff eat *Eisbein* (pig's knuckle) alternating
with a Schnitzel or a Bratwurst, as the Consul-General
first relayed the jokes he had heard from all and sundry
before discussing agriculture and commercial matters
with the new apprentice.

Wolff's jokes were of a crude variety. Often he
spoke so loudly that he had the young secretaries
crossing and re-crossing their silk-stocking-clad legs,
giggling as they tapped their golden cigarette holders
nonchalantly over a matchbox ashtray. While his direct
boss was too preoccupied at home with his sickly child
and too immersed in preparing lectures, Jack listened
attentively to Consul-General Wolff, followed his
advice gratefully, and helped Joustra by writing reports,
commenting on the trade wars, and corresponding
with food-producing enterprises in Holland about the
annual *Gruene Woche* (green week), the agricultural
exhibit held annually in the great exhibition halls
around the Funkturm, that *langer Lulatsch* (beanpole of
a radio tower, symbol of the New Berlin after inflation).

Jack was given a chance, and he made the best of it.
The chance from 1928 was that of being an official on

*Club
Nederland
& Oranje,
Berlin*

the payroll of the Ministry of Agriculture in The Hague, with the task of assisting the attaché of agriculture at the Royal Netherlands Legation in the metropolis of Berlin. He busied himself with work, learned the tricky language of German, which resembled his own Dutch, though not at all his Brabant dialect. He earned a salary but...where was his brilliant? Where to find her? Surely not among the Berliner Maedels (damsels). Could he find her among the very few young Dutch ladies at the clubs *Nederland & Oranje,* or the less prestigious club *Hollandia?*

CHAPTER 8 | LENI

She had no buck teeth. Had never worn a fur stole. Her name was not Margarida or Gretchen, and she had not come from Berlin, either. No *Berliner Maedel.* Her name was Leni, after her mother Helene. Leni, the spoiled one. The youngest of nine, blond, blue-eyed, loveable. A cherub equal to Lochner's angels. She had been delivered in the dark month of November, in the midst of a dark mood because the third of my grandparents' five sons had died. This was to be my grandmother's last child. She had vowed, "I'm forty-four. Enough's enough. Heinrich can go to Maria Laach, chant with the monks."

Grandmother Helene made sure none of the surviving five siblings, ranging from eighteen to two, would disturb her last, her golden child, the cheeriest and easiest of them all. No colic, no tantrums, a sound sleeper. What bliss! Leni, my grandmother's sunshine: in her very own words, *mein Sonnenscheinchen,* protected fiercely from all ills physical, emotional, and spiritual.

Leni grew up a free spirit. Uncomplicated. All around her treated her lovingly, teasingly, with laughter. Laughter, fun, and endearment were her security. My grandmother, grandfather, aunts and two uncles first showed her the cartoons of Max und Moritz and the story of the Fromme Helene (pious Helen) by Wilhelm Busch. In elementary school, the nuns concentrated on her penmanship, writing, reading, arithmetic, darning, and sewing.

When her brother Hubert, at twenty-one, went off to the Great War, Leni proudly waved the photo postcard from Vilna to all of her second grade classmates. "Look how tall my brother stands. Look at his big chest, his golden buttons."

At the end of the war, when Leni had just turned ten and Hubert had, after all, returned home in tatters and downcast, he confided to his little sister, "You darling angel, you sweetest sister of mine, don't ever love a soldier; it's the stupidest thing you can do." Leni, of course, did not understand what he meant. Because he added, "Don't tell anyone. Keep it to yourself. The horror I've seen. Now, go get me a pretty flower." He was so touchy, looked so glum that she never dared question him nor anyone in her family about this remark from her dearest brother, the soldier. She laughed and ran out to the balcony, picked a petunia, and looked beyond the apple trees to stare at the spires of the Dom cathedral. The two thin needles of towers to which she always turned, crossed herself, and genuflected whenever this uncomfortable feeling she did not understand overwhelmed her.

In secondary school Leni forgot the dark passages in Latin from the Bible, but adored the lilt of Hoelderlin, the gory treachery of Schiller, the humor in Heine. Goethe confused her: was he or wasn't he optimistic after all with his striving toward—what? His terrible *Schmerz*. And *Weltschmerz* she did not understand, and then he always longed for eternal *Ruhe* (peace, or rest, or sleep, or the other "*bourne*")? She simply didn't understand.

"Why *Ruhe*," Leni laughed at her best friends, the sisters Jannie and Ruth Stern, "when we want to cheer, sing, and yodel from every top of the Siebengebirge to let the world know how pretty the wild flowers bloom, how the wind feels against our bare legs when we do cartwheels in these mountain meadows, and how the Rhine glistens from up here like a string of pearls luring the river men around the Lorelei."

Leni loved life, and life loved Leni. Except for the nuns. They told her parents in all solemnity, "No, Lenchen is far too immature to enroll for the program of kindergarten teacher. We suggest she go to household school first."

For the first time in her eighteen years Leni was crossed by this harsh verdict. She had always had her way in the end though she had also always done what her elders and the nuns told her to do, following the rules dutifully. Of course she had poked fun at her ever-pious swirly mustached father, or had burst out in a giggle at the table because her younger brother, Josef, pinched her during a long Sunday meal and Leni got the blame. Then she would run to the balcony, genuflect, and look out over the wrought iron toward the Dom Cathedral and pray her Hail Marys, whereupon she acquitted herself of her silly sin, which never was her fault in the first place. So she always pleaded to God to forgive her brother, Josef, the sneaky one, or her serious sisters, or the nuns, those stiffened women in black who had no clue what it was like to be touched lovingly, to be caressed affectionately, to be teased humorously.

In Bonn, a quick train ride away, lived Leni's sister Anna, happily married with her two little children. Anna was twenty years older. Her husband, a violinist, was like a father to Leni, but not strict, and always willing to explain sonatas, sonatinas, and codas. In Bonn, overlooking the Rhine, on a bluff there stood the Institute of Dentistry, which was looking for "capable, healthy women to train as dentists."

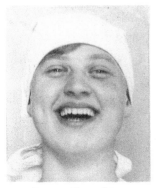

Leni was in her element when she was accepted with seven other young women to become the first female dentists in German history. Her father gave in reluctantly after repeated urging by his wife.

Leni at Dental Institute in Bonn

Quaint, intimate Bonn, with its neat park by the University, its narrow alleys winding their way steeply down to the banks of the Rhine, its staid burghers filled with Beethoven's harmonies. Bonn, where the tunes of birdsong mingled with the foghorns of barges chugging up and down the river. This bucolic town enthralled blue-eyed, cheery Leni from the big city of Koeln, in whose shadow little Bonn oftentimes felt slighted. Yet, Leni never neglected her home city. On weekends she returned to play hockey, to row the skiff, to train on the swimming team, and even to learn the martial art of fencing. But her favorite pastime was wandering, hiking with her sister Maria and their bosom friends, the sisters Jannie and Ruth. The foursome was always together, always embracing, cartwheeling in unison. Two blondes and two brunettes in the woods, in the open fields, in mountain meadows perfumed by mallow roses or honeysuckle or the *chantarella* mushrooms. They were dizzy with nostalgia—for what they then did not know.

And Leni, wherever she wandered, whether on the crowded streets of downtown Koeln, the market square of Bonn, or up on the meadow paths overlooking the meandering river, was always in the middle, smiling and embracing her female companions securely with her strong amber arms. Young and old, male and female were attracted to the unquenchable spirited gaiety that Leni radiated from her inner state of glowing love, showered on her so generously by her wise mother Helene and her pious father, Heinrich, salesman of lace and buttons.

But it could not last. Father Heinrich, on an unannounced visit to his eldest daughter, had waited for soup time, for meat and potato time, for pudding time, for grace time, all in vain—and still his Helenchen had not shown up for supper. She had been out with the boys.

It had been a miserable year back in Koeln. Leni did find work with a dentist, but only as an assistant.

Leni the ham loving life

Her hopes were dashed at becoming a full-fledged, autonomous dentist. The crash of October 1929 undid her portly father and sent him not to the monks or the spa but to the hospital. He recovered temporarily for Shrove Tuesday when he hired a window in old Koeln to watch his favorite Tanzmariechen kicking her pretty legs high as she led the carnival parade. But early on Ash Wednesday morning in 1930, just before he could cheer the marching, dancing, bouncy acrobats, agile jugglers, masqueraders, and carnival revelers, his heart failed.

The black dresses, coats, skirts, gloves, and stockings of mourning brought out Leni's delicate skin, her blue eyes, and her golden blond hair. She never bore a grudge against her stern, swirly mustached father. She forgave him as she was forgiven time and again for her own peccadilloes. Nor was she especially mournful at his passing away. She felt liberated. No longer was she admonished at mealtime to sit up straight, not to wiggle or not to speak up in spite of her twenty-two years of age. At last she could buy dresses above her knees, she could get her hair cut above her ears, she could go to the movies, go to a dance hall where a jazz band played, instead of boring waltz music. Best of all, she did not have to be the obedient daughter and listen to her father's eternal "eat your potatoes."

She began to adore her mother more and more, because so often it had been she who would caress her "sunshine" surreptitiously and tenderly whenever father Heinrich raised his voice. As he aged and saw his son Hubert seek company with only women and his son Josef not head for a bishopric but for ugly commerce, and saw Germany take on strange configurations like weasels in the sky, Heinrich's temper became shorter and more unpredictable. Leni happened to be around to catch the blame from a father who himself had been brought up with the rod, the book of rules, and the Old Testament more than by the newer, merciful more holy book.

With her father's premature death and with her sisters' and mother's consent, plus an excellent recommendation from Professor Kantorovitch of the Bonn Dental Institute, Leni accepted the perfect job in the Neu Westend of Berlin, the glitzy hub of that rumble bumble of a city. Berlin—where the zombies are, the *Verrueckten*, only she did not know it then. She overflowed with the excitement of earning a salary, and at new friendships. Who knows, perhaps love too. But at twenty-two she had no yen to bind herself to anything or to anyone. She craved freedom, space, light like the summer air on the Wannsee, flaming September, lantern-lit beer gardens, the dazzling strobe lights of the Resi dancing bar, and the starlit winter skies on the bustling Kurfuerstendamm near where she had rented a room with a dear white Russian émigré lady, Frau Avakoff, who loved her like the only daughter she had lost in the Revolution and who had introduced her to Pet Mackie, an aspiring journalist; Margot Otto, a bookseller; Trude Heckhausen, a swimming instructor: Emma Litzenrath, a photographer aspiring to become a filmmaker.

Together with new friends and with her very own income, Leni—smooth-limbed, amber-tanned, lovable Leni—immersed herself in the fast lane of Berlin. What she didn't know was that she was running headlong into the sickest patient in Europe on the verge of a total breakdown, with an aftermath that now rings virtually unreal to any person who was not part of it.

CHAPTER 9 | BERLIN 1933 -1934

On a Monday morning on the thirtieth day of the inhospitable month of two-faced January, in 1933, Adolf Hitler came to power by the standard process of constitutional democracy. He became the Fuehrer legitimately. In four out of the five elections held the previous year, he had steadily gained votes.

Hitler was forty-three and filled with resentment and the desire for revenge (*Rache*). Illegitimacy, incest, monorchism, abuse were the givens he grew up with. Three half siblings had died before he was born; the fourth he had buried himself when he was eleven. Klara, his mother, and Alois Schickelgruber, his father, could not make it to the funeral. At eighteen Hitler was an orphan, and he blamed the Jewish physician for the death of his mother due to cancer. Twice Hitler was rejected by the Academy of Arts in Vienna. He learned that four of the seven examiners were Jewish. At age seventeen he had seen Wagner's opera Rienzi. From that moment he knew, "I am the Messiah." He was born one day before Easter, April 20, 1889. From dysfunction, isolation, neglect, rejection, and four long years in the trenches of World War I he fashioned the whip with which he was to flog peoples and nations to death.

Just two weeks before Hitler came to power, approximately one hundred and fifty thousand workers from all the districts of Berlin streamed together in Lichterfelde to commemorate the fourteenth anniversary of the deaths of their leaders and freedom fighters: Karl Liebknecht and Rosa Luxemburg. It was freezing weather. Streets with their endless rows of drab tenement houses were uniformly gray. Flags, Communist flags the color of blood, struck out ominously against the early morning gloom. The song of Liebknecht and Luxemburg echoed through cold streets – both broad and narrow as all workers, from both the Socialists and the Democrats, united in ever-growing force. Tens of thousands of the six million unemployed in all of Germany marched in towns and cities in unison. In Berlin, for a brief moment, those demonstrators gave a flicker of hope to those who so fervently wished to avert catastrophe.

On that cold January morning, two weeks before Hitler became the new Chancellor, the police showed up with rifles, clubs, horses, pistols, whips, leather boots, spiked helmets, armored trucks, and tanks. For several streets long the workers took no notice, they swelled in numbers, filling the broad streets, the avenues, the boulevards as they headed for the center of Berlin merging in from a sea of tattered, singing, flag-waving, desperate men, women, and children anxious for work, a piece of meat, milk. And for a brief spell there seemed to be the assurance, even the certainty that these workers, united, would go on marching to the Reichstag (parliament) to occupy it and all the ministries. They would take the reins in hand, restore Germany to its proper and diligent petit-bourgeois place on earth.

But, suddenly, just as the swell of a tsunami finally crests and crashes, the marching masses dispersed and receded back into the streets they had come from, back to their fractious and listless social Democratic and Communist parties. Never again did the twain converge—until after January 1933, when these same leaders and fighters were incarcerated in the first concentration camps of Sachsenhausen (northwest of Berlin) and Dachau, near Munich.

Jacq slept through it all. To him it was just another one of those marching bands with flags, drums, and shrill singing that constantly caused traffic jams, fistfights, riots, and shoot-outs with Brownshirts, black shirts, police on horseback, police in armored trucks, storm troopers, and thugs. Seeking relief from the increasingly heavy burden of keeping up with the piles of economic and agricultural regulations and decrees from his homeland and his host country,

Neuer See

he took Saturday afternoon off to go skating on the Neuer See, in the Tiergarten around the corner from his office. Wearing a hat, a trim dark suit, and with a shawl nonchalantly flung around his neck, he held on gracefully to an equally trimly dressed young woman in a fur-collared suit and muff. They smiled. They made an elegant pair. Their skates, with the wooden toe ends curled up, attracted attention from the clumsy skaters around them. Both tilted sideways as they swerved in caracoles along the smooth black ice in the somber air with its naked trees starkly lining the pond.

It was Margarida. Margarida with the buck teeth. She had grown restless in Durban. Had journeyed home on a luxury liner to her estate in Denmark, grown bored there, and had been longing for her Jack ever since his farewell on the Perfect Day, now five years ago. No matter how hard Jack tried, no matter how handsome a couple they made on the ice, he still could not warm up to her; moreover, he did not at all like her political outlook. She seemed to sympathize with all those in uniform, whether Prussian, diplomatic, brown-shirted, or black-shirted. Even the young folk wearing neckerchiefs looked attractive to her. She urged Jack on that Saturday afternoon: "Do get us tickets to the Press Ball. Please do. There must be one out of the many Dutch journalists who could buy some extra tickets."

But Jacq would have nothing of press balls, receptions, soirees outside of his very own dear club, Nederland & Oranje, established in 1887, with her Majesty the Queen as Protectress. It was in this association that he found good fellowship as well as relief from the stacks of reports he had to sift through and write summaries of and mine for proposals. Every

Thursday night he would walk over to the club and play billiards or join a foursome, where he soon learned to finesse at bridge, keeping easy count of fifty-two cards. He skipped musical evenings because of his difficulty hearing; instead, he would retreat to the reading room of the club to catch up on general news from the Netherlands and to check the books and accounts, since he served on the library committee as well as on the board of the club. The one hundred twenty-odd members bonded in patriotic spirit even more as the 1930s sank more deeply into the darkness.

The ball in honor of the Queen's Birthday was the highlight of the ever-growing Dutch community, and it was this occasion that was Jacq's pet project. He made sure he was on the organizing end of this grand and gala event. The protocol of the seating arrangement for the banquet was no puzzle for Jacq. It was like home: first the elders and their guests, the siblings according to age and achievement, and last the knaves. Simple enough. In Berlin at Nederland & Oranje he had only to look at ministerial epaulets, medals, and rankings of the nobility to place them in the correct order and company.

Saturday evening, after Jacq had shown off his skating skills on the Neuer See, he looked forward to journeying vicariously back to Africa at the club. Not South Africa, but the land of pyramids. Margarida, miffed at Jacq's refusal to get tickets for Berlin's most prized ball, refused to join him that night.

"The images of the lantern slides were so beautiful that they transported each one as far beyond as if they belonged to the real traveler … After the main film a few short ones followed, which provided a good introduction for a further cozy evening of good fellowship and fun."

This was the write-up in the annual report of that evening, when Jacq was happy to be on his own and free to mingle with colleagues, friends, and charming ladies amongst whom he still hoped to find his brilliant: a sister, a niece, a governess, even a pretty secretary might do from any of the dozen Dutch shipping agencies represented in Berlin.

As a result of the night before, Jacq, blissfully deaf, slept through the last German mass demonstration of marching and singing, snuffing out hope for a last chance at decency.

Nearby, Leni, a dental assistant, had woken up early that Sunday morning. She heard the drums, the Rosa song. She jumped out from under her puffy comforter, drew the curtains aside, and shouted to her roommate: "Wake up, let's join them."

Dark-eyed Trude drawled sleepily: "Leni, you're crazy, go back to bed. You'll get arrested, killed."

At his office, Jacq's immediate boss, Joustra, and the head of trade and commerce, Wolff, demanded more and more information from their assistant on

A. Millenaar Assistant to Dutch Agricultural Attaché at Royal Netherlands Embassy

the new protectionist rules and regulations the Hitler regime was imposing on the agricultural policy of his "Greater German Reich." These strictures caused neighboring trading partners to restrict production of fruits, vegetables, and dairy goods. When the fat-necked second-in-command, Hermann Goering, decreed, "Guns are better than butter," a trade war erupted between Germany and the Netherlands. It was called the "butter boycott."

Overnight, Germany had fixed import quotas of butter from all of its neighbors. For the Dutch and Danish dairy industry this meant disaster, as they were forced to slaughter thousands of cows whose products couldn't be sold, whereas other countries were able to increase their cattle herds. Netherlanders were so outraged that dealers in agricultural machinery stopped purchasing German brands.

Dr. Joustra and Jacq were literally caught in the middle of this boycott. Why? Well, butter was to the Dutch and the Germans as apple pie is to Yankees. In Holland, as well as in Germany, two of the three daily meals consisted of eating four to six—if not eight—slices of bread, spread first with butter. Always butter first. The amount of butter spread depended on how much butter there was in a household. On Jacq's home visits to Babylonbrook in the 1930s, the butter dish always seemed more full at the end of each meal. As mother Antonia grew older and her farm hands thinner, they scraped the butter on their slices of bread more slowly and more deliberately. And as each year went by, the more everyone scraped, the more the butter mixed with the crumbs, and the fuller the butter dish became.

Far away from the homestead, Jacq and Joustra wracked their brains: how to approach the German ministry of agriculture to request a mitigation of the stringent measures on this staple good with its manifold functions, such as equipment for butter production, dealers, milkmen, truckers?

It was Jacq's task to keep track of, and analyze, the rapid changes on the agricultural trading front. As a rule, Joustra would peruse Jacq's conclusions quickly, and only if he disagreed would he check it with the ministry for food and agriculture. Jacq became adept at viewing the advantages and disadvantages for his fellow farming brethren in the Netherlands, and pointed them out honestly and persuasively to his two superiors, who in turn would catch either flak or praise from the ambassador, or even a top official at the German ministry. Jacq did not shy away from cashing in praise, and much later he loved to brag about it. After all, at the time he still had no permanent position at the embassy, he was a mere assistant diligently proving himself amongst aristocrats, career diplomats, and PhDs.

The Netherlands, for the most part, was still an agricultural nation, and Germany was its main trading and export partner. Since Jacq and Joustra agreed on most policies, and since they favored the farmer in Holland, they gave the ministry in The Hague plenty of early warnings about the regulatory production, marketing, and processing objectives set up by the Reich's minister of food and agriculture, Walther Darré, an agronomist and a National Socialist. Under Darré, the German farmer was to increase his production, receive a 20% rise in prices, and thereby contribute towards self-sufficiency for Germany. Moreover, the German farmer and his successor were guaranteed to inherit the farm, as legislated by the *Blut und Boden* (Blood and Soil) Hereditary Farm Law of September, 1933.

Consul-General Wolff, the diamond in the rough and head of commerce, though mostly agreeing with Joustra and Jacq's views, had the larger economic picture of Holland in mind, and saw how the middle class was suffering by paying higher food prices because of the subsidies that were raised on behalf of the protectionists.

When Wolff asked Jacq to check a long report he had been assigned to write for the head of commerce at the Ministry of Economic Affairs, and after Wolff had requested the Dutch consuls all over Germany to inform him on the local economic situation, Wolff said to Jacq: "Here, read this and give me your opinion. You're not leaving before you've read the whole report."

It was an elaborate analysis, and it took Jacq quite some time to read it.

"So," Wolff said, "what do you think?"

After a while, Jacq said: "It's a well-documented piece," then he hesitated momentarily before saying, "but I totally disagree with your conclusion, and it's against your own conviction too."

"God damn it, what's wrong with it, and where does it clash with my own opinion?"

Furious as Wolff had been, he forced Jacq to tell him crisply and clearly where the flaw in his reasoning lay.

Jacq's answer was, "Mr. Wolff, you agree with me that the Germans are preparing for war, and they're constantly restricting import and raising tariffs. Every single day we have to report to the ministry that one or another product from Holland is restricted price- wise, and you as well as Joustra and myself are absolutely certain that we are merely at the beginning of these protectionist measures imposed by the Nazis. You circumvent this danger in your conclusion, whereas it's your duty as head of the commerce department to point it out emphatically. You daren't defend your own position for fear of crossing the ambassador and the top gentlemen at the ministries in The Hague."

Wolff was livid. "How dare you insult me, accuse me of dishonesty? What's gotten into you to criticize my report?" He flung more such reproaches at his assistant who, because he knew Wolff inside out (after all he had had lunch with him almost daily for over five years) did not flinch and reminded him icily that he had wanted Jacq's honest opinion.

"Get the hell out of here," Consul-General Wolff yelled at Jacq. After he calmed down somewhat Wolff said, "I'll think about it and perhaps I'll change my conclusion."

Meanwhile, the clock had turned well past office hours. Jacq walked home, and Wolff stayed behind in the embassy. The following morning, Jacq had hardly warmed his office chair when Wolff entered, saying, "I changed the conclusion. There, read it."

Whereupon Jacq Millenaar did so. On returning the report, he said, "Well, now it's a report the Netherlands can benefit from. My compliments."

"Oh, to hell with you," was Wolff's reaction. "O.K., I'll now pass it on to the ambassador."

After an hour or so, Jacq was summoned to come downstairs to the first floor, where Wolff had his polished parquet office with leather armchairs and a mahogany desk. Large office windows looked out on the quiet, dead-end Rauchstrasse. Jacq heard by the tone of his boss's voice that something was amiss. Without a *goedemorgen* (good morning), Wolff flung his report on the desk and roared, "Read the last page and look at the mess you've gotten me in."

Jacq leafed through the report to the last page, where he saw how the ambassador had marked the entire page in pencil with one big diagonal line and in the margin was written, "Here you've gone crazy."

Jacq, calm and collected, answered, "Mr. Wolff, who is head of the commerce department, you or the ambassador? If I were you, I wouldn't take it. In your case I would maintain your own conclusion and ask the ambassador to write down his vision separately and enclose it with your report to the ministry."

"I can't do that. Things aren't going well between the ambassador and me anyway, and if I follow your advice, things will only go downhill even faster."

Jacq finally kept his counsel. He was not ready to jeopardize his friendship with Wolff any further. It did strengthen his belief that prestige was often won from proper and honest information, so vital to Dutch wellbeing. And partly on the basis of his altercation with Wolff, Jacq decided to seek information himself outside his office work via the press. He resolved to fight for the interests of Dutch agriculture on his own accord.

The tidal wave that had started as a ripple in a Munich beer hall as early as 1920, when the German Workers' Party, with Hitler as its seventh member, proclaimed their Party Program. One of its twenty-five points was to deny office and citizenship to Jews. That wave rolled on in a brown, black, and bloody mass to swallow up the Weimar Republic. It crushed state governments and their parliaments, eliminated political parties and labor unions and democratic associations; it wiped out the independence of civil courts and emasculated Jews in high positions, Jews in low positions, Jews because they were a chosen people, Jews because they killed

Hitler's mother, Jews because they rejected Hitler at the Vienna Art School, Jews the scapegoat, Jews to blame, Jews because they were. Just as earth's brittle crust smolders beneath the turbulent sea floor deep down in its asthenosphere and at unexpected times has to erupt to let off its gaseous steam thereby triggering tsunamis, so Germany's tectonic plate shifted and cracked into faults unforeseen in early 1933 by any average decent-thinking person.

Jacq had encountered small samples of warped and broken mentalities on the riverboat to school in Gorkum and during his apprenticeships, and then briefly in the diamond fields of Africa. From 1933 on he began to witness worse. That spring and throughout the summer Jacq anxiously avoided the Brownshirts who roamed the streets arresting, clobbering, kicking to death, and shooting those who would not salute. The terror was actively encouraged by Hitler and his lieutenants.

Margarida would not see the dangers. She was enthralled by the glitter and fanfare of the newly established Gestapo (Hitler's secret state police as of April 1933), the SD (*Sicherheitsdienst*, the intelligence branch of the SS), and the *Totenkopfverbände* (death squads, with twelve years of training).

After hearing about book burnings, Jacq read Hitler's "peace speech" on May 17, 1933, the day after Roosevelt announced his plan for disarmament: "… Germany would also be ready to disband her entire military establishment … if neighboring countries will do the same … Germany is prepared to agree to any solemn pact of non-aggression because she doesn't think of attacking but only of acquiring security … Germany did not want war … War was 'unlimited madness'... Nazi Germany had no wish to Germanize other peoples ..."

Jacq was so nauseated by the lies of this speech, and so sick of Margarida's clinging, that he said to her the following day: "I'm going to take you to Babylonbrook. There you can see I'm not made for you. I'm of farming stock, not a diplomat, in spite of my double-breasted suit, and I will never be one. You think Germany and Hitler are great. I think the opposite. Go home to Denmark. Go back to Durban. Forget about me." He did not add how repulsed he was at the blatant sexual advances she was making every time he dropped her off at her apartment door.

Many years later, on one of my summer visits to Babylonbrook, on a dismal rainy day, when the Millenaar clan gathered for an annual birthday of an astronomically distant aunt, I had the honor of sitting next to her. She said: "You never knew? He never told you? My dear, she committed suicide. She went back to her estate, and at the beginning of June your father received a letter from Margarida's mother informing him Margarida could not deal with unrequited love. Jaakie, your father, was devastated. Couldn't understand. 'Course he couldn't. She was an atheist, you know. Your father a firm believer. Suicide was a sin. The worst sin. A true Christian couldn't do that."

I was curious and asked, "Tell me about her, did you ever meet her?"

"Well, she was pretty and she wasn't. And she wore a strange fur thing around her neck. But the craziest thing was, the night she arrived with your father from that long train journey and the ferry crossings, and the buggy ride, she asked to have a bath. You should've seen her eyes when immediately after all the hellos and introductions and the late meal of plain rice pudding with Bible readings before and after, your uncles carried in an oval metal tub from the cow barn, and dropped it onto the cold kitchen flagstones. Your aunts and your grandmother urged Margarida to get undressed, never mind all the bystanders, because the water from the pump outdoors mixed with some hot water from the kettle hanging over the kitchen fireplace was cooling off fast. Margarida stared, and stood stock still, begging Jaak to get her stole before she shut her eyes tight and started to shriek all sorts of things in Danish. Early next morning your father and your grandmother had the horses ready, accompanied her on the ferry, put her on the train to Kopenhagen. Your father was sad and confused. But, by the time he left for Berlin he seemed relieved, even happy. You know, he loved his job. He just loved working there ... He never told you?"

As events overtook Berliners in ever more rapid succession, so did events catch up with Jacq. His nervous twitches had returned. He worked harder and forced Margarida's suicide from his mind. That spring of 1933, he hardly noticed the linden leaves unfurl, nor could he hear the robin, thrush, finch, or starling (*Amsel, Drossel, Fink, und Star*, as the German nursery rhyme goes) twitter their amorous song. Much later, in his retirement days, on my annual summer's visit to him in Brabant, I asked how he got to know my mother, a German woman, in 1933. He had answered with a gleam in his eye: "Adrianneke, it's a strange story, but we fell in love. It's as plain as that."

"How did you meet?"

"We met," and here he looked me so mischievously in the eyes and said, "we met in the street."

"In the street? The streets of Berlin?"

I was horrified, aghast, embarrassed. Born in Berlin from a mother he met in the street?

"In the streets. We met in the street." I looked at the dark, double-breasted suit he wore as he sat erect and calm in his upholstered chair. Looking mischievous and with the glint still in his blue eyes, he proceeded to tell me the following

"On my walk to and from the office, I kept seeing this beauty, this absolutely gorgeous young woman. Healthy, slim, and sporty with a bounce in her stride. She looked as if she came from a well-to-do farming family. I died to get to know her. Day in, day out, we passed each other on the *Tauenntzienstrasse*. I never got beyond a shy nod in her direction. She never returned it. One evening I saw her with a friend, enter a dancing bar, the Kakadu. I thought, 'Here's my chance.' I followed them. The dancing bar was chock full. I couldn't find a place near them. Every time I stood up to ask her to dance, another guy had preceded me. Then, suddenly, after an hour, the ladies got up to leave. I hurried to beckon a waiter to pay my bill. I ran out of the bar, and outside I caught a glimpse of the ladies just as they entered the hotel Eden, a few steps from the *Joachimsthalerstrasse*. This dancing hall was on the top floor of a roof garden. I was turned away at the entrance: 'Gentlemen have to wear a smoking jacket.' Disappointed and bitter, I walked back home."

From the pocket of his double-breasted suit jacket he pulled out the handkerchief that matched his polka-dotted tie and wiped a bead of perspiration or perhaps a tear. "Well, on one of the following days, our paths crossed again, and from the blushing on the cheeks of my sweet passer-by I could read that she certainly had noticed my attempts to approach her in the Kakadu. Whether the blushing betrayed feelings of regret or *Schadenfreude*, I couldn't make out."

"What do you mean by *Schadenfreude*? Why should she feel happy at giving you so much pain? Of course, she had regrets. You must have tantalized her being so persistent, and you probably looked foreign to her in your Dutch suit with a butterfly tie."

The cows were bleating in the field, and a June drizzle had started. It was hot and stuffy in my father's polished apartment, and I could hear the trays rattling, announcing lunchtime—a hot lunch at one in the afternoon. My father looked out the window. He had been a widower for over ten years. He was a lonely man then. Very much a homebody. He disliked traveling. He loved his *genever*. As every father loves his daughter too much, so my father clung to his "Adrianneke." He watched the gentle rain come down on the cow pasture, and continued: "But it still took days, and it seemed like weeks to me, before I finally succeeded in getting her attention. For some reason I had left the club on a Thursday night around 10 PM to turn homeward on foot. It drizzled, just as it's doing now. I had my umbrella with me. In the *Martin Lutherstrasse* I suddenly saw my long-sought-after sweetheart appear. I thought, 'Now or never.' I crossed the street, headed straight for her, donned my hat, and said, 'Good evening, *Gnaediges Fräulein*, may I introduce myself and accompany you?'

'No thanks, I'm almost home,' was her not-quite-unfriendly response. 'I'll do it anyway,' I said. She lived near the clubhouse and not far from the *Taverne*, the famous café restaurant where all the foreign correspondents gathered to discuss politics and feel unobserved and free to talk about anything for a few precious hours. I often dropped in with friends after the club had closed."

"When on earth did you ever get any sleep? It seems you were always up," I interrupted.

"You remember the Berlin air, the Berliner *Luft*: nobody needed any sleep in that city. Nobody could sleep anyway with all the Nazi stuff going on. ... Ugh, that vermin." He clenched his teeth, twitched his lips, his eyes looked sad and distant again.

My father continued: "But that night, I struck out. The drizzle got worse. Full of expectation, I fell into step with her. She was carrying a book under her arm. We were close to the *Taverne*, and I asked her to come and have a drink there. But all my attempts were in vain, though she never quickened her pace. After trying a few more hollow phrases, I involuntarily pulled the book out from under her arm and gushed out, 'If you want your book back, you've got to come to the *Taverne* with me.' After quite some hesitation she surrendered and went in. We sat at a corner table. I ordered a glass of wine for two, and after a clumsy start our tongues finally loosened. We soon told each other where we came from, what we were doing in Berlin, where we lived. In the turmoil of Berlin, I quickly broached the subject of politics. I let her know exactly where I stood with respect to National Socialism and asked my guest what her political affiliation was.

'I'm a communist,' she answered. I was shocked. Utterly stunned, and my heart sank to my shoes. On the other hand, I was happy to hear she was not a Nazi. When I posed my next question about her religious denomination, she lowered her voice and looked with her pretty blue eyes at me and said, 'Roman Catholic.' I said, 'Well, in that case we're miles apart politically as well as religiously for I'm a Protestant.' My dream had vanished. I was dumbstruck. I remained silent for an eternity. When she woke me up out of my stupor she asked about my parents. We soon found out that our fathers had died in the same year, in the same month at the same age. This brought us a little closer. But then another hope was dashed when I found out that she wasn't the wealthy farmer's daughter I had hoped for. When I inquired once more how she could be Catholic and a communist, she confessed; 'I'm not a communist, but it just isn't proper to go out with a stranger.' My heart leaped. "This was our first encounter. I was already head-over-heels in love. Your mother was a beauty. So sporty. She sparkled. She radiated warmth. She understood me, my work, my antipathy to the Nazis. And she was funny—the way she had said, 'I'm a communist.' Just the way she later told me she'd acted Brunhilde and cited Schiller and Goethe in a deep, grave tone.

"Before we left the *Taverne*, we agreed to have a *rendezvous* on Ascension Day, the following Sunday. There was no doubt in my mind that it was she with whom I wanted to spend the rest of my life. And when I saw her in a straw hat that following Sunday morning, I knew I had at long last found my brilliant. As we set out for the *Müggelsee* we addressed each other immediately by our first names: '*Tag Leni, 'tag Jacq.*' At that moment I knew for sure we were made for each other."

Dusk had set in when my father ended his story. The cows in the field had retreated in clusters under a willow tree. The drizzle had stopped. My father blinked a tear away.

And my mother? What had she thought of this stranger? Leni, who loved life, life with her girlfriends, lavishing the money she earned as a dentist's assistant on movies, theatres, dancing, and swimming in the many lakes in and around Berlin. After she met Jacq, her sparkle turned into a permanent glow. She too had been swept off her feet by this young foreigner who smiled shyly, smoked a pipe with fragrant tobacco, had an odd accent, wore a double-breasted suit even in summer, donned his hat with a flair. At times she felt he seemed melancholic. She soon found out about Margarida and her self-inflicted tragedy. Talking about it as they sat in cafés, strolling in the woods or parks, or dancing to a difficult waltz because jazz had by then been forbidden, all this had helped Jacq overcome the guilt and incomprehension that had made his nervous twitches come back. Leni saw a gentleman in him; he had a noble air that she had never come across in any of her German friends. Yet, he puzzled her. In a park he would suddenly kneel down and rip out a few weeds from in-between the rose beds, or he would tell her, "Last night I sat up for hours and wrote a poem for my beloved sister, who just gave birth to her fifth child. I wished I could write a poem for you in German. But that language is so difficult. You must learn Dutch."

In August, 1933, Leni wrote a postcard home to Cologne. It had a picture of Goethe's idyllic garden house in Weimar. On the back she had written: "Dear Folks, Congratulations on your Names Day.

Tomorrow ... it is at last time again to go homeward
...Love, Leni"
She mentioned no names. No Jacq. No doctor
dentist Wolff, who had to give up his profession
because he was a Jew. The following year, at the end of August 1934,
Jacq at last had his Jill. Political matters, religious
problems, linguistic hurdles were ironed out. My
Dutch grandmother, Antonia Adriana, and my father's
favorite sister, Adriana Antonia, gave their consent, to
Jacq's great relief. My German grandmother, Helene,
and my mother's three sisters, Anna, Lisbeth, Maria,
persuaded my two German uncles to agree to Leni's
marriage to a foreigner of whom they were wary.
These uncles lacked the imagination and the trust that
an outsider, a temporary employee in their greater
Reich, could understand, and therefore take proper
care of, their fondest little sister, their dear possession,
their mother's *Sonnenscheinchen*. Jacq assured my uncles
Hubert and Josef, "Don't worry; I am now officially
a civil servant in the Dutch government and will be
paid retroactively for all the years I've served as the
agricultural assistant."

In midsummer, Jacq and Leni were married before
the civil registry in the *Schoeneberger Rathaus*—where
three decades later John F. Kennedy would stand to
say, "*Ich bin 'ein' Berliner!*" Jacq did not understand a
word of what the civil registrar had said on his wedding
day in German, and he answered with a "thank you" to
the hilarity of Leni and their two witnesses and friends.

In late summer, the church ceremony took place in
Ermelo, Holland. The minister admitted he was baffled.
Never had he blessed a mixed marriage. Furthermore,

*Leni and Jacq: Civil Registry
Schoeneberg, 1934*

the ceremony turned out to be a double wedding. My father, a Brabander, to a German citizen and my father's youngest brother, Hendrik, to my Dutch aunt Willemien. Never had a photographer been permitted to take photos inside his holy Protestant church, and marrying two couples simultaneously was also new to him. Jacq and his youngest brother both had thought it expedient and far cheaper to let their aging mother and the many relatives make a long journey just one time. A warm summer's sun shone its blessings on the two young smiling brides. Each held a bouquet of twenty-one white carnations against their long flowing white silken gowns, and my father slipped his right hand into my mother's arm. Only Leni and Jacq looked each other in the eye, smiling timidly but expectantly, while the other forty family members and guests looked straight at the camera. They posed stiffly, but with amused expressions. The hem of my mother's wedding dress hung crooked. One white high-heeled shoe could be seen; the other, not. But then, all the hems of the dresses of the young women in the front row hung crooked except for my two grandmothers'—their hemlines were trim and parallel to the privet hedge. My father wore two carnations in his buttonhole, the only lapel out of the twenty with a white carnation to match his white butterfly tie and his white gloves. The white set off so neatly the black coat tails with the black top hat he had rented for the day. The brick building of the rectory behind the wedding party had the name BOSCHHOEK above the narrow door entry, and next to it a big plaque read: BIBLES OBTAINABLE HERE.

The sermon had pleased everyone and had edified the guests on that warm summer's day. My mother had followed the words carefully and confided to my father later that she had been grateful to have tied the bond with him in a non-Catholic church, and that she had loved the sermon: Genesis 28, verses 3 and 6: "And God Almighty bless thee, and make thee fruitful, and multiply thee, that thou mayest be a multitude of people ..."

Double wedding. N. Brabant: Leni and Jack, August 1934

CHAPTER 10 | BLOOMSDAY

I was told I was conceived on a Bloomsday, not far from the Bleibtreustrasse, where Poldy Bloom traveled in his dreams to negotiate riches with a dealer in lemons grown in the land of the citron. Leni had finally succeeded, with the help of professional counseling, books, and patience, in getting her Jacq relaxed, confident, and ready for the moment supreme on that warm June night in the Keithstrasse in 1937. Or perhaps it was on the shores of the Wannsee under the protective branches of a weeping willow tree, where Stephen Spender had frolicked and where Leni and Jacq found an irresistibly loving moment as the lake water lapped.

Nineteen thirty-seven had been a relatively quiet year. That is to say, correspondent William Shirer, as well as the society reporter, Bella Fromm, spent few pages in their journals on that year. It was Hitler's fifth year in power. He had been inaugurated in peacetime. In the last "democratic" election, held in March 1933, his National Socialist Party had gained five-and-one-half million votes. He personally led with over seventeen million votes, the Centrist Party got four-and-one-half million votes, the Social Democrats seven million, the Communists almost five million, and the nationalists received three million votes. He had come out of the trenches of World War I with nothing to his name—no address, no profession, no German nationality—but he had been given an Iron Cross and the rank of corporal—and had served a prison term. While in prison he had written a book, *Mein Kampf*, which, in 1933, had sold one million copies. With the help of Joseph Goebbels, Hermann Goering, Heinrich Himmler, and Reinhard Heydrich, Hitler had nazified Germany. He had not even been able to acquire German citizenship until 1932. In a few years of frantic activity, the National Socialists, or Nazis, consolidated power by terror, intimidation, suppression, incarceration, elimination, assassination, execution, and by whipping the German peoples into their goose-step while hustling the noncompliant off the streets and into prison camps, of which there were fifty-five as early as 1933.

Jacq had a taste early in the summer of 1933 of what that meant. After an evening's stroll to a restaurant in the surroundings of the Tiergarten district, Jacq and a young friend, Rijsbergen, stepped out of an omnibus to walk home. It was around eight o'clock. The air was pleasant. A big rally of the S.A. had just taken place in the Sportpalast. Hundreds of S.A. storm troopers marched by as Jacq and young Rijsbergen hurried down their street. A band of Brownshirts stopped them. With their chests puffed up, a dozen thugs clubbed and kicked the two innocent passersby. In pain, Jacq yelled, *"Was haben wir gemacht?"* (What did we do?) The answer was bellowed back, *"Sie haben die Fahnen nicht gegruesst."* (You didn't salute the flags.)

The thugs beat Jacq and Rijsbergen until they bled, and left them to lie semiconscious beside the gutter on the stones of the sidewalk. When the brutes had satisfied their sadistic rage they joined the rest of the hundreds of brawling S.A. troopers. As Jacq came to, bleeding from his nose, his cheeks, his hands, sore and stunned at the outrage of being pummeled and knocked out, he had the presence of mind to suggest to his friend they go to the nearest police station to report the violence committed against them. After identifying themselves as Netherlanders—one an employee of the Dutch embassy—the police officers listened to Jacq's request for an official report. The following day at the embassy, Jacq's bosses, Joustra and Consul General Wolff, suggested that he brief the ambassador. His Excellency told the young agricultural assistant: "I shall try to get the report in hand as soon as possible and take measures accordingly."

Meanwhile, the dozen or so Dutch correspondents posted in Berlin had heard of the assault. All day they overwhelmed Jacq with questions. The following day the leading newspapers in the Netherlands carried elaborate articles about the attack on their compatriots. Rijsbergen's parents were in shock. Mr. Rijsbergen senior, a chief engineer of the Dutch railroads, phoned the embassy to inquire after their one-and-only son. Jacq, who had met them on several occasions, was able to reassure Rijsbergen senior of his son's continually improving condition.

The ambassador's intervention was successful. The Auswaertige Amt (Foreign Office) issued an official excuse, assuring his Excellency that in the future the German people should never commit an atrocity such as done to these two decent Netherlanders!

That bludgeoning occurred after Hitler had been in power only a few months. From then on the "incidents" took on a life of their own—a metastasis, which in this case infected at least seventeen million Germans. "National Socialists" sounds harmless. "Nazis" meant annihilation, leading from the streets to the gas ovens. Nazis. They wiped out the legislative and judicial governing bodies and the trade unions. To blame were the Jew. The "bolshevik-Jewish conspiracy." A culprit had to be found. It was always *"der Jude steckt dahinter"* (the Jew is behind it), because in the German language every child was brought up with the idea *"etwas steckt dahinter"* (something is behind it). For adults it was easy to substitute *etwas* with *der Jude*, because the average German had long heard it ring in their ears.

Jacq turned more ardently, and with a greater feeling of patriotism, to writing detailed reports back to the ministry of agriculture in The Hague. As the restrictions regarding import duties and contingencies increased, he and Joustra had more and more newly issued regulations to analyze, summarize, and relay to the minister.

In a contest sponsored by the Royal Netherlands Agricultural Commission on "which course to take to adjust Dutch agricultural policy to the new circumstances," Jacq showed his annoyance at many of the Dutch experts who adhered to the concept of free trade. Not that he was against it, but he felt the Netherlands had to prepare to become self-sufficient in the event of a German blockade. He held that since the Netherlands was already self-sufficient with respect to dairy, cattle, food, and even textile products, all it lacked was the staple of grain on which the Dutch agriculture depended. Yet, free trade had been basic to this small nation since its Golden Age. However, no one seemed ready to hand a prize to young Jacq, or to heed the warnings he sounded in his reports. Chagrined at being ignored, he began to write more openly, even brazenly, in periodicals and newspapers, until his boss received a reprimand: It did not behoove a subordinate of the agricultural department at Her Majesty's embassy to write articles against the official policy of the Netherlands.

For a while Jacq stopped writing articles. But it was hard for him to restrain himself as he saw Hitler preparing for rearmament and observed the Germans eyeing neighboring territory as new *Lebensraum*: a new word in the German vocabulary. And he loved the attention his articles received through the many responses from readers in Holland. It was similar to the attention he received from his colleagues at the embassy when one day he showed up with a shining black Dodge cabriolet. He had been able to purchase this rare vehicle for a mere few hundred Reichsmark. But the *Strassenkreuzer* (street cruiser) had aroused jealousy, especially in Dr. Joustra's wife. She reproached her husband, saying that it was improper for a subordinate to own a car whereas he, the head of the agricultural department at her Majesty's Royal Embassy, had to bicycle through the metropolis to work, or ride on a bumpy double-decker bus full of smelly Berliners. Soon Jacq, the farmer's boy who was learning city manners and had exchanged his strong Brabant dialect for the high Dutch spoken by his superiors, could not refrain from sending warning signals to his fellow Dutchmen. Thereafter he wrote under the pseudonym "Z."

He turned down an offer to become editor-in-chief of the important periodical, *De Groene Post*, with the excuse that he had just been given official civil servant status in the Dutch government, with retroactive salary. He would not dream of giving up this preciously earned post, which guaranteed a pension with health and retirement benefits—especially since he had just married and longed to start a family. He felt honored to have been asked to take the editorship. Yet even when urged to take it at a far higher salary, and with assurances that he would have to write only one main editorial a week, he declined, feeling flattered but proud that he had resisted the tempting offer of mammon and unfettered ambition.

When a certain Mr. Oppenheim, a wealthy landowner and internationally known trader in cattle, who had moved from Berlin to The Hague sometime in the 1930s, pressed Jacq to take the job by offering to open a bank account with 25,000 Reichsmark in it, Jacq answered, "Even if you double that amount, I refuse to give up my newly acquired post." Oppenheim knew Jacq Millenaar to be a fervent hater of the Nazi regime. When Millenaar turned down the editorship again, he played him a nasty trick.

Oppenheim must have believed that with his money and his possessions in Germany, he could buy time and influence from ministers in The Hague. Oppenheim marched up to the Prime Minister himself and proposed that he fire the minister of agriculture and have Adrianus Millenaar succeed him. When Oppenheim informed Millenaar that he should show up at the Prime Minister's, my father burst out in fury. "God damn it, what's gotten into you to play such tricks? I certainly won't have an audience with our Prime Minister. You'll clean up the mess yourself, make excuses, and tell His Excellency to pardon me, who had nothing to do with the measures you undertook unbeknownst to me. There's not a hair on my head that has ever dreamt of seeking the office of minister of agriculture. Tell him also that my views on the Dutch agricultural policy diverge so much from the present one that I wouldn't last more than a week in that office."

Now Oppenheim was outraged, but he beseeched Jacq to quickly smooth things over with the minister of agriculture. Millenaar did so, not out of pity for Oppenheim, but rather to explain to his ultimate boss the ins and outs of the foolish affair brought about without Millenaar's knowledge. The minister seemed receptive and was happy to get acquainted with the man in Berlin who so fervently defended the farmers in Holland in his publications. He urged Millenaar to forget the Oppenheim business.

How had it come about that the influential, wealthy Oppenheim had gone out of his way to insist that young Jacq Millenaar first take on a chief editorship of *De Groene Post* and, when that failed, to then suggest to the Prime Minister he fire the minister of agriculture and place Millenaar in that office? Of course, Oppenheim, like my father, saw the *Mene Tekl* on the wall. But, why did Oppenheim go further—all the way up to the Prime Minister, a conservative, strict Calvinist disciplinarian? Had my father, at a luncheon at the Hofjaeger together with Consul General Wolff, who had introduced the hardworking, forthright, opinionated, and politically astute young assistant to the wealthy Jew, been so flattered by all the attention given to him, or had he had one glass of wine too many, bragging, "Well, if I were minister of agriculture, I'd know how to tackle those Hitler sycophants and change our government's blind policy."

Years later, as I grew up in Berlin after the war, in the Berlin divided into sectors, when the military occupation of four mighty nations vied to display their power through parades, luncheon parties, cocktail parties, dinner parties, and balls celebrating the control these allied forces had, I well remember how whiskey, champagne, Scotch, vodka, and *genever* flowed, tax free. I also remember the times my father, by that time the Consul-General of the Netherlands and Acting Head of the Netherlands Military Mission, would clatter noisily up the stairs, my mother trying to hold him upright, sobbing and whispering almost inaudibly, "Zhjecq, you promised me ..."

The next morning my mother's soft-boiled egg under the yellow knitted woolen hood would get cold. She would not appear in her breakfast armchair until the coast was cleared of husband and children. She had another headache. And later that same afternoon, when I came home at five, excited and flushed from another thrilling day at the British Armed Forces School, my mother would be waiting for me in her living room armchair, her beautiful face drawn, her soft blue eyes sad. She would stare out of the wide window at the linden tree, her fingers yellow from smoking Du Mauriers and her book open to page one.

Sometimes the book my mother held on her lap was *Krieg und Frieden*, then again *Oorlog en Vrede*, occasionally War and Peace. What was she doing? Comparing family life? Practicing her English? Trying to understand the nuances and shades of Dutch? And then, late at night, after the dinner guests had left, as my father wobbled down our walkway to the front gate where a chauffeur pulled up a Ford Fairlane or a Humber, I would hear him brag, "If I were Eisenhower or Truman, I'd push that button, get rid of the Communists."

So who knows what Jacq Millenaar might have said at the Hofjaeger luncheons after 1928 in the presence of Consul-General Wolff and Oppenheim, with an extra glass of Berliner Kindl and times tense. He had smiled at the tempting offer of the editorship, but the undertakings by Oppenheim had infuriated and embarrassed Jacq, though he still delighted in all the attention he had been getting.

Soon after the Germans invaded and occupied the Netherlands, the Dutch nationalist Socialist Movement (N.S.B.) took control of *De Groene Post*. Needless to say, Jacq was more than relieved that he had stuck with his position at the embassy. Of course, he also soon realized that none of his ideas set forth in articles or submitted for a grand competition would have made a dent in Nazi-occupied Netherlands. The Dutch staple goods were requisitioned to feed Hitler's army, and the Dutch starved to death.

Those who persevered in growing from childhood to adulthood, acquired jobs, married, and found a rhythm in life, must have found it hard to imagine the boredom, the anger, the despair, the senselessness and hopelessness of all those who landed with the street gangs, the homeless, and the disempowered. For the jobless, the hopeless, and the aimless, it may have been easy to drift into an amorphous band or a tattered uniformed troupe where brotherhood and equality supply license to act like those riverboat ruffians Jaakie had encountered in his school days in Brabant. Perhaps they all joined the N.S.B. (Nazi party) under Mussert in the Netherlands.

On May 1, 1933, the airship Graf Zeppelin flew over Berlin as part of the May 1 celebration *"Tag der Nationalen Arbeit"* (Day of National Labor). Jacq and his Leni were walking arm in arm to Unter den Linden, where they wanted to see the airship. By the time they stepped under the Brandenburg Gate and approached the opera building, dusk had turned to night. The throng of Berliners thickened. Their voices lowered, then silenced in mounting expectation. As the airship glided within view and hung over the masses of heads, the crowd exploded in jubilant cheers, rejoicing at yet another Germanic miracle. From a distance the deep tones of *Deutschland ueber Alles* caught on like drumbeats from a jungle. Suddenly, before the last verse of the German national anthem ended, Jacq felt a heavy blow on the back of his head. He could not see his hat fly over the heads of the people out in front of him. But he did feel a fist from behind knock his scalp with brutal force. He blacked out and lost his balance. Leni pulled him upright with the help of a pale and apologetic-looking bystander. Hardly had Jacq come to his senses when he turned around and saw a band of SS soldiers fidgeting and tapping their boots behind him. He clutched his Leni, tightly wrapping his hand around her arm as the vermin shouted: *"Hut ab du Schuft und gruessen (hat off you scum, and salute)."* Leni pressed her hand reassuringly around my father's hand, turned to the black-shirted SS and informed them, with an accent, in a dignified manner: *"Wir sind Holländer (We are Dutch)."* Leni heard the SS soldiers mutter, *"die bloeden Auslaender wissen nicht besser"* (Those stupid foreigners don't know any better.) A man who had caught Jacq's Borsolino hat hurried after them and whispered in Jacq's ear, "You are no scum, it's the black shirts who are." It was the last time Jacq attended any kind of mass demonstration.

He turned to church affairs. In May 1934 he helped establish the Foundation of the Netherlands Church in Berlin. At the time, over two thousand Netherlanders resided in the city. Most of them were either members of the club Hollandia or of the far more posh club Nederland & Oranje. The club members of Hollandia had taken the initiative to set up a Protestant community with the goal of having regular services in the Dutch language, conducting a catechism, organizing a youth center, starting a fund to support the needy, and providing lessons in the Dutch language and history. The first seven names in the Book of Baptismal Records were entered in September, 1934. The baptisms were performed in the American church on the Motzstrasse, off the Kurfuerstendamm. Only five more names follow: No. 8: Adriana Helena Millenaar, baptized on May 22, 1938; No. 11: Bastiaan Hendrik Millenaar, baptized on February 2, 1940. The last entry is on November 11, 1944: Hendrik Gijsbert Millenaar. The three of us were all baptized by the Reverend Heinrich Grueber, a German pastor in Berlin who spoke Dutch, which he had learned from his Dutch grandmother. He was incarcerated several times when he spoke out against Hitler, and openly helped Jews, the Dutch, and anti-Nazis. (In 1961, Heinrich Grueber was to testify against Adolf Eichmann at the historic trial in Jerusalem.)

As it turned out, my younger brother was the last Dutch man to be baptized amongst the ruins of Berlin. In the years before, my mother learned to speak a properDutch from an instructor who had been designated to teach that guttural language through the Foundation of the Dutch church. She had been an obedient and eager student. She still loved life in spite of Jacq's outrage in the aftermath of having been physically assaulted for a second time. True, she detested the Nazis, but she glossed it over as a temporary aberration. And she was so grateful that her brothers had decent jobs again, that girlfriends and sisters were marrying men gainfully employed after the slump of the early thirties. Her brothers and two brothers-in-law earned enough to help support mother Korsten in Cologne. Leni could now buy a toaster, that miracle gadget that roasted soft white bread without burning it if you remembered to take the slice out in time. She could not wait to buy a steel-tubed tea trolley in Karstadt, the biggest, most modern department store. She had to have one, with all the visits they received from friends—her German friends, their Dutch friends. In and out they came for morning coffee, afternoon tea for the Dutch, Kaffee mit Kuchen for the German friends, both for the mixed couples, and wine and beer for the evenings.

On Jacq's thirty-sixth birthday, Leni's mother, Helene Korsten wrote to her youngest son in Cologne:

Berlin, den 10. January, 1935

"…My stay here is very nice. I encountered a well kept household by Leni, and Jacq also has the characteristics of a caring husband. The apartment is beautiful, located quite near the embassy. Of course they have to complete their furnishings, how could this not be the case? They engage in a very cozy (*gemütlichen*) companionship, naturally with mostly Dutch friends, who come over at around eight o'clock …

Last Saturday I went with Leni to Karstadt; one must see that, It cannot be described; but I will not go there a second time."
For now many greetings, in love
Mother

Later that year, on September 15, 1935, the Nuremberg Laws were promulgated: Jews could not have German citizenship; they were forbidden to marry Aryans; they were forbidden to have extramarital relationships. By 1936 there were thirteen decrees by which Jews were excluded. Signs went up all over Germany: *JUDE RAUS*.

Three days before these laws were announced, Leni's best friend, Jannie, her childhood friend from around the corner of the Everhardstrasse in Cologne— Jannie, with whom my mother had wandered over the seven ridges of the Siebengebirge, always Jannie and Leni together with their sisters, entangled in loving life, adventure, and laughter as if there were no tomorrow— Jannie had come to visit Leni and Jacq in Berlin. On

Kakadu: the biggest bar of Berlin

November 11, 1935, just after Leni's twenty-fifth birthday, the three signed their names to a postcard displaying a picture of the most elegant bar in Berlin, the Kakadu. The card shows, in sepia color, an intimate bar, small round tables. Two or three club chairs face a round, polished parquet dance floor. There are starched white tablecloths only a bored old veteran waiter could have draped in perfect, equidistant folds. Each table shows off exactly six white carnations in a vase and two fluted champagne glasses turned upside down lest dust specks alight during a slack time. Champagne coolers stand glistening between the two club chairs; there is music on the grand piano stand next to the drum set. It is hard to distinguish the elongated, swerving figure embossed in white in the center of the dance floor. It could be a mermaid; it looks like a slender female torso. On the menu cards the comb of a snow-white paradise bird is discernible. On the reverse side of the postcard, with a Hindenburg stamp, my father wrote to his new brother-in-law, a violinist in the Bonn orchestra:

Dear Wilhelm,
   We have once again landed in the Kakadu and we especially enjoy the wonderful memory of your company. For Anna and the babies my very best wishes,
Yours, Jacq.

Dear Ones,
   It is still exactly like it was then, also the girl [read Bar woman] who had danced with you is still here and she sends you her affectionate wishes.
Best, your Leni
Besten Gruss, (best greetings) Jannie Stern

Three days later, Leni and Jannie buy *Mein Kampf* and start reading. Mr. Stern, an engineer with the big electric company AEG in Cologne, is dismissed from his job.

Jacq read more and more newspapers, wrote more and more articles, took more and more minutes for the community of the Dutch church in Berlin, and used every opportunity to spend evenings at Nederland & Oranje.

One more time, for one last global fling, the Olympics of 1936 lulled the crowds into suspended disbelief. Newspapers, tabloids, radios, megaphones, microphones announced the who's who for gold, silver, bronze. In the sultry August heat, flags, swastikas and formations of white uniformed gymnasts camouflaged what was later to slouch forth. The spectacle the Germans pulled off for the whole world to see was dazzling. My mother, Leni, only two years married to Jacq, proudly underlined the snapshots she took of the *Fuehrerstandarde* (Fuehrer's flag(pole), *der deutsche Fahnentraeger* (German flag bearer*)*, *die deutschen Teilnehmer* (German participants), *alle gruessen die Fuehrerloge* (All salute the Fuehrer's box), *Hitler begibt sich zur Fuehrerloge* (Hitler goes to the Fuehrer's box), *Blick vom Platz auf die Fuehrerloge* (View from the place

At the Olympic Games, 1936

on the Fuehrer's box), *eine Goldene fuer Deutschland* (A gold one for Germany), *4x100 Staffel* (Relay), *vorläufig Deutschland fuehrt* (Germany leads for the time being). At the end, after snapshots of the giant complex of playing fields, swimming areas, basketball courts, hockey fields, the *Maifeld*, my mother, her sister Maria, my uncle Josef's young wife, Martha, and my pale, hatted father, chatted in front of the forest of flags before the Berlin palace. Along *Unter den Linden* three rows of blood-red swastikas hung in the distance, banners limp. Women strode by, smiling on high-heeled pumps with white or flowery dresses to match and light raincoats over their arms. Chilly weather had been forecast. (On the last night of the Olympics, U.S. Ambassador William Dodd told Bella Fromm, the Jewish society reporter, that he and his family had stood in the park with heavy coats on trying to catch some warmth from the fire pots and that they had taken pity on the ballerinas, who, with hardly anything on, and blue in the face, had executed a dance.)

For sixteen days, Olympic fever crowded out the fact that, from February on, every building in Germany had to have a bomb cellar, that thirty thousand soldiers had marched into the Rhineland, that Germany was deceiving the whole world by masterminding an Olympic spectacle in its capital. My mother took only three photos of Jacq. His smile was tentative, and wan. He knew better. His work was pressing. In Nuremberg, on the party day, Hitler announced he was making Germany independent of raw materials from abroad; and Germany and Japan signed a pact.

When I was conceived on a mid June afternoon or warm night not too far from the *Bleibtreustrasse* or under the Wannsee weeping willow tree, Leni and Jacq overflowed with love. Love fit to bestow on a newborn. After four years of matrimony, a reward. "And this shall breathe life to thee." Because in March 1938, it was not only I—Adriana for my father, Helena for my mother—who was born in the city where soon all hell would break loose. From then on, from the sick brains of Hitler, Himmler, Goering, Goebbels, and their lackeys was born evil that a demon would have been hard-pressed to invent.

CHAPTER 11 | 1938—1939

In June of 1938, as the Brown Shirts vandalized and plundered Jewish businesses, Jacq and Leni, downcast but simultaneously distracted by me, their darling baby, introduced me to their mothers. Helene Korsten-Stockhausen had to be fetched from the St. Gereon church where she knelt daily before the altar, praying that the good Germany would get the upper hand. Antonia Adriana had grown frail, was cloistered with her poetry and the folio Staten-Bijbel. On that visit the meadows in Babylonbrook were lush. The hay in the barn was high and healthy. A cuckoo called in the distance from the willow tree near the river by the dyke. Leni loved these low lands and their unending skies filled with the fragrance of hawthorns in bloom. She loved Jacq. This was another moment supreme. Far away from violence, S.A., S.S., Gestapo, *Verboten, Jude Raus.* Leni wished she could stay in these Netherlands forever. Here was a land that had been neutral during the Great War, a land that was still not taking sides, though its Queen had staked her hopes on England and France soon retaliating for Hitler's lies and terror. Little news of Berlin, Vienna or Prague reached bucolic Brabant. Certainly Jacq did not talk politics. Nor did his family show any interest. It was

a vacation. Jacq showed Leni where the riverboat had
anchored, where he and his brother had escaped the
fiery stallions, where his grandfather on a stormy night
had drowned in a billabong when he had misled horse
and buggy off the slippery dyke. Jacq and Leni strolled
with mother Antonia and her thirteenth grandchild
through the apple orchard. Mother Antonia, in spite of
her frailty, stood tall and erect as a candle. It was to be
Jacq's last time with his beloved mother.

When she died, in December, he dared not attend
her funeral. Kristallnacht had just happened and
shaken him to his core. His Leni was over five months
pregnant. His Adrianneke was only nine months old.
But worse, his work was piling up and the threat of
war was imminent, in spite of Chamberlain's weak
stance toward Hitler, the devil incarnate, according to
Jacq's all-too-close observations. He was heartbroken,
not only at his mother's death, but also he felt sick
and baffled by the events occurring around him. His
Calvinistic heart, his upbringing on the farm where
each season brought pride coupled with humility in
what had been sown, weeded, reaped, and plowed, could
not comprehend the destruction of the synagogue near
them and the shattering of windows and destruction
of Jewish stores on the night of November ninth and
tenth on the Kurfürstendamm, in all of Berlin and all of
Germany, as he read later that day. He understood that
one 17-year old Herschel Gruenspan had had to do
something with his anger. But did he have to shoot an
employee at the German Embassy in Paris? That was
incomprehensible. Yet, when Jacq had heard that the
youth's father had been deported and that ten thousand
Jews had been rounded up, pushed into boxcars and

sent to Poland during June, July, and August of 1938, its meaning barely penetrated his decent mind.

On that dark November evening the dire reality was brought home to him. Several Jews were members of Nederland & Oranje. They often had asked Jacq for help. Other than sharing ration cards with them and picking them up for evenings to and from the club, Jacq was not able to do much for them. True, he had tried to help Oppenheim, once with a nephew whose nails were being pulled out in the Buchenwald concentration camp. Jacq could not believe this, but had boarded a train to The Hague in order to get an affidavit of 10,000 guilders to free the nephew, with the possibility of having him emigrate to the U.S. The offense of Oppenheim's nephew was unclear. Jacq persuaded a notary to sign the affidavit, which would be sent to the Berlin embassy in a few short days. Jacq boarded the night train back to Berlin. Two days after returning to work, Jacq received notice that the nephew had died.

On the dismal night of shattered glass in November, Jacq had driven to the posh district of Schöneberg where the brothers Dr. Arthur and Dr. Eugen Goldschmidt lived. For sixteen years they had been loyal and enthusiastic members of Nederland & Oranje. Jacq had rarely experienced human beings with the innate nobility of these two men. They had given generously each year to the poor fund. They had donated many Marks to the club. They remained loyal to Queen Wilhelmina and sang Wilhelmus passionately. But, they had become cautious. In the evenings they dared not go out on the streets. Jacq fetched them, sharing their delight to move about freely among their Dutch compatriots, to play billiards and bridge, or just chat for some peaceful moments. The night of the ninth, on driving them back home, Eugen said to Jacq: "You've never visited our apartment. Let us show it to you. Won't you come upstairs with us for a little while?" Jacq was in awe at the luxuriously furnished rooms, including the two bedroom suites. On each nightstand, however, Jacq noticed small bottles that aroused his suspicion. He asked them: "What's in there?" to which they promptly replied in unison, "That's poison and as soon as we see no way out, we will take it." Jacq walked from bedroom to bedroom, snatched the bottles and threw them out of the window saying: "Have you gone mad? You've still got the club. I'm still there to take you out every Thursday and if you feel like spending an evening with my wife and me, just phone—phone me anytime and I'll come and pick you up. Anytime."

"Dear Millenaar," they said, "we're grateful to you for inviting us and we'd love to take you up on it. Come and visit us more often and bring Mrs. Millenaar along." But my father was naïve. At age thirty-nine he did not see the pattern. In hindsight, how could he? Before Jacq left the brothers Arthur and Eugen, he said emphatically: "Do not give up hope. Don't." The following morning, the chairman of the club phoned Jacq at the embassy, informing him that brothers Dr. Arthur and Dr. Eugen Goldschmidt/Goudsmit had taken their own lives that night. They each had left big sums to the club.

Years later my father told me of another incident that happened the same night. "You were just a baby, there was loud knocking on the door that startled you from sleep. It was Simon den Hartog and the Catses. I rushed them to the bathroom." He swallowed. I could hardly hear what he said. I had never seen real tears in his eyes. "Blood was streaming down their cheeks, their hands dripped with it, their bodies were bent over in convulsive pain. They groaned. They tried to suppress their screams. Washcloths, towels became drenched in blood. The washbasin, the bathtub, the tiles were spattered. Den Hartog's wife screamed, fell, fainted. It was then that I saw glass splinters in her jet black hair, a shard sparkled on her woolen dress."

"So it was during that night the brothers Goldschmidt drank the poison?" I asked. "Yes, and many others committed suicide. From then on the Dutch and most of the Jews who belonged to the clubs left Berlin, or tried to leave, tried to emigrate, tried to go into hiding. Some committed suicide. Embassies were inundated with visa requests. Hitler, Goebbels, Goering, Himmler, Heydrich decreed: 'Jews are to be excluded from schools, theaters, movies, resorts, public places, libraries.'

"And do you know what?" my father had asked with fury in his voice, "Neither church leaders nor generals nor any other decent Germans in high places protested. Not a voice said, 'Enough's enough.' Not a peep. Not even your mother's brother Joseph. Hubert, Maria, your grandmother, they protested, but only within their living room walls. Do you think they would have marched? Joined a demonstration? None of that. Where were the protest marchers? Were they intimidated when they'd seen synagogues burn, storefronts smashed, people stoned, dragged out from their houses and apartments, beaten and kicked until they bled, were knocked unconscious, killed, taken off in boxcars to camps? No one protested in all of Germany. Now they say, 'Well the Socialists and the Bolsjewicks had already been locked up, silenced.' But where were the thousands and *aber-*

tausenden who could have taken to the streets following a church leader, a strong-willed general, a minister yelling NO to the Nazi vermin?" Instead, it had all been England's fault, England was to blame and had refused peace. Soon after the Reichskristallnacht Hitler signed a pact with France. People talked of Czechoslovakia.

On my first birthday, March 14, 1939, there was hardly any celebration in the Keithstrasse. Jacq and Leni's moods were down. Jacq's because he feared Hitler would walk over Czechoslovakia. He was disgusted at the thought that France and England would let Hitler get away with breaking yet another treaty. Leni's mood was at its lowest, she was to give birth any day. She worried about the small apartment, how she was to handle two babies while Jacq was overworked. Her two brothers in Cologne were a problem. True, Hubert detested Hitler and his lies, but at least he ought to find a job and stay away from women. Joseph favored every step the Nazis undertook. In his mind, marching into Austria, Czechoslovakia, even Poland, perhaps Russia, was justified. The Treaty of Versailles had to be undone. Germany had to take its revenge, repossess her lands. Hitler was the guy. Of course, brother Joseph had said this all in secret and would not let his mother know, for he knew that she had rejected the golden cross honoring her as an "Aryan" mother procreating seven healthy, blond-blue-eyed Aryan sons and daughters. Joseph knew she prayed every day at the St. Gereon, beseeching her God that her Germany would conquer Hitler's evil. Moreover, from her Dutch son-in-law and her *Sonnenscheinchen* she learned regularly of what really went on in Germany. She did not want to live through another war. She did not want her five grandchildren to starve, hear guns, see bloodshed on streets. Leni did not trust her youngest brother, but his wife, the demure, neat Martha, had promised to help Leni once she gave birth. Martha had been married to Joseph for over six years, but they still had no children. Martha was desperate to become pregnant. But Joseph stayed out so late after his work, always with the excuse: *"Na ja,* we had to discuss the *Polensache* (the Polish matter)." Martha would respond tersely, "and another round of *Skat* (a card game)."

On March 28, 1939, Martha stands next to Jacq at a party celebrating the birth of his son, my little brother, Bastiaan Hendrik. The party looks like a carnival, half the party goers are dressed up. My father is the only one with a tall hat and a black overcoat with a fur collar. It's a mixed crowd, Dutch and German. Some are in smoking jackets, ladies in taffeta and lacy evening gowns. Some are smiling, some laughing. Jacq smiles straight at the camera, proud a son is born to him. But it is a faint smile, cautious, not elated. An unruly strand of hair falls over his forehead. Too much *chiripico?* Too much anxiety about the future? Too much confusion? He had found a larger apartment. A longer walk to the embassy, but still off the Kurfürstendamm. It overlooked the Nestorpark. The big advantage was a real *Luftschutzkeller* (air-raid cellar). Leni secretly hoped Nestor, wisest of the Trojan War Greeks, would protect her. A double protection: Jacq, her beloved Dutchman, and through him her precious Dutch passport. They could move to Brabant, live on the family farm. She'd have nine rows of beans. Tulips. Beehives. Outings to the seashore. Zeeland. Thrilling. Jannie, Ruth, Carola, Margot, Emma, Martha, they could all visit her. She would load them with bushels of apples from the apple orchard, bulbs to grow in their city parks.

My mother Leni continued to build herself glorious sandcastles. In spite of the terror around her, in spite of what she read in the German and Dutch newspapers, in spite of what she heard over their newest acquisition, the shining wireless, she remained naïve and kept repeating to Jacq: "But Hitler wants peace, he keeps talking of peace." Jacq answered in exasperation: "Don't you see what happened to Czechoslovakia. *Meml?* The whole world knows he wants Danzig, then Poland and—who knows—the Ukraine. The Italians have swallowed up Albania."

Leni countered, "But why are England and France keeping silent? They believe Hitler. Come on, Jacq, think positive. We must go on our vacation. You need it. You're pale and so thin. We've got to show little Basje to his great-uncle Bastiaan. He'll be so proud. We can stay at Anton and Ella's on the seashore in Scheveningen. I've never seen The Hague, Haarlem, Delft, Gouda, Edam. You must show me those provinces, South and North Holland. Amsterdam. Rembrandt's city. And doesn't Spinoza come from there?"

"Who's he," Jacq, the farmer's son, asked.

"The philosopher," Leni, the city daughter, answered.

"Wasn't Homerus or Erasmus the philosopher?"

"Oh Jacq, you don't know your own history."

"And you Leni, you're blind to what's going on in your very own country."

In Holland, near Scheveningen, Anton, Elly and Leni had persuaded Jacq to go to the Garda Lake in Italy, where Anton wanted to liquidate his Italian bank account. Anton worked in Berlin for the Dutch Central Horticultural Auctioneer Bureau. Once a year a Grüne Woche—an agricultural fair—attracted world agronomists to its metropolis. Jacq had become close friends with ever-smiling Anton, who saw life through rosy glasses. Leni loved Elly for her repartee and crazy German sentence structure. They lived nearby and both strolled their prams in the Nestorpark, where

Vladimir Nabokov strolled Vera's and his little toddler, Dimitri, from 1933 to 1937.

In Jacq's shiny cabriolet the two couples arrived in Zell am See, Austria, early in the afternoon. Clammy from the heat, they first changed into clean clothes. Leni and Elly, the goodly housewives they were, gathered the underwear, sock suspenders, corsets, brassieres and all. Including four handkerchiefs, the underwear list numbered over twenty-two items.

In the Nestorpark with my father

Leni asked the hotel manager to drop it off at the local laundry. No sooner had they had their *Kaffee mit Kuchen* than they pulled on their woolen bathing suits, hurried out over the hotel terrace and stretched out in deck chairs to soak up the flaming September sun. Long car rides did not become Leni. Overjoyed after the insufferable journey, she sighed, "It's idyllic. This is where we'll stay. Anton, forget Italy. We'll stay here for the fortnight." In her exuberance, Leni jumped up and ran toward the beach, her bronzed arms glinting in the sun. She bounded into the water, disappearing for almost twenty-five meters underneath. Soon she was a mermaid bobbing her head above the smooth liquid mirror with the mountain peaks gazing down benignly. The Rhine had taught her not only how to row in a skiff against eddying currents, but also how to hold her breath and swim under a chugging barge she had missed seeing. In between, she sang at the top of her voice.

Refreshed and quite rosy from soaking up the late afternoon sun, the two couples sat down in the hotel dining room and started arguing again, in Dutch, whether to stay or continue on to Italy. Anton was determined to drive on, see Venice, exchange his Liras. Elly could be persuaded either way. Jacq was uncomfortable with both choices. He had not wanted to leave Holland in the first place. He was annoyed that he had been talked into driving so far from Holland, where he should have insisted on spending his precious vacation days. They sat at the bay window overlooking the lake. Not a ripple disturbed the glistening surface. The mountains darkened into their own shadow. Three waiters appeared from the kitchen, each balancing a large silver tray. They strode up to three of the dozen tables. With practiced flair, they deposited the *Abendbrot* platters between the shoulders of the hungry dinner guests. They gestured in unison, like trained soldiers.

Before Leni had time to pass the basket of bread, the chatter of a dozen lazy summer sojourners stopped dead. A loud voice over a radio near the kitchen door announced: "Hitler marched into Poland yesterday, Friday."

CHAPTER 12 | WAR

Was Jacq Millenaar still naïve on May 10, 1940, when the Nazis invaded the Netherlands? Along with thirty-two members of the Dutch embassy Jacq was locked up by the Gestapo in the Tiergarten embassy building before midnight on Saturday, May 11, the weekend of Pentecost, celebrated by my Protestant father for as long as he could remember in his forty-one years. Did he foresee the horror that was to be unleashed by the Nazi-Germans and their sympathizers on all five continents? How was he to know that the Allies would have to set up listening posts in the Arctic, allies in Australia would have to mobilize regiments, because the Nazis would electrocute, execute, gass human beings?

His first reaction to the Envoy Extraordinary and Minister Plenipotentiary Jonkheer E. Michiels van Verduynen's request that Millenaar stay in Berlin had been "No." His instinct told him to flee the capricious violence he had experienced on the Berlin streets for the last seven years. His intuition bade him protect his one year-old son and me, his two-year old daughter, and our amber-armed mother, his wife Leni. His pride at fatherhood, at having attained the status of a full-fledged human being complete with a newly established family, was at the root of his initial refusal.

So why did he stay? Did he believe his German wife, together with her clan of relatives, would give him immunity? Was he so low in the hierarchy of the plenipotentiary ministerial establishment in metropolis Berlin that he could be ignored? Was he more easily persuaded—or ordered—to stay than a chancellor, a first secretary or second embassy secretary? Had Millenaar become too fanatical a patriot who would therefore vehemently defend Dutch interests in Nazi-Germany? Or had his involvement in the club *Nederland & Oranje* and in setting up a Dutch church community in Berlin qualified him to continue looking out for Dutch citizens in a lion's den?

Soon after World War II had broken out. On September 1, 1939 Germans marched into Poland. On September 3, 1939 Britain and France declared war on Germany. The German-imposed restrictions on trade and agriculture had diminished the workload at the agricultural department at the Dutch legation. Jacq was asked to shift his responsibilities and work under the political chargé d'affaires to help supervise the allocation of food rationing for the *corps diplomatique*. He gladly took on this new task, felt competent as his mother Antonia's image appeared before him, doling out equal portions three times a day to her growing brood and hungry farmhands. Had it been his enthusiasm in accepting this latest assignment that led Van Haersma de With, her majesty Queen Wilhelmina's envoy, to leave Millenaar behind as the thirty-one members of the embassy staff were finally escorted by the Gestapo to Switzerland for repatriation on May 20, 1940?

My father might have been shocked at first by the request that he stay, but he may also have been flattered, since it came from "higher up." He always saw himself a 'farmer's boy' and it always nagged at him that he had dropped out of high school. I remember him as always in awe of nobility, titles, and rankings. Perhaps vanity played a part in his eventual response.

My father recounted later that the ambassador had told him, before the evacuation, "You with your German wife and two little kids will be a real drag *(blok aan't been)* on us, especially since we have no idea of our final destination."

Normally, in dealing with this kind of situation, the chancellor would stay behind, or perhaps a chargé d'affaires, or a first or second secretary. In this case, the ambassador explained from the Dutch embassy in Bern, Switzerland on May 22, 1940: "It was decided that Mr. Millenaar, assistant to the agricultural attaché and Mrs. Van der Kroon, employed at the Consulate-General, were to stay behind in order to work and cooperate with the Swedish embassy ..."

My father cried and my mother cried when, on May 14, all members of the Netherlands embassy departed by special train from the Anhalter Bahnhof to the German-Swiss border. Jacq and Leni had been certain they could return to the Netherlands, where Jacq would continue work at the Ministry of Agriculture in The Hague. Instead they had to carry out a policy that had been decided on by the Swedish and Netherlands governments in 1939. The policy provided that Sweden, as a neutral nation, in the case of war would agree to act as a Protecting Power and in this capacity take over Dutch interests in Germany. During World War One the Swedes had functioned as a Protecting Power for Germany in Russia. It was at that time that the Swedish

Ministry of Foreign Affairs established a B-department for serving the interests of certain belligerent nations. The institution of a Protecting Power had been validated after World War I, in international treaties ensuring protection of combatants in the field, prisoners of war, and to a lesser extent, civilians in war zones. The most important of these treaties was the so-called Convention of Geneva in 1929. It is here that first mention was made of a Protecting Power that would mediate between p.o.w.s and the military authorities imprisoning them.

How and why did Sweden remain neutral? Why did it not experience an invasion such as happened to Norway and Denmark in April 1940? In World War I Sweden had remained neutral, as had the Netherlands. The Swedes had been pro-German in their outlook. Economically, Swedish industry did well in German markets. Culturally, the Swedes had been influenced preeminently by Germany, by German values and traditions. Politically, the Swedes had pursued an active neutrality policy and prided themselves on the humanitarian aspects of their task as a protecting power, first for Poland, and then for Netherlands' interests in Belgium and France.

When the Germans trampled over Holland and forced it to go to war before capitulating on May 15, 'economic' and 'humanitarian' considerations coalesced in determining the neutral position of Sweden. The Dutch scholar Louis de Jong introduces his volumes on The Royal Kingdom of the Netherlands in the Second World War by observing that: "History is simple only afterwards."

Iron ore was Sweden's economic lifeline. The import and export of iron ore and steel was central in Hitler's economic strategy. He feared the Allies might cut off access to this precious mineral that was essential to making ball-bearings for tanks, airplane motors, automobiles, guns and other war materials. Good reason to invade Norway and Denmark and thus to have domination of the Baltic and the choppy North Sea. Surrounded by these waters, Sweden's position depended on Hitler's every whim from then on.

Joseph P. Kennedy, father of the future American president, John F. Kennedy, wrote as U.S. ambassador from London, on June 7, 1940, to his Dutch colleague in London, the Envoy Extraordinary and Minister Plenipotentiary, Jonkheer E. Michiels van Verduynen, the following:

> Mr. Minister:
> I have the honor to acknowledge the receipt of your note… in which you were so kind as to advise me that arrangements had been made for the Swedish Minister at Brussels to assume charge of Netherlands interests in Belgium. I have conveyed to my Government the suggestion that the American Ambassador at Brussels be instructed to transfer protection of Netherlands interests to the Swedish Minister, and will not fail to advise you when I am informed that the transfer has taken place.

> I also have the honor to advise you on the receipt of a further telegram from my Government stating that the German Government has now requested that arrangements be made to have the interests of a given belligerent represented by the same Government throughout the area under German occupation. In view of the German Government's attitude, my Government would not be in a position to assume representation of Netherlands interests in any other country which might be invaded by Germany ...
>
> *signed: Joseph P. Kennedy*

Does this letter give proof that, so early in the game, America avoided protecting the interests of neutral powers? Did Joseph Kennedy, Sr. and President Roosevelt hope they could persuade the isolationist Congress to declare war on Hitler Germany soon? No, Kennedy was opposed at that time to Britain's going to war against Germany.

One month earlier, in the British Parliament on May 7, 1940, a great battle raged. Cromwell's words were being quoted by Churchill to Prime Minister Chamberlain:

"You have sat too long here for any good you have been doing. Depart, I say, and let us have done with you. In the name of God, go!"

On May 8, a 'Vote of Censure,' was held by the British Parliament. Churchill, still First Lord of the Admiralty, spoke:

"I take complete responsibility for everything that has been done by the Admiralty, and I take my full share of the burden." Churchill writes in his first volume The Gathering Storm, "... because of the exceptionally prominent part I had played in the use of our inadequate forces during our forlorn attempt to succour Norway."

May 9, 1940, was fuzzy in Churchill's mind (too much *chiripico*, or perhaps brandy?) and he writes:

> "It was a bright, sunny afternoon, and Lord Halifax and I sat for a while on a seat in the garden of Number 10 (Downing St.) and talked about nothing in particular. I then returned to the Admiralty and was occupied during the eve and a large part of the night in heavy business."

Chamberlain, on May 10, 1940, finally relinquished his Prime Ministership as he realized he could not form a national government and as it finally dawned on him that he was not capable of confronting the latest crisis, the invasion of the low countries. The Netherlands and Belgium were stepping stones for Hitler's thrust into France. Churchill's warnings about Hitler's intention had been thrown to the wind for six long years. Now, on that May 10, Churchill's heart beat fast when he was called for an audience with King George VI.

Meanwhile, in The Hague, the Dutch government was taken by complete surprise early on Friday morning of May 10, 1940. Major Sas, the military attaché at the Netherlands embassy in Berlin, had taken it upon himself to pick up the phone on the eve of May 10, and to call the Ministry of Defense. For a long twenty minutes the nervous Major Sas sweated it out before he could tell the A.D.C. (Aide-de-Camp) to the minister of Defense in a garbled and coded message that an invasion in the West was imminent. The major had been given regular information by German Colonel Hans Oster at the department *Abwehr* of the *Oberkommando* who had told him: "Dear friend, it's really finished ... The swine has departed for the West. *Wehrmacht* (O.K.W.) Colonel Oster had dined with Major Sas on May 9 ..."

When Major Sas, for the nineteenth time, warned the ministers of Defense and the Foreign Office in The Hague, they waved it aside as yet 'another war of nerves.' After so many false alarms, the conscientious and overly agitated Major Sas was not believed, though his warnings would prove to be well grounded. Hitler had left Berlin the afternoon of May 9, but so as not to cause alarm, the rest of the high-ranking Nazis stayed behind. Goering and Goebbels attended a premiere of the play *Cavour*. The playwright was named Mussolini.

An offensive in the West? An invasion of the Netherlands? Hearts did not yet stand still on that bright sunny early morning in the low lands after the third night of a new moon. The Dutch, in deep slumber, thought the planes some of them heard might be on the way to attack England. Had not Von Ribbentropp, Reichsminister of the Auswaertige Amt notified the Belgian and Dutch governments by way of a phony memo that French and English troops were poised to march into the Ruhr area via the Netherlands and Belgium? A second report supporting this lie was sent by the Reichsfuehrer of the SS, Heinrich Himmler. By 3 p.m. however, the Dutch Minister of Foreign Affairs,

Van Kleffens and the Dutch Minister of Colonial Affairs, Welters, had been on a precarious flight to England and had made their way to the British Foreign Office to announce that their neutral kingdom had now become an ally of the British Isles, and to request that British troops help out the Dutch military forces. Churchill, as of that May 10 Prime Minister, wrote:

> "Even with the recent overrunning of Norway and Denmark in their minds, the Dutch ministers seemed unable to understand how the great German nation, which up to the night before (May 9) had professed nothing but friendship, should suddenly have made this frightful and brutal onslaught."

Hitler, on May 10, shouted to the masses over the radio: "The fight which starts today ... shall decide the destiny of the *deutsche Volk* in the next *Tausend Jahre*."

That morning at 3:55, two airports in the Netherlands were bombed. Hitler had started his invasion. In The Hague government there was great confusion, but Foreign Minister Van Kleffens and the Minister of Colonies flew to England to plead in vain for reinforcements from the British military. Churchill was unprepared to send a division. On Saturday, May 11, the confusion among top leaders in the Netherlands turned into ever-increasing nervousness until the Minister of Justice took leadership and stayed in close contact with the chief of the military. German motorized units and tanks penetrated Jaakie's beloved province of Brabant, and not a Dutch unit could halt their advance. The French army, which tried to advance against the Nazi troops, ordered the Brabanders of Breda to evacuate. Dutch forces retreated. German troops pushed forward to Rotterdam, where the harbor was the proud gateway to the great trading nation. In the Westland, where Jaakie had served his final apprenticeship and where he had learned how sour grapes could be, the Germans had landed air force units. They overran hamlets, villages, towns, meadows. Like a stampeding herd of mad elephants they crushed every upright thing in their blind charge, as Hitler sent an ultimatum: surrender Rotterdam.

Crown Princess Juliana, her consort Prince Bernhard and their two baby daughters attempted to get to England. They succeeded, on the third try, on the evening of May 12, the eve of Pentecost. The journey was dangerous and slow, not only because of the Queen's one-and-only offspring (Holland's guarantee as a monarchy), but also because of the gold bars the Netherlands Bank wanted transported to England. The British torpedo boat with its precious cargo reached Harwich on May 13. On that same Whitsuntide Sunday, the ministers in The Hague could not agree on whether to stay or to leave. In vain they consulted the constitution, which was of no help: "Never can the seat of government be transferred outside of the kingdom" (article 21,ii). The divided ministers overlooked the fact that, in case of an emergency, the cabinet was permitted by the constitution to go abroad.

In the course of the same day, the chief of staff, General Winkelman, was fast becoming discouraged. In London the ministers Van Kleffens and Welters negotiated with Churchill, who offered a few torpedo boats. The night of May 12-13, the Germans bombed the Waalhaven airport a second time. The Luftwaffe was in command of all the northern regions of the Netherlands. Great confusion reigned among the Dutch ministers. Queen Wilhelmina phoned King George VI, getting him out of bed, to beg him to send air force units. Surprised by being woken in the middle of the night, he said he would pass on the message before going back to sleep. One of her Majesty's officers found her in tears when he unexpectedly entered the air raid shelter in her palace where she had taken refuge. On the morning of May 13, the Queen decided for herself to leave the country, follow her child, the Crown Princess Juliana, to London and govern from there. By May 14, she and all of her ministers had arrived, separately, in London. The Queen had no inkling what her cabinet was up to, nor vice versa. It happened that both parties, after agonizing deliberation, great conflict of conscience and utter despair and doubt, had decided to flee the country and govern their kingdom from elsewhere.

The fighting in all directions grew worse. General Winkelman, along with the majority of Netherlanders, was shattered when, on the morning of May 14, they heard over the radio that their Queen, as well as her ministers, had abandoned them. Hitler was getting impatient; his demand had been immediate capitulation. If not, he threatened destruction of the Netherlands. On Tuesday, May 14, his ultimatum was issued to the military commander, the burgomaster and the aldermen of Rotterdam: Capitulate or Goering's Luftwaffe will destroy not only Rotterdam, but also Utrecht, The Hague, Amsterdam and Haarlem.

Shortly after noon on Tuesday, the center of Rotterdam had its heart bombed out. In the evening the wind turned into a nasty gale from the east. The city that had stood strong for six centuries, since 1340 A.D., was ablaze. Fire and black smoke filled the night. Crackling wood, explosions from electric wiring, flames sparking like lightning, deafened tens of thousands of inhabitants who fled the carnage—utterly stunned and outraged.

By Tuesday evening of May 14, it was clear that the Netherlands' representative, General Winkelman, had to enter a capitulation agreement with the enemy forces. This agreement was officially signed on the morning of May 15. Soon after, the general announced it on the radio. By afternoon the majority of nine million Dutch inhabitants were in shock, as were Jacq and Leni in Berlin. My father twitched uncontrollably, pleading at the top of his voice with my mother: "Leni, eight hundred of our men, Dutch men, eight hundred good, honest Dutch citizens leading decent lives here in Berlin have been rounded up, herded like cattle, incarcerated in the cellar of the police station at the Alexanderplatz. They have no food, no sanitation, no beds, nothing. Strobe lights are shining on them twenty-four hours a day. They can't even sit down. I've got to help them."

My mother's pitch was even higher than my father's, "But Zhjeck, I have no potatoes, there's no milk, no soap for the diapers."

Nevertheless, it was clear that Jacq Millenaar was determined to put up a Herculean fight. He was going to liberate the Dutch in whatever way he could. He prayed for God's mercy and recited a psalm as he hurried over to the Alex prison, talked to guards, ran to the *Auswärtige Amt* to protest on behalf of the eight-hundred prisoners incarcerated involuntarily and for no reason.

"They are civilians, have Dutch passports, and I am accredited to the Swedish Protecting Power and I am here to tell you to let my people go. Do you understand. Here is my card."

DER KOENIGLICH SCHWEDISCHEN
BOTSCHAFT ZUGETEILT

It took several weeks, but those eight hundred men were freed. As soon as my father had informed the Swedish legation counsel, Tor Wistrand—who kept strictly to diplomatic rules—about the plight of the prisoners, Wistrand pleaded at the Auswärtige Amt for their liberty, and together with the secretary, Charlotte van der Kroon, (through marriage a Dutch citizen employed by the Swedish Consulate-General,) Wistrand, Millenaar, and Van der Kroon succeeded in freeing the Dutch men. In all, it had been a relatively easy task to free these men who had resided and worked or studied in Berlin for many years. However, the effort included following official routes to the Auswärtige Amt, arranging meetings with *Reichshauptstellenmeister* responsible at the *Aussenpolitisches Amt* of the NSDAP for the Nordic Lands. Millenaar had to ask his Swedish superiors for permission to participate in meetings held by Nazi authorities. He had to come up with written proof that none of the Dutchmen had been communists, were Jews, or had dealt in subversive acts against the Nazi regime. A German lawyer had to be engaged to negotiate for the Netherlands via the Swedish Protecting Power for the eight hundred prisoners.

"Understand clearly," the Nazi-lawyer told Millenaar, "it'll cost your head, should your statements turn out false." Eight hundred declarations had to be notarized. After several weeks the majority were freed. This was the easy part.

Naturally, my mother understood. My German mother with her Dutch passport, automatically a Dutch citizen by Dutch law on her wedding day, was in agreement with my father. For seven long years she had witnessed the arbitrariness, the cruelty, the anomie on Berlin streets. To my father, who saw to it that we continued receiving our daily bread, she had simply said: *"Ja. Ja, natuurlijk, Zhjeck."* From then on I strained my ears to understand Dutch, which my father and mother whispered to each other, believing I was out of earshot.

In May, 1940, around twenty-thousand Dutch prisoners of war were trucked off to camps in the river Main region. The prisoners were clubbed, bludgeoned into obedience, and cut off from family and friends for several weeks. Hitler had decreed that if these captives signed a declaration of loyalty to him, these soldiers would be allowed to return home to Occupied Netherlands where, in all probability, the same men would have to serve Hitler. Fourteen thousand prisoners signed and were let go. All career officers were imprisoned again in May, 1942.

By the time Queen Wilhelmina and her cabinet had established themselves in the British Isles under the protective wings of King George VI and Prime Minister Winston Churchill, and the day after Belgium capitulated, a new authority took over the administration of the Netherlands. A doctor of law, Arthur Seyss-Inquart, had become the Reichskommissar of the occupied Netherlands. He was born in Sudeten-

Deutschland, an enclave in Czechoslovakia, of a Catholic father who taught classical languages and of a Lutheran mother who was even more nationalistic than her husband. Seyss-Inquart had studied law in Vienna, had joined the *Deutsche Gemeinschaft* (community), an anti-Marxist, anti-Jewish association. In 1938 he had helped undermine the Austrian prime minister, Schuschnigg, and had become his successor when Hitler marched into Austria the day before I was born. A year later, in the fall of 1939, Seyss-Inquart became Generalgouverneur in Cracow, formerly Poland, and for eight months he supervised the deportations of Poles and Jews. In a farewell speech in Cracow he professed his credo: "... in the belief in the national socialist trinity as our highest commandment: the German people, Volk, the power of the Reich, and the will of the Fuehrer ..."

It was this lover of classical music and admirer of architecture, who became the suppressor of the Poles because "all humans to the East of Germany were inferior." This reserved man who prided himself on keeping all emotional feeling under control, presided over the Netherlands in a sly, insidiously paradoxical yet seemingly rational manner. His mission was to persuade the Netherlanders to gradually yield to National Socialism and Aryianism, to come into the fold of the *Deutschtum* of the *Herrenvolk* and quietly accept the idea of a new *Lebensraum*, a New Order under Hitler. The secretaries-general left in charge of government as their ministers formed a government in exile in London were convinced of Germany's eventual victory and cooperated with Seyss-Inquart for the first few months of occupation. But they all had miscalculated: the

Dutch would be tenacious, resist tyranny, and remain independent. They would follow the motto inscribed on their coat of arms: *JE MAINTIENDRAI*. The fight would take five long years.

And Jacq Millenaar in Berlin would see what Seyss-Inquart and his 'little Reichskommissare' in the twelve Dutch provinces was up to. In fact, they were rounding up males, earmarking any man 16 or older, taking them prisoner, accusing females who dared express anti-Nazi sentiments or who had become resistance fighters in the underground. Anyone attempting to thwart Seyss-Inquart and his so-called "enabling" policies was bound for prison camp. First to Vught, Scheveningen, Haaren, Westerbork, then shoved into trucks, buses, box cars, detention camps, labor camps, concentration camps, annihilation camps. More and more prisoners were dragged off to camps: camps with barbed wire, electric wire, barracks, planks for bunk beds with space only for the multiplying lice, barracks with no sanitation, no heat, no privacy, no books. Watchtowers with trigger-happy guards pointing spotlights. Any captive who protested, who failed to salute, who let out a swear word, was removed from camp premises to special punishment camps where they were tortured. Millenaar was to see the camps, visit them not as a captive, but by the grace of the goodwill of some Gestapo Hauptstellenleiter, as an assistant 'accredited to the Swedish Embassy.'

Years later, when time was running out on my father and when he had come to the last of his stories for his six grand-children scattered so far from his beloved Babylonbrook, I found the scribble below on an unnumbered note sheet on what was otherwise an orderly stack of handwritten note pads saved in an old chocolate box covered with a transparent lid. Notepads, box, and memories were held together with a thin elastic band. The text on this yellowed unlined note pad, at times written in the third person, reads as follows:

ONDERMAANS BESTAAN (sublunar existence)

From May 1940 onward the march of prisoner after prisoner, group of prisoners after group of prisoners from Holland to German camps took on surreal proportions that no nightmare could equal, not even the apocalypse. For that horror merely portrayed mythical, unimaginable tales one read in books. And these tales always happened in remote times, biblical, classical, historical. Even the Great War had become historical, unreal. But from May 1940, Jacq Millenaar a petty little assistant was saddled with a task as incomprehensible and untrodden as history's ineluctible march forward can only be. To unravel the history of World War II is best done in a spectrum of hindsight, and by one story at a time. The only thread Jaakie clutched on to for five long sublunary years, was: "what would happen to my children, to my Leni."

By the time the year 1940 had passed into 1941, one cruel event after another exploded into an exponential torrent of random cruelty. All proportion, perspective, rationale were lost. For seven long years Hitler had been given license to remove, incarcerate, torture or liquidate socialists, communists and Jews from his own Germania. From May 1940 on, the same rules were applied to the Netherlands. In Germany the amputation of the good members worked one-hundred percent. In the feisty little Netherlands, always looking seaward, the attempted amputation failed. The Netherlandish lion reared.

Leni and Jacq in their Nestorstrasse apartment were dejected on New Year's Eve of 1940. There was nothing to celebrate. All they wished for was no disruption: no sirens, no air raids, no bombs, no having to wake me and my brother from our restless slumber. My father did not want to hum the New Year's Eve song: *"uren, dagen, maanden, jaren,"* (hours, days, months, years) in the cellar in Dutch. Nor did he want to meet the pushy neighbor, who during the last heavy bombing just before Christmas, had said loudly to him: "One thing you have to admit, Herr Millenaar, if God ever had had a son, then it would have been Adolf Hitler."

My parents wanted peace, to just read a little, first to us. Later, Leni asked Jacq: "Can you read your favorite psalm to me?"

Jacq had asked Leni, " Only if you read *Kennst Du das Land* …" (Do you know the land...Goethe)

That Sylvester night the Allies were kind. Leni and Jacq went to bed before midnight. They held each other lovingly, passionately, dreading the New Year.

CHAPTER 13 | 1940 — 1942

During a short respite in Switzerland, Jacq encountered sunlight, warmth, and had time to compose a rhyme in the guest book of Pieter Kerdel in Arosa:

> There's sunlight in the mountain
> There's sunlight in the dale
> There's sunlight in my soul
> There's sunlight everywhere.
>
> Then the sun went down
> Yet the warmth in me remained.
> In the "Holland Hus" at Kerdel's
> My heart regained its strength.
>
> With fatherlandish enthusiasm
> I so firmly rely
> On the Netherlands' rising
> From an abyss never to die.
>
> With this warmth in my soul
> Strengthened with new force
> I shall fulfill the task
> Awaiting me in the hell of Berlin

Until once again our red, white and blue
Shall wave from every Dutch pole
As Netherlands' glory
Shall shine like the sunlight in our soul.
Arosa, February 1942

How was it possible that Adrianus Millenaar was
allowed to set foot outside Nazi Germany in February
1942, when barely two months earlier the Soviet
counter offensive had begun and the United States
had suddenly been forced by Japan to enter the war?
Did the Auswaertige Amt issue an exit visa in the
hope they could get rid of this persistent Dutchman,
who under the protection of Sweden's embassy, pried
his inquisitive way into Gestapo agencies on behalf
of Holland's prisoners? Did certain Nazis really wish
Millenaar would flee the coop? Choose freedom,
leave his beloved Leni and his children in the care
of *Grossmutter* Korsten until my grandmother's sons,
her sons-in-law, her nephews, her male friends had
conquered all in the name of a Third Reich? Had the
neutral nations, Switzerland and Sweden, made one of
their customary financial deals with Nazi Germany in
return for exit visas to merchants like Paul de Gruyter,
director of a Dutch grocery chain with an affiliate in
Berlin, and a multiple travel visa? He was a dear friend
of Jacq's.

Paul de Gruyter, as I remember him after the war
on a rare visit back to military-occupied West Berlin,
was a soft-spoken Roman Catholic gentleman who
held my hand in his and who looked kindly at me
with melancholic eyes from his smoothly shaven, pale,
elongated face. A long, narrow nose pointed toward
smiling sensual lips. His dark blond hair, cropped above
his ears, was parted, neatly brushed to the side and

held there with shining cream. The lilt of his Dutch sounded like my father's. Both were Brabanders. Both were patriots, courageous and determined to alleviate their countrymen's plight. My mother, my father, and I—who had teenage flutterings—all hoped Paul would marry Anneke. Anneke—a charming, ethereal, witty, and attractive young lady. Her parents were both of good Dutch trading stock and her father was a wealthy man who had set up his business in the early thirties in Berlin. They had a villa built in the Dutch architectural style, a villa we would live in after the war. A villa that had been completed in the late thirties, just in time for an important Nazi to occupy. Paul and Anneke were two sophisticated souls of Dutch nationality who had survived Berlin in their young adulthood. But their union was not to be. Paul entered a Roman Catholic seminary. Anneke became a secretary to the Roman Catholic bureau in The Hague.

On her deathbed on a very hot June day in 1996 in The Hague, when I was researching the archives at the Foreign Office and found my father's poem "Sunlight" attached to his twenty-seven-page legal-sized report written in Bern, Switzerland on February 23, 1942, Anneke slowly answered the question I had never dared ask her until that hot June day. But I bit my lips before I forced the question out. After an endless pause she lowered her weak voice even lower and whispered:

"No, I wasn't raped. Mother was. I lay curled up in a laundry basket covered by sheets and towels. I heard it. I saw it through the cracks of the wicker. The Russians outside were shooting from the *Wilden Eber*, and the Russians inside our house raped Mother over and over again."

The official reason for my father's leave in free Switzerland in February 1942, was that Her Majesty's government-in-exile had granted Jacq Millenaar a paid vacation in the Swiss mountain air. The Dutch foreign minister in London, Van Kleffens, wanted to hear first hand what Millenaar knew about prisoners and their whereabouts, whether the Swedes at the Protecting Power in Berlin were trustworthy in actively pursuing aid and freedom for those thousands of Dutch prisoners. They wanted to know why it was that Millenaar was so anxious to keep issuing the old-type passports and why he was loath to hand out the required new kind of identification papers. They questioned his constant need of more money without proper accounting for it.

Millenaar himself had given three reasons for accepting the invitation to visit free Switzerland after two and a half years of nonstop work. He worried that, sooner or later, Seyss-Inquart would make way for a Quisling, as happened in Norway. When the pro-Nazi Norwegian, Vidkun Quisling, became Prime Minister of Norway, the Swedes had to relinquish their position as Protecting Power for their neighbors, the Norwegians. If Mussert, the pro-Nazi leader of the Dutch *Nationaal Socialistische Beweging* (the infamous NSB), was given free reign to govern over the Netherlands, the Swedes would be deprived of its Protecting Power authority. Then where would Millenaar go? What would happen to Netherlands' state property in Berlin? What would Mrs. Van der Kroon, who did the bookkeeping, much translating, and helped with passport division, do?

The Swedish Legation Counsel, Erik de Laval, was a hardworking, keenly observant and courageous Swedish lawyer and military attaché who headed the Protecting Power's Legation B after Wistrand. Undaunted, he set out to help and visit the Dutch whenever and wherever he could. De Laval was going on a vacation himself at the end of February, and Millenaar needed to be back to continue the unrelenting search on behalf of his desperate compatriots entrapped in camps and living not only in dread but also with little hope. Millenaar's third reason for having taken the vacation offer sooner rather than later was that he feared that the bombing of Berlin would start again in the early spring. He did not want to leave his family alone then.

For almost a whole year, my father had carried my bicycle down our unlit apartment staircase to take me to nearby Nestorpark. Once there he proudly watched over me as I mounted my steel horse and wheeled myself around the paths. I had learned to ride it the same day my parents gave it to me. It had been on my third birthday in 1941. The weather was still nippy. Spring and chirping birds seemed far away. I wore a thick fluffy fur coat with a tight woolen cap to cover my curly hair. I looked like a teddy bear in my bulky woolen knickerbockers. When my father finally helped me get seated on the saddle of this two-wheeled magic vehicle,

My father with brother Bastiaan and me in the Nestorpark

he gave me a little push and said: "Look straight ahead, Adrianneke, and keep pedaling."
I did as I was told.

****

At the end of his long report from free Switzerland, my father wrote:

> "The bombing of Berlin has often been severe, yet the question is whether the bombs had any effect. Personally I'm not convinced. ... My own apartment building was hit by a time bomb which exploded the night after. Not a windowpane was whole and the house was damaged from the outside. And yet, within twice twenty-four hours no one could see anything had happened. Also, the other houses in my immediate neighborhood, where fifteen bombs had fallen, were restored after a few days ..."

In his opinion, the tremendous cost and energy of the Allied flights over Berlin would only work either with a mass bombing attack à la Rotterdam, devastating the inner city into blazing ruins, or with the sending of just a few fighter planes all day and all night long. This would get the Berliners out of bed constantly and thus make them even more irritable and nervous than they already were. It would rob them of energy and cripple their ability to function.

He continued:

"It's about four weeks ago that a few English planes were to be expected. That announcement of flights had a great useful effect because all work and traffic was interrupted. Such air raids are to be recommended."

And this while I pedaled on. We, too, were in dire need of a vacation from the endless air raids, blackouts, food rations, clothing rations, and panic. I picked up more strange words when Pappie came home and whispered agitatedly to my mother: "prisoners, *concentratiekampen, joden,* Mauthausen, *Indische gijzelaars* (hostages), Buchenwald, Professor Regout, Rector Rooyackers. *Ik moet ze zien* (I must see them)."

The real reason for my father's leave was perhaps that he had come close to a nervous breakdown. He had gained enough self-knowledge to recognize that his twitches had gone out of control. Scenes of the ruffians on the riverboat with the copper wiring knocking the steward unconscious flashed through his mind as he saw the barbed wire in the concentration camps. The nightmare of the battle between the champion horses Champi and Emigrant recurred as he saw punishment camps, the police prison, the Alex, where increasing numbers of Dutch citizens were tortured before they were sent off to the camps. He needed a rest. A break from the constant search for his compatriots rounded up in Holland, deported to Germany, and robbed of freedom, dignity, and hope.

Leni, my mother, had urged: "Zhjek, we'll be all right. Mutter and Martha will help me, perhaps Josef.

My grandmother Helene, Adriana, Tante Maria Korsten, my mother at the Funkturm

Maria can come. I could stay with Anna in Bonn. There are Carola, Margot, Pet right here in Berlin. You must go. You must tell them in Switzerland what's really happening, what you see and what unbelievable things you hear. Go Zhjeck. Tell them how the Gestapo sends you from *het kastje naar de muur* (hither and thither) whenever you inquire about the whereabouts of a countryman."

Six Dutch Roman Catholics, including Professor Mr. Dr. Robert H.W. Regout, a professor of international law at the University of Nijmegen (not far from where Jaakie had apprenticed at Summer's Joy) was arrested by the Sicherheitspolizei on July 1, 1940. Regout was being held presumably because he had published an article about the legal status of the Netherlands under occupation. He had traveled to The Hague and other cities, warning academicians and legal authorities about their rights vis-à-vis the Nazis. Jacq was able to visit Professor Regout in the Alexanderplatz prison for a first time.

Since the Swedes had no command of the Dutch language, the incoming mail was first read by Millenaar. Hardly a day passed without a notice about a delicate case dealing with a Dutch person. The only recourse the Swedes had was to take action via official channels. Any other way to lend help was gladly left to Millenaar. So, one day in mid-August 1940, his friend Paul de Gruyter informed Jacq: "Six eminent Roman Catholics have been moved by the Gestapo from prisons in Holland to Germany. The bishop of Den Bosch (the capital of the province of Brabant) asked me to do everything possible to find out where they are."

Most of these distinguished Roman Catholics had been in touch with the German Jesuit priest Dr. Friedrich Mueckermann, who had published regularly against Fascism and warned against Hitler. As early as May 1939, an article had appeared in a German as well as in a Dutch periodical warning against the Himmlerplan. The idea of this grand plan was to abolish the monasteries, sentence prominent Roman Catholics, and execute them. Lists with names had been prepared. Half of the priests would be sent to factories and state-run companies, and the other half would change their diocese. Any form of religious practice would be prohibited. The Gestapo was after not only Mueckermann but also everyone who had been in touch with him or his writings.

Jacq brainstormed, made phone calls, wrote letters, traveled by any means to make contact with a Gestapo agency and inquire who could be responsible for an imprisoned Dutchman. Once Millenaar had traced someone in the Gestapo hierarchy even vaguely willing to listen to him, or had found out who was responsible for internees from the Netherlands, he used his every strand of diplomacy and wit to ask, first: in which prison the Dutchman was held, second: would the Gestapo give Millenaar permission to see the prisoner, third: would it be at all possible for the prisoner to receive letters, packages of food and clothing, reading material, cigarettes, or perhaps money to buy extra food?

In his long report from Bern, Millenaar wrote: "I have broken off virtually all contact with my German friends and acquaintances ..." But how did he look for anyone in that vast metropolis with interminable bureaucratic acronymic agencies such as SS, SD, RHSD, OKW, AA, etc., needling his way into a Nazi haystack?

True, the officials of the Auswaertige Amt were ready to help the Swedes. But only in the case of Dutch POWs could they actually do so, resorting to the Geneva Convention. The Swedes were otherwise tight-lipped, mostly ignorant, and scared of wiretapping and eavesdroppers. Scared of tipping the balance and provoking an incident, a pretext for the Nazis to march into Sweden, occupy it, and deprive it of its neutrality and therefore pride in its altruistic position, if altruism was truly at its root. Remember the ball-bearings made of iron ore? Yet, the main reason for rejecting help on behalf of the Dutch by the Auswaertige Amt was: wherever the Gestapo had been responsible for incarceration, it was not in their domain to intervene. Civil servants at the Auswaertige Amt could not provide any information on civilian prisoners.

And did not the AAAIII (*Abwehr Abteilung* [espionage department at the Auswaertige Amt]) send out a notice stamped *GEHEIM* (secret): "...urgently interested in the personality of this Dutchman ..." The Dutchman was Millenaar at the Swedish Legation. His name was still not known, by the end of March 1941, at this department of the Nazi Foreign Office. They estimated his age to be thirty-five and described him as very hard of hearing and speaking a very good German.

There was, of course, my mother. My German mother. Well, she did have a Dutch passport; thus she was a Dutch citizen who had sworn allegiance to Her

Amt Ausl/Abw **Geheim** Berlin, den 27. März 1941

Abt.Abw III Nr.4524/3.41 g.(III F)

XII 132

An

V A A (über Ausland)

DRB Ausl Meldesammelstelle

Auswärtiges Amt
Protokoll
A 06050
XIV 132
Eing. 2 APR. 1 9.41
Anl.

In der schwedischen Gesandtschaft Berlin, welche angeb-
lich die Interessen der Niederlande wahrnimmt, soll sich
ein Niederländer befinden, der mit diesen Geschäften be-
auftragt ist. Der Niederländer, dessen Name nicht bekannt
ist, wird als 35 Jahre alt und sehr schwerhörig beschrieben;
er spricht sehr gut deutsch.

Abw III ist dringend interessiert an der Per-
sönlichkeit dieses Niederländers und bittet um Hergabe
aller dort über ihn bekannten Daten.

Im Auftrage:

POLITISCHES ARCHIV DES
AUSWÄRTIGEN AMTS
Protokoll

AKTENZEICHEN:
XIV 132
BAND:
R 119111

... urgently interested in personality of this Dutchman

Majesty Queen Wilhelmina. And true, my mother felt closer to the Netherlands, where her beloved river, the Rhine, flowed so freely into the open sea, so far from the dull and bloody Spree in Berlin. My mother had hoped to live in Holland, not the occupied Netherlands. And when my father left for a so-called vacation for free Switzerland, she secretly hoped her Zhjeck would also plead on her behalf to get her and her toddlers out of Berlin and off to the freedom and the mountains of Switzerland. Before my father boarded the train with his precious exit visa, my mother whispered: "Get us out of here. I can't stand it anymore."

She had her friends. She had relatives. I had aunts, uncles, cousins. I called them: "Tante Carola, Onkel Heinz, Tante Margot, Tante Pet, Onkel Jupp, Hella," and somewhere there was "Heinz Otto." Tante Pet was a mysterious figure with pitch black, curly hair, bushy dark eyebrows. She was always smiling. She swung me up in the air, holding me with pudgy fingers and short arms in photographs taken on Easter day in 1942. This Tante Pet Mecki was always in uniform of some kind. In one photo she stands next to my mother, dressed in a Scots plaid pleated skirt with a field hockey stick; in another she leans against the Dodge 1939 cabriolet in a tight leather coat full of pockets. As she swings me up in the air she wears a tightly buttoned woolen dress with two pockets above her sturdy bosom. Even her bathing suit looks like a uniform, tight and trim.

On one of my annual pilgrimages back to my father, when I sat opposite him looking at the cows in the distance mooing in the lush summer field and inhaling the scent of mallow roses drifting through his wide-open window, my cousin Gilbert and his wife Emy were also visiting. Emy, so full of humor and tall tales. My cousin

Gilbert, survivor of the Klinker, a punishment camp of the concentration camp Sachsenhausen. A camp near where we would move after my father returned from his lucky sojourn in free Switzerland.

The Klinker existed for political resistance fighters. The purpose of the Klinker was to work the prisoners to death. The survival rate was next to nil. My cousin Gilbert was exceptional. Out of my more than two dozen Dutch first cousins, he was my dearest, my closest, my most understanding cousin, because he opened up late, as I uncovered late, what had happened to him as a young adult during that time.

Cousin Gilbert said to my father on that summer's day: "I'll never forget: Pet Mecki would say, 'Jacq, I feel sorry for you because Hitler will win,' and you, *Oom* Jaak, always shot back, 'Pet, I feel so sorry for you, because we the Allies will absolutely win.'"

My Tante Maria in Cologne told me: "Pet Mecki? She was a *hohes Biest* (high beast) in the Nazi *Frauenpartei* (Women's Party). She wrote a book. A wonderful person. A Ph.D. An ideologue, totally wrong. Yet, your father liked her. They liked each other. She helped him a lot."

A *hohes Biest*, a friend of my mother's. An aid to my father. He grit his teeth, had his Leni invite her hockey friend, Pet Mecki, many a time. She would swing me in her arms and settle me down on our red couch, and he would ask her:

"Pet, I need to know who is responsible in your SS party for Dutch citizens. Can you find out where Dutch hostages are held?"

Most of the time Millenaar was forced to resort through her to others, because the Protecting Power, Legation B of the Swedish Embassy, had never received official notification of any civilian cases of arrest or internment by the Reichs government itself.

In most cases, Millenaar heard from private sources or from a small group of Dutch free citizens in Berlin or Germany who spied for any piece of information. Someone would let him know a compatriot was arrested, interned, put behind barbed wire or in a cell to be tortured. Immediately he would inform his Swedish chief. In 1940-1941 it was Wistrand, the legation counsel, a reserved, correct and willing diplomat ready to do anything in his legal power to help protect the Dutch. Between May 1940 and the end of his term at the Legation in Berlin, before his new post in Washington D.C., he visited Buchenwald concentration camp and the POW camp Hohnstein. My father was given permission to accompany him.

In August 1940, Millenaar finally got to see the handful of Roman Catholics in the Alexander prison. Dr. K.H. Hoffmann, a "high beast" in the Gestapo and responsible for the Dutch civilian prisoners in Germany, had shown an unexpectedly friendly attitude toward Millenaar when presented with his calling card inscribed with the German words "accredited to the Royal Swedish Embassy ..." Dr. Hoffmann snubbed the gentle, aristocratic-looking Paul de Gruyter, saying: "You have no business here, get out."

That very first time Millenaar held out his hand to one of the six prisoners, the guard accompanying him stepped forward, stopped my father's reaching arm, and commanded: *"Nein, verboten."* (Handshakes were forbidden.) It was also forbidden to speak about the cause of their arrest. Nor was Millenaar allowed to inquire about their treatment in prison. But the faces of these distinguished Roman Catholic gentlemen, after their initial surprise at a visit from a Dutchman, lit up as soon as Millenaar said: "Mr. De Gruyter sends his best wishes."

The mention of the name De Gruyter meant that the prisoners understood contact had been established with their families, their friends, and the bishopric, Den Bosch, the capital of the province of Brabant. In the course of his brief conversations with the prisoners, my father would slip back into the lilt of his Brabant dialect. And from then on, a twinkle in the eyes of these dignified captives would appear, and a bond was tied worth so much more than the *verboten* handshake.

Not until years after the war was Millenaar's friend De Gruyter told by one of the two survivors, the monseigneur Rooyackers, that they always knew a visit by Millenaar was imminent because they were ordered to shave and wash their clothes. They also were given extra food so as to make a decent impression on the representative from the Swedish embassy. Of course, the ulterior motive of allowing an official visit by a "foreigner" was to give to the outside world the impression of "well-run" prisons and camps. Millenaar was even allowed to hand the prisoners chocolate, cigars, cigarettes, and some food. These precious luxuries were collected and lovingly wrapped into packages by my mother and the wife of the chief clerk at De Gruyter's grocery company.

The slender, keen-eyed Jesuit priest and professor of international law, Robert Regout, was the soul and sustenance of this small group of Dutch prisoners in the Alex prison. He led gymnastics exercises, he listened intently to any grief they wanted to share, he had a way of turning their sad mood into a positive one. On Queen Wilhelmina's birthday, August 31, 1940, he held a sermon emphasizing "how proud we should be in bearing our exile like the Royal Family is doing for the sake of God and fatherland." In the Alex prison these first Dutch prisoners had been beaten, kicked, and whipped regularly. Rector Rooyackers was made to stand in a corner for hours on end. Hoeben was tortured in his isolated cell. Once a week they were "aired" for fifteen minutes in a tiny inner courtyard.

Just before these six eminent Dutchmen were transported to the concentration camp of Sachsenhausen in the city of Oranienburg, thirty-five kilometers northwest of Berlin, Professor Regout preached: "Wherever we shall celebrate Christmas, here or at home, it can be merciful for us wherever we are, and perhaps this Christmas feast is more merciful for us than ever before."

That same afternoon, December 16, 1940, Regout, Rooyackers, Van Lierop, Hoeben, and Kusters were transported as the first group of Netherlanders to Sachsenhausen, where on the big stucco square entry building beneath a clock tower, the letters stand: *Schutzhaftlager*. On the iron gates stand the words *Arbeit macht frei* (Work Liberates).

The thousands of prisoners who marched abreast in rows of three or more through this stucco square entry saw a long rectangular building with two-story windows, with a third set of windows under the clock tower. Straight ahead, at a distance of approximately twenty-five feet, was a gallows with rope hanging ready and waiting. An almost nine-foot-high wall met their eyes wherever they looked, punctuated at intervals by nine watch towers. Atop the wall, electric wire was strung from post to post for another two feet. In front of the gray wall was a four-foot scroll of barbed wire. It was electrified. It was just high enough, and the scroll just thick and rounded enough, for a prisoner to fling his body, with arms and legs outstretched, into the instant shock of death.

"On the first Christmas Day, that morning, we found two of our prisoners dead in the electric wire. They had committed suicide: without religion and faith such a Christmas was unbearable." This is what Rector Rooyackers, the superintendent of an agricultural school and one of the five eminent Roman Catholics, wrote about his first Christmas in Sachsenhausen in 1940.

The Sachsenhausen concentration camp, thirty-five kilometers northwest of Berlin, was ready for use by the end of 1937. It was one of the six official camps built between 1933 and 1939, with each of these camps having an *Aussenstelle*, a satellite camp. It was a triangle of 388 hectare with barracks for one hundred forty-six prisoners each. The SS forced five hundred into one barracks. Before 1939 the camp held mostly German socialists and communists. In December 1939 there were over fifty-eight thousand prisoners in the Sachsenhausen camp itself, not counting the Klinker punishment Kommando, and the approximately one hundred satellite camps in and around Berlin.

My family would soon move away from the deadly center of Berlin to just twenty-five kilometers east of this camp to a benign little village called Biesenthal.

Nestor Strasse 13, Berlin

It took my father a mere ten to fifteen minutes on his Swedish motorcycle to ride over to Sachsenhausen. One of these *Aussenlager*, satellite camps was literally under my bedroom window in the farmhouse we went to live in at Easter time 1942. Shortly after my father returned from Switzerland, my mother refused to believe she had to stay in Berlin. She was sure her Zhjeck would negotiate exit visas for us. She was not only disappointed; but also angry when her Zhjeck said: "Leni, how is it possible for you to think that I would ever desert my countrymen? Who would do anything for them if I weren't here? Who would wrap packages if you didn't do it?"

My mother answered icily: "Shouldn't you think of your family first, the safety of us, your children? What are your priorities?"

She forgot that she had begged him to help the Dutch prisoners. But three weeks on her own with us, in spite of my Tante Carola's visits and my *Grossmutter's* stay, had been too much for her. It had been bitterly cold during my father's absence, and there was no coal for heat, no milk.

My father, energized from the Swiss sunlight and the Dutch he had spoken freely, responded optimistically: "Leni, you know what, we'll take up Freule Wttewael van Stoetwegen's offer to move into her country house in Biesenthal. Remember when she left Berlin just before war broke out, and she had said I could always go and live there. So that's what we'll do. The ambassador in Bern informed Minister Van Kleffens in London and my work will be harder than ever. More and more prisoners are being deported from Holland. Hitler wants workers for his war machinery. I heard of a Westerbork camp. Things are getting worse and worse. And I told you the rumor Minister Rickert heard from a German pilot about the killings near Kiev. Three, four thousands of Jews shot in one day. ... Leni, we've got to stay. We'll have a garden. I'll grow beans. There are cherry trees the Freule told me."

The spring and the summer of 1941 were generally chilly and rainy in most of Germany and Holland. Mid-August 1941 Jacq finally managed to get permission to visit the Sachsenhausen concentration camp for a second time. The head of the Protecting Power submitted a written request, and after repeated telephone calls, Millenaar was allowed to see three out of the five Dutch *Schutzhaeftlinge*, the euphemism for political—that is, criminal—prisoners for whom execution awaited at the end of the line.

Officially the Swedes were not allowed to have any dealings with these prisoners. To be taken into *Schutzhaft* (Schutz meaning protection, care) was to protect the power and the privileges of the Nazi regime. Thus, the Gestapo. The SS, the SD (*Sicherheitsdienst -* security service), the criminal police could at will arrest anyone who was a danger to the Reich. Besides ordinary criminals, anyone who opposed Hitler was arrested, including gypsies, homosexuals, and "anti-socials"—that is, the mentally handicapped or retarded. Any expression of a tinge of doubt about Hitler or Germany not winning the war was reason enough to arrest for *Schutzhaft*.

Millenaar, after having written a quite optimistic official report in German to the Dutch ambassador in Stockholm, who in turn relegated it to the minister of foreign affairs in exile in London, sent a hurried handwritten letter about his August 1941 visit to Sachsenhausen in Dutch to the bishop of Den Bosch:

"The gentlemen looked great, were even cheerful and of course exceptionally happy with our visit ... I was allowed to offer the gentlemen a cigar and later the rest of the cigar box as well as the rolls I brought with me. We could speak fairly freely. They have to do light 'housework' and are very often out in the fresh air... They are allowed to read ... Food was decent....I think I wrote you at the time that their transference [from the Alex prison] to Sachsenhausen would mean a step forward, and I'm happy to say I have heard this expressed by the prisoners themselves. They looked 'splendid' and have again and again reiterated that things weren't that bad for them ... My companion and I therefore returned quite satisfied from our trip. And the gentlemen have repeatedly asked us to send this favorable news 'home' as quickly as possible. ...every possibility to liberate them will be undertaken and I will shortly submit a request for another permit to speak to them. ..."

Dr. Frans Govers, who has researched the book *Stemmen Uit Dachau* (Voices out of Dachau), "In honor of the dead and as a warning to the living," writes at the end of Millenaar's optimistic account: "Commentary can be short: this kind of information could have concerned a vacation colony; the naïveté will have penetrated the recipients: archbishop De Jong and bishop Diepen."

Was Jacq Millenaar still naïve? Was he in denial when he could not articulate the horror? Had he verbalized it to his Dutch friends in Switzerland? Or was he learning to be diplomatic, just as he had learned

Concentration Camp Sachsenhausen: Appelplatz (roll call)

to use his deafness to his advantage? Was he overly
cautious, sticking to the camp rules so he could continue
to request permits not only to speak and hand over
cigarettes to Rooyackers, Van Lierop, and the janitor
J. Kusters, but also to see other Dutchmen forced to
march through the gate to the *Schutzhaftlager*?

According to a countryman who was let go after
eleven months in Sachsenhausen, there were over a
dozen other Dutchmen there. He had information on
only two of them, but begged Millenaar not to ask any
further details, presumably in connection with a sworn
oath of silence on his dismissal. Nevertheless, Millenaar
could make out from his informant's generalizations
that horrendous scenes were taking place in this camp
of thousands of prisoners.

What Millenaar probably did not know on his
visits to Sachsenhausen was that, at the end of the
long triangle of the several acre compound was a
Genickschussecke (literally "neck shot corner"), with a
Station Z, a crematorium. Nor did he know that two

of the barracks were for the Jews. He did not get to see the *Sonderhäuser* (special houses) for prisoners of a "special kind." He might have heard that prisoners were tortured on special tables with special apparatus in the places opposite where they were murdered.

Between the summers of 1941 and 1943, eighteen thousand Russian prisoners of war and another five thousand were assassinated, cremated, or worked to death. If loud music was played through amplifiers while he was permitted to spend time with his countrymen, Millenaar perhaps could not distinguish the steady shooting going on in the background. Did Regout, Rooyackers, Van Lierop, and Schmutzer know?

On May 3, 1942, seventy-two Dutch men were shot by this method. Did my father know of the *Stehkommandos*, where those men who did not belong to a work unit had to stand upright, pressed by the hundreds against each other on the *Appelplatz* (where roll was called) from morning at 5 a.m. until evening? There were eavesdroppers around him whenever he talked to a prisoner. The more he was allowed to penetrate the darkness of any prisoner's captivity, the more his deep-seated empathy told him to walk on eggshells lest he be deprived of his precious contact in the den of the beasts.

"More and more men break down; the dying and dead lie on the ground. No one removes their corpses. We're not allowed to take the sick to an infirmary or their barracks... On this day seventy-eight died and in the night of January 18 another sixty-seven died," writes Harry Naujok in My Life in Sachsenhausen. Naujok was a *Lageraeltester* (camp commander) incarcerated as early as 1936.

The alluvial Netherlands is a small nation of nine million inhabitants of all ages, from all strata of the aristocracy, bourgeoisie, peasantry, and seafaring, artisan and professional folk. All of these factions came together as one as soon as they realized that their neighbors, the *Herrenvolk*, were pursuing a relentlessly merciless war to annihilate every single human being who did not look, think, or act like an Aryan as defined in *Mein Kampf,* Himmler's writings, or the SS handbook of rules and regulations. The terror the Nazis had unleashed within Germany by incarcerating even their own German-speaking citizens took on ever more surreal proportions in the abruptly awakened Netherlands. As Nazi boots trampled all over these Netherlands, Hitler's government appropriated and copied every list of Dutch citizens registered in every municipality of the twelve provinces (and sent copies of these lists to Berlin's headquarters, the *Reichshauptsicherheitsdienst,* RHSD). The aim was to spot the slightest opposition against the Teutonic *Blut und Boden,* including men, women, and children. The goal was not to retrain or brainwash them, but to wipe them off the face of the earth.

The men, the women, adolescents, children, and specified groups of people from the Netherlands that were deported to Germany during the summer, fall, and winter of 1940 included the POWs, the military commanders, the Colditz group, the Stanislau/Neu-Brandenburg-group; hostages from the East Indies. On and on the list stretched: political prisoners: illegal Germans who immigrated to the Netherlands (women and children included), Dutch inhabitants who demonstrated on the birthdays of members of the Royal family (including adolescents); laborers who organized and participated in the strikes of February 1941 (women, adolescents included); clergy who publicly denounced National Socialism, young men who refused to join the labor force under Nazi occupation, students who would not sign the declaration of loyalty toward the Hitler regime or Seyss-Inquart's policy; ordinary citizens who had not handed in their radios; entrepreneurs; prominent people of Dutch society; the men and women who possessed weapons, ammunition, and explosives; men, women, and adolescents who had listened to forbidden radio stations; those who had worked for forbidden political parties, those who had published pamphlets and newspapers illegally; and finally, the spies.

As the winters of 1940 and 1941 imposed shortages of electricity and food, the Dutch fighting spirit was aroused. They were ready to navigate treacherous waters. They would unsheathe their lion's claws. They would drive out tyranny. They would abide by their motto, *Je maintiendrai* (I shall endure/prevail). And my father would pray fervently, *Mijn schild ende betrouwe zijt Gij oh God mijn Heer* (My shield and my refuge art Thou, O God my Lord).

On May 20, 1941, the Swedish Legation Counsel, Erik de Laval, and my father left Buchenwald. As they walked alongside the barbed wire that fenced off the barracks where two hundred-and-thirty-two Dutch hostages were kept prisoner, one of them, the president of the Dutch railways, Goudriaan, stepped in stride with my father. He called out to him and pleaded in Dutch: "Mr. Millenaar, Mr. Millenaar, do what you can. We can't stand it here any longer."

The group to which Goudriaan belonged was called the "Indian hostages." When the Nazis unexpectedly and ruthlessly overran the Netherlands on May 10, 1940, the governor general of the East Indies (now Indonesia) took every German resident living in that Dutch colony prisoner. Over two thousand members of Reichs Germans, who worked and traded mostly in arms manufacturing contracts in Indonesia under Dutch rule, were shipped off to the jungle island of Sumatra.

A struggle ensued as to how the German side would retaliate. Seyss-Inquart in The Hague wanted to proceed cautiously and not incarcerate too many prominent Dutch businessmen, and this risked thwarting his tactic of winning the Dutch over gradually. Hitler meddled. His instructions: "For each German in Indonesia, lock up ten Netherlanders." Hitler demanded that *Reichskommissar* Seyss-Inquart prepare a list of thousands of Dutchmen (thirty-thousand for around the three thousand Germans in East as well as the West Indies). Seyss-Inquart reluctantly delivered a list, albeit a short one. He did not want to ruffle the Dutch general public. Moreover, he first needed to get the signature of every Dutch military career officer. Each officer would have to sign a declaration of unequivocal loyalty to National Socialism. Only then would the officers be released from their POW camps. And only then would Seyss-Inquart work on collecting thousands of names in retaliation for the imprisonment of Reichs Germans in the Indies.

On July 19 and 20, 1940, a group of Dutch school teachers, clerks, and government officials on home leave from their jobs in Dutch East India had been bused to the Buchenwald concentration camp. Among these hostages, fifteen women were taken directly to Ravensbrück. Among the men there were also some office holders at the royal court of the House of Orange. A second group of so-called "Indian hostages" followed. This time the hostages consisted mainly of one hundred and sixteen highly professional and prominent members of Dutch society. They arrived at the Buchenwald camp in October 1940. For those who survived and were not dismissed because of age or sickness, most were imprisoned for four years. Because these prisoners were "hostages" and not *Schutzhaeftlinge* (political-criminal prisoners), their status under international law and the Convention of Geneva was murky. The Swedish Protecting Power in Berlin did its utmost to press the Auswaertige Amt to give permission for inspection visits.

Complications resulted from disagreements between the governor-general in Batavia (now Djakarta, Indonesia) and the Dutch minister of colonies and the Dutch minister of foreign affairs in London. The question was: should they free the two thousand Reichs Germans? There were also disagreements between the foreign minister in Berlin, Von Ribbentropp, and Reichskommisar Seyss-Inquart in The Hague.

Meanwhile, I just could not understand why my father was not coming home for suppertime in the warm weather with the birds twittering so loudly. I was itching to go to the *Nestorpark* and ride my birthday bicycle. My mother was full of excuses: "I'm writing *Oma* (grandmother), and I'm darning socks. Go draw me a flower."

She would stroke my brother's hair. He always played right where she was. And she would say to him, "Little prince of mine, what a pretty tower you're building."

And she would continue writing the letter to my *Grossmutter* or my Tante Anna or Tante Martha, asking one of them to come to Berlin right away to help out because her Zhjeck was away so much. This time he had gone to Weimar overnight and Grete, the maid, just did not know how to boil potatoes and she came home with dog meat. (The maid from the country was employed in the city through the *Bund der Deutschen Maedel* [the league of German girls]). My mother would talk on the phone often. She would talk for hours to her best friend in Halensee. It was my Tante Carola; a tall, slender, impeccably dressed woman with resounding, playful laughter. Her daughter was supposed to be my friend. Instead, Rola, a year younger than I was, was my brother's playmate. Those two were always together, giggling and playing with blocks or making a castle in the sandbox of the Nestorpark or a snowman on my bicycle path.

When my father returned from his visit in May to Buchenwald, I jumped into his open arms. "What's Buchenwald?" I queried.

"A forest of beech trees," my mother quickly explained when I could not stop kissing my father and chattered: "Pappie, let's go biking. Tell Mammie about Buchenwald later. And what is Buchenwald and why are you so sad, and why do you and Mammie whisper?"

My father pressed me close to his chest, flung me a bit up in the air, held me tight again before putting me down on the polished parquet floor. In his lilting Brabant accent he said softly: "Adrianneke, on Sunday we'll go to the park, all day, I promise."

"But Pappie," I shouted, so he would really hear me, "why not Saturday, why not tomorrow?"

I tried to pronounce *maandag, dinsdag, morgen* ... I got confused with *Montag, Dienstag* ... and twirled around on the tips of my shoes, ran to the couch, grabbed the pretty cushion, hugged it, squeezed my eyelids tight. The tears did not show.

Two earlier visits by Swedes from the Protecting Power Legation to the "Indian hostages" in the Buchenwald concentration camp had preceded my father and De Laval's visit. Now, on a Tuesday in May 1941, Millenaar and De Laval personally spoke to the hostages and heard from them that they now were allowed to wear their own underwear again; wedding rings and photographs and small personal objects were returned to them; they were permitted to study and play chess. But, as far as packages and letters were concerned, they were still given permission to receive only one package and letter a month and write only one letter home per month. They were grateful for the woolen blankets they had received from the Swedish Red Cross. The drinking water was still bad. It was contaminated. Nutrition was insufficient. It weakened them, and lately large numbers of men had gotten sick and died.

Shoes were a big problem. Even for German citizens the repair of shoes and finding new soles for them was difficult. The hostages were given clogs, but they were of a German type with an open heel, and they were of odd sizes. The result was that walking was awkward, especially on the muddy paths in the camp, so they could hardly make use of the opportunity to get fresh air and exercise on the field available to them once a day. The Dutch Red Cross had been informed and had taken foot sizes in order to provide proper shoes.

After their visit to the hostages, my father and De Laval requested that the camp commander, Koch, allow them to see the Dutch Jews. In February 1941, the German police in Amsterdam had arrested about four hundred Jewish men between twenty and thirty-five years of age on the pretext that they had been carrying weapons, which they were supposed to have relinquished. According to German authorities, the young men were to be treated as hostages. No sooner had they arrived behind the barbed wire of Buchenwald, than their status was changed to political prisoner, which meant their treatment was equal to that of political criminals, thus implying no packages, no correspondence, forced labor, torture, death. Millenaar and De Laval wanted to visit these Jews. Their request was denied. Standartenfuehrer Koch told them the Jews had recently been transported

1940 — 1942 [163]

elsewhere, to near Mauthausen. De Laval had put in a new request at the Auswaertige Amt for permission to visit the Mauthausen camp. Millenaar and De Laval in Buchenwald had heard from one of the hostages that the number of deaths among the Jews had risen to fifty-two.

Nor did my father and Erik De Laval get to see the two hundred *Geuzen*, illegal workers who had distributed anti-Nazi literature and planned sabotage. (*Geuzen* named after the sea beggars who fought in the Eighty Year War against the Spaniards, who had occupied the Netherlands during the Inquisition.) The organization of the *Geuzen* expanded too rapidly. They were unaware that the Nazi secret police in the Netherlands were often aided and abetted by Dutch informers. At the beginning of 1941, one hundred and fifty-seven of its members were sent to Buchenwald, where Millenaar and De Laval were refused permission to speak to them. "They are not hostages. They are political criminals," was the explanation given.

In a summary on the "Indian hostages" of the May 1941 visit, De Laval wrote: "...They seem to bear their difficulties with patience, in many cases with wondrous good humor and in other cases with resignation. A transfer to an internment camp in the Netherlands would undoubtedly be an improvement ..."

Just before the representatives from the Protecting Power left the barracks, the hostage Goudriaan had whispered so desperately: "Mr. Millenaar, Mr. Millenaar, do what you can. We can't stand it any longer."

An SS officer marched up to them to accompany the two foreign delegates to the gate. A man passed them. The SS officer pointed at him and told them it was one of the *Geuzen* who had just been released from the camp. When Millenaar and De Laval approached the liberated Dutchman walking down the Etterberg

Road lined with beech trees, my father asked De Laval to have the chauffeur stop and give the man a lift. When my father, in Dutch, offered the man a ride, the fellow bolted. Another trap. A Nazi able to speak Dutch?

From then on, from when the birds started twittering so busily and when the blossoms in the *Nestorpark* fell and the tiny leaves and catkins changed shape so miraculously, my Pappie very often did not come home at night for his evening meal. My bicycle stood waiting. My mother was on the phone, at her desk, with little Bastiaantje nearby. Whenever my Pappie did come home that spring and summer of 1941, he sat down at my mother's desk. He wrote letter after letter after he had written report after report, phoned, taken trolleys, buses, or was chauffeured through greater Berlin to an SS, SD *(Sicherheitsdienst,)* AA *(Auswaertiges Amt,)* Gestapo station and had penetrated the Alex prison. Sometimes I would stamp my feet on the parquet floor and yell: "Pappie you promised, my bicycle waits to pedal."

" ... In spite of our deliberations, in spite of our fervent prayers, the drama took its course ..." my father wrote in a report. There were seven hundred and forty Dutch Jews in the Mauthausen concentration camp. My father and De Laval were dismissed from seeing them by Auswaertige Amt officials with the excuse that they were political prisoners. A Gestapo member told my father repeatedly that the German police would never imprison anyone who had not deserved it. My father complained in his Bern report that, "regarding these prisoners (the Jews) the Protecting Power had never sent the Auswaertige Amt a serious, official letter of protest." Just before Jacq Millenaar left for Switzerland, he had written to the Auswaertige Amt requesting that the "certificates of death" of all the Jews in Mauthausen be sent to the Swedish embassy. He did

Annual Booklet

Celebration at Nederland & Oranje

not expect an answer, since in the past no response was ever given. Moreover, he wrote: "the Jew in Germany no longer counts, ... Berlin is supposedly to be free of Jews before April 1942 ..." The mass deportations to Litzmanstadt (Lodz) were taking place. The number of suicides amongst the Jews in Berlin was high.

Throughout the year of 1941 my father visited prisons, POW camps, and concentration camps on an average of twice a month. The Dutch prisoners he met, the scenes they surreptitiously reported, either by gesture, facial expression, or a whispered Brabant idiom, were stored in his ever-expanding, incredulous mind. He had little time for reflection. He needed to act. At the Legation B in the Rauchstrasse, he wrote note after note reporting on his findings. He wrote notes to the government in exile, to relatives of the prisoners he has spoken to. He usually walked home dodging bombs. The half an hour's walk from office to home often took hours as he was forced to seek shelter. Once at home, the first thing he did, while holding me in his arms, then again my brother, then me again, was to tell his Leni what awful things he has heard and seen. My mother, Jacq's sole confidante, got the full load; she saw his twitches worsen; she heard his voice quaver. And just as I felt their agony flow into my shivering body, another air raid alarm would sound its long, shrill screech. Basje and I would be hurried down the dark stairs. My father would push the cellar door. The cellar would be full of people standing, sitting huddled. Some would hold gas masks in their hands or on their laps. My father would push his way to a wall. My mother would have to elbow herself through a throng of mumbling people. Reluctantly they would make way for her with Basje in her arms, he sobbing, I shaken, but feeling safe close to my father. His arms

were strong and calm. He would find a space against the
cold wall and slide down. My mother would slide down
next to him. We would wait. The mutterings of the
people, mostly women, would stop. There is the far-
away sound of an explosion. My father does not flinch.
He has turned off his hearing aid, that strange black
shiny apparatus he has been wearing lately. In his arms,
on his lap, I feel him fiddle with a knob of his battery.
He moves closer to my mother. I catch the scent of
her perfume. I lean over to kiss her. The mysterious
liquid she dabs on just before my father comes home
is heavenly. Like the roses in the Nestorpark. The
smell hangs about the dark cellar walls, mixed with the
odor of sweaty inhabitants. Suddenly, in the midst of
the huddled human mass in the dark cellar with the
flying fortresses booming overhead, I stop kissing my
mother. I wiggle loose from my father's arms. I try to
stand up. I want to twirl on my toes. I scream: "Pappie,
you promised to bicycle with me."

On a cold Saturday, January 3, 1942, one week before
Adrianus Millenaar turned forty-three years of age, and
one month before he left us for Switzerland, he gave a
farewell speech to his beloved club Nederland & Oranje,
that "little piece of our Fatherland," where the Dutch
spirit sang, played, celebrated so gloriously for over fifty
decades. The Gestapo had ordered the club disbanded
and its possessions requisitioned. After long wrangling,
the Protecting Power managed to get responsibility for
its funds and furnishings. In his short farewell speech,
Millenaar said: "The future is concealed. Yet we have
kept something, namely the ineluctable wish that God
will soon return to the world the peace and thereby the
freedom to our beloved Fatherland."

CHAPTER 14 | 1942

From the beginning of the year 1942 to the very end of that eternally long year, activity increased exponentially on all fronts, in all parts of the world. The "final solution" was drafted in a villa on the Wannsee in Berlin, a villa near where my father and his Swedish colleagues would find new lodgings after the Rauchstrasse Embassy was bombed. From the *Teppichlegen* (carpet) bombing beginning that infamous day of January 2, 1942, until the day of a general strike by students in the Netherlands in December of that same year, there was fear. Fear of the knock on the door of a Gestapo agent, the panic of a misstep, a wrong utterance, forgetting to draw a blind, passing a piece of bread or a note to a Jew. There was fear of a phosphorous bomb burning you up long after it had landed, a craving for a lump of sugar, the dread of tuberculosis, the crippling fear, and always the hope for an end soon, the deliverance from evil. From that New Year's Day until the end of 1942, the horror marched on ceaselessly, brutally, incomprehensibly. Each side, every faction, dug in its heels. The terror surrounding young, old and middle-aged blunted the soul. The daily terror narrowed everyone's vision to mere survival: just one day, one hour, one next minute.

It was the young men on both sides who dug in. In America they became soldiers, ninety-day wonders; in Holland they went underground, like my dearest cousin Gilbert who became a resistance fighter. On the other side, in Germany

Biesenthal, Neue Muehle (New Mill)

where I grew to school age, my cousin Heinz-Otto was ordered to the East front, first with courage and fanfare, but soon discouraged when, on a home leave, he heard the truth from his sister Hella, who heard from her Dutch uncle through her aunt, my mother, what Hitler really was like. My mother informed her of the Reichskristallnacht and how my mother had removed glass splinters, dressed the bleeding cuts, held a weeping Ruth, Sarah, and Bram in her arms. Leni had just turned thirty. My mother mumbled something about mass evacuations, and she had used the word 'killing.' But if Hella's brother, my cousin Heinz-Otto, refused to sacrifice himself for the Reich's *Blut und Boden*, he could end up in Zweibruecken, the Klinker in Sachsenhausen. So he dug in his heels in the mud of Stalingrad where twenty-two Soviet divisions dug in their heels in the trenches on the other side, with successful outcome.

That spring of 1942, shortly after we had moved to what my parents thought was a bomb-free bucolic town, the first phase of deportations of the Jews from

Amsterdam had begun its spiraling suction into the sealed wagons, trucks, and train loads en route to Sheol. The Jews from the cities of Rotterdam, Groningen, Utrecht followed. The deportations took place at night, during curfew, first to the north to Westerbork in the peat bogs of the province of Drente.

My father had heard about these deportations, as he had perhaps heard from a secretary or an attaché, the rumor of mass murders of Jews in Kiev. He had seen Jews being evacuated from his neighborhood in Berlin on his walks home late at night. At the same time he was weighted down with new reports of Dutch students, Dutch laborers, and Dutch illegal workers being deported to prison camps inside Nazi Germany. He felt discouraged and disappointed at the little he was able to do on behalf of any of his Dutch compatriots. He was desperate more often than not. He had a hard time keeping up his courage.

In one report he writes:

> "It is far from me to consider my ambitions for our Dutch cause as a merit. It was to be considered as a very serious lack of duty if—in these so difficult times for our country and our people—I were not to put all of the strength available to me in the service of the good cause ..."

He talked himself into courage as he braced himself for further hardship: the physical and spiritual torture yet to come from a people gone awry. In his heart he knew that "finding oneself in a state of suffering befinds hope ..."

He was angry at the endless officialdom of the three embassies he had to deal with. The diplomats needed to read every text in their own tongue as well as in French, the diplomatic language. (In Stockholm the Swedish text was translated into French, sent to Her Majesty the Queen Wilhelmina's minister in Stockholm, who had the text translated into Dutch to be sent to London and vice versa.) These texts were typed by secretaries, Dutch and Swedish. Did they gossip about what they read? One of them typed what Envoy Arvid Rickert wrote about what a German pilot had witnessed near Kiev: three to four thousand Jews shot in mass graves.

In London the Dutch diplomats in exile more often than not used French as their diplomatic language. Letters often had long introductions and endings of irrelevant politesse that diplomatic etiquette required. In addition, my father was furious at the way financial matters were handled. The Dutch government was at first reluctant, then downright refused, to dole out state money for Dutch workers or prisoners in Nazi Germany. There was confusion about where the money came from: was it from a special aid fund collected by Dutch clubs and individuals within Germany before the occupation of the Netherlands? Or was the money part of a subsidy given by the Dutch government to Swedish consulates protecting Dutch interests? Whatever the case, Millenaar emphasized how "impossible it is to send some people, knocking on our door for help, away empty-handed and it is of national interest that we help, because most of our countrymen in difficulties are not by any means the worst kind caught in Germany ...."

He had to urge high Dutch officials in London via *note verbale* (memo) to send thank-you-notes to the

Swedish diplomats in Berlin for all the willingness they displayed in assisting the ever growing numbers shipped off to Nazi Germany. These Swedish diplomats did not seem to last long at their difficult posts. They represented their neutral nation in fulfilling the obligations of relieving the Dutch from the hell they were in. The least that these Swedes could do was inspect camps and badger the Auswaertige Amt for information, and point out to them the rules of the Geneva Convention. The least the Dutch envoy in exile in London could do was to continue praising the Swedes in Berlin for the hazardous, thankless job they kept performing on behalf of their protection power task.

The least my father could do was to listen closely to every bit of information from sources—aboveboard or not—and act upon this information by passing it on by word of courier mouth or by sending it on by written documentation. And the very most Jacq Millenaar could do was to get permission to visit his incarcerated countrymen, speak to them personally so they could see with their unbelieving eyes that there was someone in enemy territory looking out for them, assuring them that there was a glimmer of hope. For the Jews the door was closed. The majority vanished. Millenaar was helpless. 'Nothing, nothing, nothing …' could be done for them:"…it is beyond any human concept of cruelty. I dare not give any examples here, which have been reported to me by eyewitnesses … Seven hundred and forty Jews …Nothing, but nothing."

Nothing was done for the Jews in the way of official steps, he complained. Nothing could be done except end the war, which my father thought might be over at the end of 1943, at the latest.

Just before Easter 1942, we had moved to the Neue Muehle (new mill) in Biesenthal. Biesen meaning rushes, thatch, and Thal is dale, valley. Biesenthal was a relief after Berlin-Mitte (Berlin center): Tiergarten district, Nestorpark. We lived in a rambling farmhouse owned by a Dutch aristocrat, Freule R.Wttewaal van Stoetwegen. She had been a member of the club Nederland & Oranje ever since she moved from St. Petersburg to Berlin. She knew my father as the fervent organizer and secretary of that club. She knew he had a passion for gardening, not for fowl, which was her hobby.

At the outbreak of war she had left for the Netherlands and had said to my father: "Millenaar, whenever you feel like it, move to my estate with your family. It's all yours."

Part of this long, rectangular three-storied farmhouse had become one of the many *Aussenlager* (satellite camps) in which approximately forty Yugoslav Serbs were kept prisoner. A Gestapo officer in charge of these Serb p.o.w.s lived in a garret room overlooking the front yard and the big patch of grass bordered by the brook. The comings and goings of my father, my mother and her many German friends could be easily observed from that tiny window on the third floor. My mother's best friend, Tante Carola, her husband Heinz and their daughter, Rola, came to live with us in the guise of my mother needing help and company, with my father absent so much.

On the weekend of Palm Sunday, 1942, between moving us to Biesenthal and carving a wooden boat for my brother Basje's third birthday, my father managed to visit two convict prisons, Luettinghausen and Zweibruecken, forty kilometers northeast of

Cologne. How did he do it? No one was to gain entry
to punishment camps except criminals of the highest
order. What personal contact did Millenaar have?
Well, the neutral Swedes relied upon consulates,
Swedish churches in several German ports, and had
Swedish correspondents in Germany as well as in
Poland. Freiherr (count) Kurt von Schroeder had been
the Consul-General for Sweden in Cologne. He was a
prominent banker, had a high position in the Nazi party
and was one of the 'first personalities' in the Rhineland
with substantial influence. He had given a subordinate
in his consulate, Dr. Keller, permission to visit these
two convict camps.

Dr. Keller had reported in person to the Swedes
at the Legation in Berlin on two previous visits
to Luettinghausen and Zweibruecken. Millenaar
requested to accompany Dr. Keller on his next visit.
Jacq had known from a mother in Holland (Eindhoven)
that her high school age son had been sentenced by the
Kriegsgericht (war tribunal) to two years punishment
camp for possession of forbidden arms. What Millenaar
did not know was that the young Reinier de Jongh
shared this fate with over fifty Dutch countrymen, and
that the very same day Millenaar was allowed in the
Luettinghausen camp, ten more Dutchmen had been
delivered there. Had Millenaar known the names of
these fifty, now sixty, compatriots, the camp director
would have had 'no objection' to parading the convicts
before Millenaar and Dr. Keller. The forthcoming
camp director had understood that these Dutchmen
were not criminals, and he was quite satisfied with their
behavior. They were allowed to receive Dutch Bibles,
and every six weeks they were permitted to write to

their relatives. Once in four months they could have visitors (Millenaar's visit not included). The Dutch were allowed to work together as a group on the farms in and around their camp. Occasionally, a farmer would give them an extra piece of bread or some milk to lessen their hunger during the ten hour work day. Young Reinier looked rosy and healthy and expressed contentment with the treatment in the punishment camp and was 'optimistic' for the future. His attitude was convincing and forthcoming. Millenaar and Keller then went to inspect the very well-taken-care-of camp building with pleasing views of the surroundings.

The following day, in the Zweibruecken camps, the Oberregierungsrat Schulz, the director, emphasized the great distinction between the usual criminals and the twenty-three Dutchmen with whom he was so pleased. He hoped for their sake amnesty would be granted them soon. Were they to refrain from any attempt at escape, their good reputations would not be spoiled. However, Millenaar was asked to admonish one of his recalcitrant compatriots, a twenty year old former clerk from Amsterdam (Davies) who refused to do any work, even peel potatoes, which he said was a woman's task. And so Millenaar took this young fellow to task and impressed upon the obstinate Amsterdammer that he must behave himself, do his duty for his country's sake, so as not to endanger his life and the lives of his twenty-three fellow workers.

His hosts at Luettinghausen and Zweibruecken had put on quite a show, but Millenaar had not been fooled. A 'friendly' church, a 'friendly' camp inspection, a pretty environment, healthy, rosy-cheeked young Dutchmen (called the *Geuzen*, sea beggars), and a 'friendly' reprimand by Adrianus Millenaar, member of Legation-B, accredited to the Swedish Embassy, accompanied by Dr. Keller, attached to the Royal Swedish Consulate-General in Cologne. Cologne, where my mother was born and bred. Cologne where my *Grossmutter* lived with her daughters Maria and Lisbeth, the latter married to the one-armed Paul Keller, veteran of World War I, and daughter-in-law Martha, whose maiden name was Schroeder. My Tante Martha, who claimed she was of nobility, from the island of Ruegen in the Baltic—perhaps a Von Schroeder? Maria, Lisbeth, Martha, Anna, my German Tantes, Onkel Paul Keller, a German uncle.

On that Palm Sunday when my father returned home from Cologne to Biesenthal, he was in an unfriendly mood. He unloaded the burden of what he had seen and heard in Luettinghausen and Zweibruecken on my mother. He complained to her about the nefarious obsequiousness of the Freiherr Von Schroeder, Dr. Keller, and the camp directors. That week he motorcycled forty kilometers back to Berlin, to the Tiergarten district, to read the incoming mail from desperate mothers and wives from Holland, official *notes verbales* from the ministry in London, the embassy in Stockholm; inquiries on the status of the 'Indian hostages,' the 'Stijkel group,' the Roman Catholics, the former Prime Minister, Dr. Colijn, a Miss Kolkman in a single cell, the 'Geuzen' group, the Jews; cannot he do anything for them in Mauthausen, in Buchenwald, in Ravensbrueck, and what about Theresienstadt, and a new name, Auschwitz? He wrote hurried letters to relatives of prisoners, answered as many inquiries as he could, composed new reports.

My mother asked her Zhjeck late that Palm Sunday evening: "And what about *Mutter*. Did she say when she would come? Did you tell her we'll have peas here soon?"

Jacq answered, "Leni, your mother said she'd come in August with Hella for your names day. She wants to spend Easter with Martha, Anna, Maria, Lisbeth and the three grandchildren there."

I had to wait one long week for my Pappie, six long days before Easter Sunday, before he would play with me, show me the rows of beans. And when he did come, on a windy, cold Saturday late afternoon, I ran up to him, jumped in his arms and said: "Pappie, you promised to bring me my bicycle."

He was so sad, his face so wan, his arms so thin, his hands pale, slender. I did not wait for his answer. I stuttered in half German, half Dutch, "Show me the beans, *die Karotten*."

Gardening in Biesenthal

He smiled, picked me up in his arms. I kissed him all over his prickly cheeks, I smothered him in kisses, I wrapped my arms around his neck. He swung me up in the crisp spring air, danced around holding me tight, and started to hum a tune, a distant tune in a different language. Something like 'Perfect Day.'

My mother appeared from the doorway of the farmhouse with Basje holding on to her flowery dress. She walked over to us, took hold of my father's arm. She fell in tune with her Zhjeck. Perhaps the melody was something about May till September? I can't remember.

For me, Biesenthal was a perpetual garden where the grass was high, where there were wildflowers and pretty bushes full of white and pink blossoms. On Easter Sunday, April 1942, Basje, Rola and I had scurried around in chilly weather gathering a few Easter eggs amongst the shrubs. In the month of May my father took me by the hand beyond the brook over a slope past an old gnarled chestnut tree to an open field bordered by cherry trees. The sun was out. We each had two baskets dangling from our arms. The field had sprouted little green plants. "Potatoes," my father said, or rather "*aardappels,*" earth apples. But when he and I walked back hours later, our baskets were heaped with early cherries. We had climbed into the tree branches and picked those fleshy yellowish cherries with bright orange dimples such as my mother had whenever she smiled. From each of my ears four cherries tickled my cheeks as I skipped down the slope back to the brook near our big new farmhouse. My father had strung six cherries each, one pair held by his hearing apparatus, hidden with a bow under his hair. Butterflies fluttered, robins chirped, and as we wandered by the rustling brook and approached the farmhouse, the scent of poppies, daisies, and blue cornflowers overwhelmed me. I felt nauseous. My mother said: "You shouldn't have eaten so many cherries."

Basje and Rola were wet, they had preferred splashing in the brook. Basje had stumped over to my mother who stood waiting for her Zhjeck and me in the doorway.

Basje's skimpy legs muddy, his feet unsteady and far apart, he sobbed uncontrollably: "But the garden is always so far away." That night in May we were sent to bed early with only a dry piece of sourdough bread for the supper we had returned to, too late.

Rola, Adriana and Bastiaan

Since we had settled in our farmhouse in Biesenthal, I had seen my father's spirit and rosy coloring from his vacation in the free Swiss sunlight dwindle rapidly. I noticed his twitches. I felt his despair. Whenever he returned home from the Legation or from a camp inspection, he would take my mother by her arm, walk her around the patch of grass to the brook and over to the slope by the field at sundown, in moonlight, or just in the dark cold or heat of an evening and he would confide in her.

I would lie awake in my bed until I heard his footstep, his voice, or motorcycle engine. Usually I would not hear his tread. Instead I heard the Serb prisoners squabbling under my window. These Serbs were a noisy lot. Sometimes they would start to sing. That is when I would fall asleep. One of them, Milenko, was allowed to help my father with the garden. He would play the guitar on a bench just below my bedroom window. More of the forty Serbs would leave their straw mats in their flea-ridden cellar and come out into the enclosure fenced in by barbed wire. I was forbidden to lean out of that window: "You will tumble on the prickers of the *Stacheldraht*." For it was this barbed wire strung from below my window alongside the length of the farmhouse into a closed rectangle like a giant chicken coop in which the Serb p.o.w.s lived. The barbed wire was not electrified, as I found out two years later.

Whenever my Pappie came home to our farmhouse, I would not leave his side. I clung to his thinning arm, begged him to show me the rows of beans he had planted, asked him what the difference was between tomato sprigs and carrot shoots. I picked apples with him, stacked the wood he chopped, though I never watched him slaughter a sheep. It was fun to be with him, to listen to the few Dutch words he would speak to me. My mother and my Tante Carola ordered me about in German: "This is how you remove the red currants, this is how you must pit cherries, plums ..."

My *Grossmutter* at least gave me back rubs, but she, like my Pappie, stayed away for ever longer intervals.

My mother and all the Tantes who would come to visit, especially on warm weekends, would sit around in deck chairs in front of the cobbled path of the farmhouse overlooked by that small garret window. They would smoke Swedish cigarettes; bursts of laughter would shoot through the summer air. Then again, my mother and these Tantes would lean toward each other, huddle and talk in voices so low, with faces so grim that I, sitting in my favorite spot on the threshold of the doorway of the farmhouse, trying to cut out a little round cushion for the cardboard couch in the living room of my paper dollhouse, became upset at not understanding. Once, before I could walk up to my mother to ask questions, the air raid alarm went off. Basje and Rola, dripping and giggling, skipped to my mother and Tante Carola, who with the other Tantes, flew up from their deck chairs, ran to the doorway, grabbed my hands, and bolted down the cellar stairs, panting in the dark musty cellar space until the all-clear went off.

Had they been whispering about the steady 'evacuation' of Jews from Berlin? Of the suicides of the Jews they knew or had heard about? Of the Gestapo rounding up truckloads of people, bicycles for the front, blankets for the frostbitten soldiers fighting for Hitler in Russia? Had Tante Pet, Tante Margot seen the revolvers every Nazi official and clerk had to carry since an Easter ordinance? Had they found any toothpaste or a roll of toilet paper anywhere? And where had my bicycle gone? Why did it never show up in Biesenthal? Had it been handed in for the metal collection needed for the Nazi war machinery?

Just after Easter 1942, my father had been told via Th. Bakker, a Dutch lawyer from The Hague, that Hitler had ordered a mass execution for the Stijkel group.

For over a year Millenaar and others had worked to free this group of one hundred and fifty illegal Dutch workers under the leadership of Aaldrik Stijkel, a graduate of the University of Amsterdam. He was in his early thirties when he established a framework for a counter government in the event the Nazis lost. In April 1941, the strapping Anglophile fell into a trap as he prepared his escape to England with lists of names for a shadow government. He, together with one hundred and fifty illegals in his organization had been arrested, locked up for one year in the infamous Oranjehotel, a prison on the coast in Scheveningen, adjacent to The Hague. Forty-seven of these prisoners were sent to the red brick, top security Lehrterstrasse prison just north of the center of Berlin. They had arrived there at the end of March 1942. Aaldrik Stijkel and his group belonged to the *Nacht und Nebel* (night and fog) captives. These men and women were rounded up and forced into secret incarceration in isolated cells. No visitors permitted, no letters sent or received, no packages given. They had no contact with the outside world. Their cells were lit day and night. They never inhaled fresh air.

A *Reichskriegsgericht* (Reichs war tribunal) was to try these prisoners with a Berlin lawyer (a colleague of the Dutch lawyer, Bakker) quasi 'defending' these Dutchmen. This Berlin lawyer, Guenther von Rohrscheid, had informed Bakker, saying he was more than willing to help Millenaar and Bakker in their attempt to annul the death sentences of these forty-seven Dutchmen. Hitler thought that a grand public trial followed by the instant gunning down of forty-seven 'traitors' would deter future attempts to overthrow his Reich.

No matter how much effort Millenaar and Bakker put into setting the Stijkel group free, nothing seemed to work. They dreamed up an idea to have the Dutch government-in-exile in London find Nazi prisoners on death row in Britain and the U.S.A. The Auswaertige Amt agreed to wait for such a list of possible exchange "objects." Correspondence on these condemned prisoners would take months and months, piling up letter after letter in all languages. Waiting for answers was excruciating. Anxiety grew to a pitch when word leaked out to two relatives in The Hague about the pending Reich's trial. The pro-Dutch, Von Rohrscheid, in despair, felt he was under suspicion and pleaded with Millenaar. "If you don't help me, I'll hang from a tree. The Reich's court is sending someone to the two relatives in The Hague to interrogate them on who leaked the information about their father, a general, and a brother-in-law."

Von Rohrscheid, fearing for his life, had begged my father to ask the Swedes to find someone capable of making the ten-hour journey to The Hague and prompt the daughter and sister-in-law to tell the *Reichskriegsgericht* informer that it was a member of the Swedish Legation who had leaked the word on the Dutchmen. Of course it could have been my father who had done the leaking, inadvertently. But, it turned out to be the women themselves: they had applied for entry visas to Germany and had mentioned the names, in one case the father, in the other, the brother-in-law, in the faint hope they would be answered and accidentally hear of the whereabouts of their loved ones. The continuing tension of the situation would prey upon all involved for many more months.

It was the middle of the year 1942, and *Grossmutter* had finally arrived, with my cousin Hella, to celebrate their summer's names day with my mother, Leni, alias Helene. Jacq had suddenly become aware of a lessening of activity by the Swedes on behalf of Netherlands' interests. The cautious Swedish ambassador in Berlin, Arvid Rickert, had been warned by a member of the Auswaertige Amt not to draw too much attention (*ruchtbaarheid*) in aiding the Dutch protecting power work lest the Swedes be deprived of this task. Millenaar asked his superiers, in a roundabout way, what his attitude should be. He by no means wanted to see the position of the Swedes jeopardized, yet he was not convinced that slackened zeal on the part of the Swedes would pull the rug from under Sweden's neutral stance vis-à-vis the Netherlands. If the Dutch Minister-in-exile in London deemed the danger unlikely, he would urge Her Majesty's Minister to regularly inquire after the fate of Dutch p.o.w. officers, hostages, etc., which would, in turn, force the Swedes to be more active. The more actively and heinously the Nazis went about committing their evil crimes, the more energetically and deliberately the Allies garnered their forces to combat the enemy, and the less engaged the Swedes in the Stockholm foreign office and the Berlin legation became. The foreign minister (Guenther) as well as the envoy Arvid Rickert accommodated the Nazis in constant fear, whether real or imagined, of a German invasion of their territory. Swedish neutrality turned into a cautious game of diplomacy in order to keep air space and shipping lanes open so Swedish diplomats, couriers, mail, food and clothing packages could pass, censored or uncensored, between Germany's and Sweden's borders. The shipping of iron ore from Sweden to Germany's armament factories continued unhindered.

Publicly, the Swedes kept a low profile in Berlin, attending dinner parties, along with those diplomats of other neutral representatives, and together with German aristocrats, business leaders, and industrial magnates. My father had virtually no contact with the envoy Rickert, who was far too high in the hierarchy of the embassy. Jacq Millenaar was a mere former assistant at the Dutch embassy, an annoyance of little significance to the tight-lipped Swedish ambassador.

But Jacq kept his eyes and ears wide open, observed his Swedish superiors closely, and emulated their adroit tacking in the shifting winds of 1942 and 1943. Even though he watched carefully, Millenaar did not steer a middle course while he was learning diplomatic tact. On the contrary, under the guise of artful diplomacy copied from the Swedes, he collected more and more information from Dutch journalists, Dutch businessmen *à la* Paul de Gruyter, who was lucky to possess a multiple entry visa (*Dauervisum*), Dutch singers who had been left stranded in Germany, and many a Dutch citizen, like himself, who had married a German who had automatically become a Dutch citizen, but with German relatives. In Leni's case, German relatives were numerous.

My *Grossmutter*, Helene Korsten, wrote to my Tante Martha and Onkel Jupp (Josef):

Biesenthal, August, 31, 1942

Liebe Martha und Josef,
... Things are well with us here, except that Leni had an unpleasant surprise (I along with her), namely, the rationing of victuals was drastically reduced and she now stands so to say on equal footing with us. The children aren't very visible. All day long they are "outdoors" (*im Freien*), go into the swimming pool, that is the brook which flows through the garden. Three times up until now the air raid alarm went off, otherwise a heavenly peace.

Onkel Josef was my mother's youngest brother. His wife was my Tante Martha, her maiden name Schroeder. They were a childless couple, but still hoping, after years of matrimony. The dark-haired, slim Tante Martha sped to Berlin from Cologne whenever she could to help my mother with us babies-turned toddlers. *Grossmutter*, my mother, and her three sisters, my aunts Anna, Lisbeth and Maria were anxious for their salesman, Josef, to become a father. The thinking was that the more Martha and Josef visited with us little ones, the more likely Tante Martha would become pregnant. So my *Grossmutter* kept in close touch with her favorite son, who like her own husband, was continually on the road—not with buttons and lace—but with linoleum for the Deutsche Linoleum Werke. *Grossmutter* had spent the month of August with us to celebrate my mother's and her own name day, Saint Helen's. As good Roman Catholics, a name day had more meaning than the day of birth, which hinged on the will-of-the-wisp of a conception day. At the end of the letter *Grossmutter* asked Martha and Josef to come and visit while she was still in Biesenthal.

At this time, the Dutch in the Netherlands were thinking of their Queen Wilhelmina's birthday, but were no longer allowed to celebrate it. My father had just returned from visiting the p.o.w.s in yet another camp, Colditz Castle, on August 29, 1942.

Millenaar and the Swedish attaché, H. Forsberg, had agreed to divide this task.

The attaché would inspect the condition of the camp according to the guidelines of the Geneva Convention, while Millenaar was to converse with as many as he could of the seventy-five Dutch officers who had refused to pledge their word of honor to the Nazi occupier after the Netherlands had been forced to capitulate. It pleased Millenaar how well these captives were informed. Secretly, some of the four hundred English, French, and Belgian p.o.w.s passed on the news they heard through a hidden radio. It also pleased Millenaar that they were quite busy figuring out a way to flee the immense, thick fortress of Colditz. The Dutch prisoners had one big complaint: they knew they would soon be deported to Stanislau, in Poland. They could not reconcile themselves to the fact that in the Stanislau camp they would be forced to live with over fifteen thousand Dutch military men who, at the time of Netherland's capitulation, had not had the courage to refuse to sign their word of honor to the enemy.

These Dutch prisoners were of course puzzled and at first distrustful of a free Netherlander in a double-breasted suit who would step forward, shake hands and address them in their own mother tongue while an SS guard watched to pounce at any blunder Millenaar might make.

A month earlier, in the Langwasser p.o.w. camp on a hot July day, one of the Dutch officers had stared at Millenaar. He would not stretch out his hand, stood stock still at attention, ignored the perspiration trickling onto his neck and the noisy commands of camp guards in the distance. When Millenaar called out: "Yes, Schouten, it really is me, Jaak from Babylonbrook," the fellow relaxed, stood at ease, and even smiled. In the Brabant dialect my father reassured him that he would send a letter home to his folks, telling them their son, Captain A. Schouten, was doing o.k.

At the end of September 1942, when Millenaar accompanied yet another Swede, the tall and bulky Count Adolf Von Rosen, to the p.o.w. camp, Stalag 371 in Poland, another officer looked up, amazed. Captain Henk P. Zielstra had been best man at Leni and Jacq's wedding at the civil registry in Berlin before they were blessed in matrimony by the Dutch protestant minister at a ceremony attended by Jacq's Brabant family and Leni's family from Cologne. It was so long ago, at a time when concentration camps were inconceivable, yet already in existence.

After visiting these camps, Millenaar set up a continuous stream of correspondence with relatives of these officers. It was an easier and more pleasant task than sending the news to Holland of a son or a daughter imprisoned as civilians in a concentration camp or a *Zuchthaus* (punishment camp for convicts), where throughout the year of 1942, ever greater numbers of

POW Camp Stanislau in Poland 9-30-1942
Major Von Faber, Millenaar, Major Röme (O.K.W.), Count Von Rosen,
Dutch General Nauta Pieter, Dutch Major Droste

students, workers, and illegal resistance fighters were dispatched.

In January 1943, Roosevelt and Churchill conferred in far-off Casablanca on a strategy of landing troops on the Atlantic sea wall—what was to become Omaha Beach. The obstacles were overwhelming. Italy had to surrender first, Tunisia had to fall, Japan had to fall, Burma had to fall. There had to be an 'unconditional surrender,' not the wishy-washy Peace of Versailles that in the eyes of the Nazis had been a deception, the 'stab in the back' that had caused Jacq Millenaar to run himself ragged, propping up his fellow countrymen who were starving, dying, being hanged, shot, beaten, worked, and gassed to death.

The more information Adrianus Millenaar received, the more addresses of prisoners were given to him, the more letters, reports, *notes verbales* he wrote and the more money orders and food parcels he sent off. Leni and Dutch co-workers could send parcels and money orders to camps to find out whether the prisoner was still alive and, if so, the more positive a letter Millenaar could write to desperate relatives in Holland.

In May of 1943, Millenaar returned to Biesenthal earlier than expected. He was distraught. He told my mother: "One more word about the Stijkel group and I'm arrested."

Finally, on a May day in 1943, the Auswaertige Amt had demanded the list of exchange 'objects,' to be received by them within ten days. Again Millenaar pulled all strings, suggesting a fictitious list of names, sending lawyer Bakker to Stockholm, bribing a Gestapo officer with a dinner of cognac, sardines, and silk for his wife so he would willingly issue a visa for Bakker.

Once in Stockholm, he would contact the Dutch foreign ministry in exile in London to learn whether a fictitious list of Germans held by the Allies could be put together, fast.

The mission failed. My father was disappointed, disgusted, utterly exhausted. His prayers, his arrangements, his writing, his contacting Gestapo, his attempts at persuading his Swedish superiors, amongst them the elusive Swedish ambassador, Arvid Rickert, had all led to dead ends. Deeply upset, he came home to Biesenthal. That night my mother took her Zhjeck in her amber arms. They loved each other. They consoled each other, "comfort ye." They conceived. It was my youngest brother, who would be born in the worst of times.

On June 4, 1943, at four in the morning, thirty-two of the forty-seven men of the Stijkel group were summoned from their isolation prison cells and told they would be executed at eight sharp in the Tegel prison grounds. It was a half hour's truck ride north from the Lehrter prison. As promised, the execution started at eight. It ended at ten. One after the other was shot. One member of the Stijkel group had started singing the Wilhelmus, the Dutch national anthem, verses six and seven:

"My shield and my comfort
Art Thou, oh God, my Lord ..."

Thirty-two men joined in the singing of the anthem. They had not complained. Most had asked not to be blindfolded. They faced their executioners squarely. They had lifted their eyes.

For fifteen months, a German Protestant minister, Dr. H. Poelchau, had been in weekly contact with this Dutch group of *Nacht und Nebel* prisoners. He accompanied them on their last walk. A priest stood by the Roman Catholic prisoners.

My father did not personally know Dr. Poelchau, since this pastor was closely watched by the Gestapo, but via the ever helpful lawyer, Von Rohrscheid, my father was able to pass on some small packages, which the minister smuggled in by hiding them in an extra set of underwear, which he would exchange in the cell of the prisoner. In this manner, Dr. Poelchau also managed to hide a farewell letter from each member. My father wanted these letters, to send them safely back to the respective relatives in the Netherlands. But Dr. Poelchau had found a good hiding-place for these precious letters and naturally felt he could deliver them in person once the war was over.

Not one letter ever reached its destination. Aerial bombardment of Berlin dashed that plan. Only one item, a New Testament, was later found. A Berlin cleaning woman, who had been put to work in the Tegel prison by the Soviets after the war, had swept the little pocket Bible up with other rubbish. She had spotted the booklet. Had picked it up, opened it, and somehow made out it was Dutch. She brought it to my father at the Consulate-General on the Hohenzollerndamm. She would not accept remuneration for it.

Jacq was ever more troubled by the slow course of the war. In Holland, in the spring of 1943, the students at the universities were asked to sign a declaration of loyalty to the Nazi occupier. Around 85% of the students refused to sign. Some tried to go underground, others could not for fear of retaliation against their immediate relatives. They prepared for the worst: deportation to labor camps in Germany. By May 1943, Millenaar heard that all ex-military servicemen had been summoned to report for transportation to p.o.w. camps in Germany. In June 1943 he had been told of a last phase of the deportation of the Jews from Holland. Acts of sabotage were organized. The civil registry in Amsterdam was burned down, wiping out the lists of each resident in that city. It was to no avail. Resistance groups and illegal workers were rounded up, deported as *Nacht und Nebel* prisoners, and executed.

In November 1943, all hell broke loose in and around Berlin, Biesenthal included. It was called "saturation (carpet) bombing," *Teppichlegen*. Hitler was known as the *Teppichfresser*, evoking images of him squirming on the floor, mad as a hatter, biting the fringe of a carpet.

The Allied bombers flew in formation, blackening the skies. The Americans by day and the Brits by night. They bombed Nazi German cities and citizens to destroy their morale, to end insanity, to annihilate the annihilators.

CHAPTER 15 | 1943

As Jacq became ever more engrossed in his efforts to bring attention to his unfortunate countrymen being ground into pulp in the Nazi war machine, life still went on for his family, though normalcy took on its own character.

Two days before Christmas 1943, my *Grossmutter* wrote to her youngest son, my Onkel Josef, who by then had been forced to join the *Wehrmacht* (army) as a late enlister. In her narrow, Gothic script she wrote:

> "The children are playing alarm, cry like the sirens, and little Basgen is pounding against the door, then the Flak shoots. *Et* Millenaar's Adriana and *et* Weissweiler's Rola are sitting under the table with their dolls; apparently in the air raid cellar. In silent sorrow I think of the last Christmas with you ..."

Grossmutter had once again come in August to celebrate name day with the three Helenes. Actually four, since my middle name is Helena. If I was not a Korsten, at least some part of me could be named after my German blood. So my mother had insisted long before the war.

Grossmutter Helene remained with us from that summer on. My mother needed help. She had not planned to be pregnant. What could she do? She was a good Roman Catholic, and her Protestant Zhjeck was an ever more fervent believer in God, his refuge. But Zhjeck was away too much. My mother was irritable, easily downcast. She feared for Zhjeck's life, not only because an incendiary bomb could burn him up any day, but also because the Gestapo could snap him up any moment with the excuse: "Millenaar isn't neutral enough." So my mother had begged *Grossmutter* to stay on. *Grossmutter* was my center of tranquility in the midst of a cauldron of agitated women, where I was increasingly reprimanded for minor infractions: "Do you have to play on the threshold of the main door?"

Why could these adults not understand? The doorway was the best place from which to rush either to the cellar or to the brook, where an incendiary bomb could never catch me. No matter how loud the screaming of the Allied bombers through the August, September, October, November, December skies, *Grossmutter* would encourage my mother, her *Sonnenscheinchen*, to see the sun behind the clouds so my mother could face her weary Zhjeck with a smile at the end of another bad day. Recently, young men from Holland were coming in droves, forced labor for the enemy's war machine.

Grossmutter would gently clasp Basje and me by a hand, pull us away from our playing "alarm," and lead us down to the musty cellar. That is where I saw snakes and spiders crawl up cracked cold walls of concrete. I would lean against my *Grossmutter*'s well-rounded bosom. I smothered my face in her black woolen or muslin dress. I tried to drown out the eternal drone of the bombing planes, the sirens, the screeching of my aunts "Katastrophe." Always a "Katastrophe." I squeezed my eyes shut. I pretended I was picking cherries with my Pappie in my perpetual garden.

My *Grossmutter* helped my mother become a saleswoman. The fruit and vegetables my father had seeded, planted, weeded, and hoed with the help of Milenko, the Serb p.o.w. under my bedroom window, were bartered by my mother for a sheep, a pig or a calf from the neighboring farms. Friends from the city, Dutch and German and Swedes, would find their way to Biesenthal. In exchange for bad news they would be given a few more potatoes, some goose fat. Sometimes they brought a precious piece of furniture they had moved from a bombed out apartment or villa in Berlin. It would be stored in our farmhouse in the middle of forests alternating with undulating farm lands, where more and more Dutch laborers were forced to slave against their weakening will. Somehow they had heard the name "Millenaar," had found their way to Biesenthal, to our farmhouse, and were handed beans, cherries or an extra potato. My *Grossmutter* would rise from the straight chair she sat on while knitting or darning and walk up to Basje and me, take us by our hand and direct us to the brook to see if we could catch an elusive fish, or walk us up the stairs to her little bedroom and give us a bonbon she had received from her son Josef and had kept hidden. We were not supposed to talk to what seemed like friendly fellows visiting us, only to leave too soon. My mother whispered with one young Dutchman dressed in knickers that slipped off his hip bones, so thin was he. Even the suspenders had been taken away from so many of them. But, when some of these young men left, they seemed much fatter. As these dark figures showed up increasingly often, we would be shooed away hurriedly, like the flock of geese that waddled around our farmhouse. Whenever the Gestapo man living in the garret room appeared, the geese hissed, flapped their wings and off they flew. The geese were also as afraid of the black German shepherd belonging to him as we were. The dog snarled, looked like Red Riding Hood's wolf. The Gestapo man did not spend much time in his room. Where he went during the day I never knew and never asked. All I ever asked then was: "When is Pappie coming home?"

My mother was too busy bartering to answer my question. She was too busy with Tante Carola, discussing the goulash they were planning to fix for supper for Heinz and Zhjeck. They would come home later and later after dark, if they came home at all. My mother was busy talking to a young Dutch fellow I was not allowed to see, busy slicing bread for him to take on his night journey to Holland, because the factory he had worked in had been bombed. He hoped to escape if he was given proper clothes, food, and directions. Only my *Grossmutter* would take time for me and say in her soothing, calm voice: "*Mein Herzchen* (my little heart), your father will be home, truly. Just have patience."

Though patience was not something that came to me naturally, time passed. Life's rhythms, however strange, became incorporated into each new hardship. But there are events seared into my memory that would suddenly bring our situation into bald relief. Only later did I fully realize not only the precariousness of our own lives, but also the uncertain fate of entire peoples, entire nations.

One chilly day, *Grossmutter* had just put four bonbons on her nightstand when it was not the siren, nor the low hum of distant fighter planes that grabbed our attention, but the loud bark of a dog. Ethereal Anneke, who lived in Berlin with her Dutch family and who was supposed to have married the suave right hand helper of my father, Paul de Gruyter, was visiting to pick apples and early beets. My *Grossmutter*, Anneke, and I rushed to the window overlooking the cobbled path to our farmhouse. The Gestapo man, in his black leather boots, stepped up toward the front of our cobblestone path, toward the big doorway. His black dog, on a double leash, was close to his boots. I stood beside my *Grossmutter*, tightly clasping the loosened skin of her still hand. Anneke held my other hand. I stood on my toes, pressed my nose against the cold windowpane. Anneke, slim and beautiful in her red and blue checkered dress, drew me closer to her side. My hot cheek touched the belt she wore around her waist. The perspiration from under the hollow of her arm smelled a bit like perfume, but not the same scent my mother would dab on a Sunday or a special holiday. Outside, the shepherd dog barked faster and louder. I saw the Gestapo man kick another man. He then kicked the man with his other boot. I pulled my hands away from *Grossmutter* and Anneke. I covered my ears with the palms of my hands to shut out the barking. I shut my eyes, then opened them. This Gestapo man continued to kick a thin fellow in dark tunic trousers. It was a young Dutch man, a worker from a nearby factory, farm, or forestry school. My mother had probably given him some food, knickers, and a document in the Swedish, German, and Dutch languages. She had led him on this chilly day to the front door at dusk, thinking the Gestapo man would not return so early. What I saw, before I squeezed my eyes shut for good, was the young Dutch fellow, bent over double. He had fallen to the ground on the cobbles. The dog had a piece of cloth hanging from his jowls, dripping blood. It made the cobblestones black like the knickers the fellow was wearing. It was hard to see in the dusk, but I saw it: the fellow curled up on the cobbles, the dog's teeth, two black boots kicking into the crumpled up shape. The heap of a man wailed as I let go the palms of my hand from my ears. Then, suddenly, the wailing was overtaken by a different sound, a familiar one, a sound I had heard for over half my life. It was the air raid alarm. I was learning how to count, but I had forgotten to count the alarms that day. Perhaps it was the fourth, the fifth. Even though I held the palms of my hands against my ears, the siren sound was followed by the low heavy drone of fighter planes. It grew dark as *Grossmutter* put her arm over my shoulder and Anneke wrapped her sleeved arm tightly over my other one. The scent from under Anneke's arm was stronger, like the earth my father dug when he shoveled for potatoes. *Grossmutter* stood stock still as the fighter planes flew low like a dotted giant black carpet. She soothed me saying: *"Mein Herzchen*, they fly away, *keine Angst* (no fear). No matter how hard I squeezed the palms of my hands against my earlobes, the explosion invaded my head. The glass of the window against which I had just pushed my nose shuddered then exploded in front of my eyes. The fighter plane sparkled in the dark sky like the fire my father lit in the fireplace of the big hall of our farmhouse on a chilled late afternoon.

The sound of the explosion struck my ears. The flash in the sky turned black. The fighter plane dropped like a sparkling branch then was extinguished in a heap of ashes. I screamed: "What will happen to the people in the plane?" I yelled. I screeched that phrase into the dark window until I drowned out the

My father gathering kindling

panic in my heart, until Anneke, decades later, as she lay dying on her bed in The Hague, said: "Adriana, do you remember when you stood at that window and shouted, 'What will happen to the people, the people in the plane?'"

Were my parents' senses already blunted by Christmas 1943 at the misery they experienced day in, day out? Did they shut their distraught minds, doing what they could on a daily basis, waiting for relief once young energetic and rapidly trained Allied soldiers and marines reached the intractable evil? Did my father pray more fervently for liberation while lying low to escape the Gestapo's handcuffs? Frantically he wrapped packages at the Legation and sent off money orders to ever more increasing numbers of prisoners. Did my

Netherlands Embassy, Rauchstrasse 10, Berlin-Tiergarten

mother become depressed, carrying a child to term as a good Roman Catholic woman should? Was she desperate because she could not grasp the perversities her countrymen were perpetrating?

During the night of November 22-23, 1943, Allied bombs had smashed to smithereens the proud Dutch neo-classical embassy building in the Rauchstrasse 10, which until that November night had functioned as the Swedish Legation-B, the Protecting Power for the Netherlands, with Jacq Millenaar as its hub, keeping everyone engaged on behalf of his passionately beloved compatriots. At 6.30 p.m., when the building was empty except for the doorman and two chauffeurs, an incendiary bomb had lit the elevator shaft and demolished the square structure. Completely gone was this proud symbol of ex-territoriality and its diplomatic immunity. Not one scrap of a document was saved. The doorman and the chauffeurs had managed to flee the air raid shelter, but with serious wounds. Crocodiles from the nearby Berlin-Zoo had shambled into the river Spree. They were shot, and the cold Spree turned red.

Count Von Rosen, legation counsel and head of the Protecting Power, Legation-B since 1942, during inspection of the embassy ruins with Millenaar, had driven into a bomb crater and had to be flown to Sweden for treatment of severe injuries. Millenaar, unscathed, was relieved at the absence of his passive superior. A nervous, heavy-set six-footer; Von Rosen had shown little sympathy or empathy for the plight of the Dutch. Millenaar poured out his heart to one Mr. Hebbel, sent from the Stockholm foreign office to size up the damage done to the embassy and various other Swedish-occupied buildings in the Rauchstrasse and immediate neighborhood. Millenaar complained that the p.o.w.s. had been visited only eight times during the whole year of 1943. Von Rosen had inspected just two camps. For the civilian prisoners and for those who were to be executed, Count Von Rosen had paid no attention whatsoever, and left their fate to Millenaar. Nor were the forced laborers cared for. Millenaar spoke up loud and clear, pounding his fist on the table:

"It is Sweden's duty as the friend of the Netherlands to protect Dutch interests and to lend assistance in whatever way possible. After all, the Netherlands-Swedish treaty of 1939 was a binding one."

The continual bombing, the shortage of food and clothing, the worsening conditions for the thousands of prisoners and laborers, the deportations, the steady and systematic annihilation of the Jews, the despair of the 'free' Dutch citizens in Berlin and the Dutch in occupied Netherlands, had not yet quite exhausted Jacq Millenaar. In fact, he became more resolute. He gritted his teeth. He remembered Apostle Paul's words: ".. knowing that the oppression works a state of suffering; and the finding oneself in a state of suffering befinds hope ..."

He read Job, he hummed the sixth verse of his Wilhelmus. And when he came home to Biesenthal, ashen but by no means broken from the November bombing, and saw how his Leni spread her arms to lock him in a loving embrace, and when he felt the little quivers in her womb against the hollow of his stomach, he kissed her passionately, thanking the Lord in silence with "Thy Will be done." I ran up to him from under the table where Basje, Rola, and I had been playing at alarm, imitating the thrumming of bomber planes, and jumped up into his thin arms begging: "Pappie, let me light the fire."

And then soon after the bombing of my father's office, where he had worked for fifteen years, came the last Christmas we were to be together. We were happy. We sang together. We laughed together. My father performed sleight-of-hand tricks. My father loved doing magic, after the war he often entertained guests and especially kids by performing magic tricks. I don't know when or where he learned. He was good at it. Basje, Rola, and I were four and five years old. We laughed.

My mother had stooped to pick up a present from under the little tree, unwrapped it, held it to her mouth and bit into what looked like an apple. She bent over, made funny noises, slobbered from the apple-like fruit as if it were dripping all over the bulge of her tummy onto the floor. We burst out laughing all over again.

"A peach, a peach," Tante Carola and Onkel Heinz spluttered in unison. It was a wooden peach. It looked like a giant cherry, like one I had picked with my father with the yellowish pink dimple in it, like the dimple in my mother's cheek.

Grossmutter, at the head of the table, began a tune. She hummed sonorously. It was as if the silver bells on the little tree in our big hall had turned into a choir of angels, so beautiful did her soprano voice resound.

We joined in. We sang the carol together. We sang *Stille Nacht, Heilige Nacht*. We sang together for the last time. And we sang in German. A German written long before 1939, long before 1914.

To this day I sit in a front pew in church because I am as hard of hearing as my father was. I look up at the two pale chubby angels perched on a Corinthian column. Whenever tears well up, I try to laugh the way we laughed at that last Christmas together.

After that cold, snowy, happy Christmas, Basje went manic.

After that Christmas, my mother became despondent.

After that Christmas, Tante Carola kept wailing: *Eine Katastrophe*.

After that Christmas, Onkel Heinz whispered to my father: "Jacq, what if Hitler wins after all?"

After that Christmas I for the first time repeated what my father had asked me to say in Dutch: "*Onze Vader die in den Hemelen zijt, Uw Wil geschiedde ...*" (Our Father who art in Heaven.)

After that Christmas, my *Grossmutter* stayed calm, straight as a ramrod. Her name was Helene Stockhausen. After that Christmas a lump stuck within me, like a New England lyme tick. That Christmas snow fell.

In January 1944 my father's pleas were answered. His new office in another part of the Rauchstrasse was equipped with new furniture, filing cabinets, pens, paper, and a typewriter. He was given clothing to distribute amongst his Dutch assistants in the Legation and in the passport departments. The Swedes had also sent extra food. Best of all, a young, energetic and enthusiastic thirty-five-year-old Swede by the name of Börje Oesterlind had come to the Legation-B in Berlin to take over the difficult work that the shell-shocked Count Von Rosen seemed unable to perform. Oesterlind was appointed to the Legation to visit and inspect p.o.w. camps regularly. The undaunted young Swede visited the Dutch in the prisoner of war camps five times during January 1944 alone. (In the whole year of 1943 p.o.w. camps had been visited eight times.) In February 1944 Oesterlind went another four times to the Dutch p.o.w.s This bright and eager Swede knew Dutch through summer courses he had taken at The Hague's Peace Palace. Jacq Millenaar supervised the civilian prisoners and the slave laborers with help from Lagergren. They sent as many food parcels, money orders, and medicines as they could to the addresses of prisoners Jacq found via the various underground organizations sprouting up in Berlin. He relied upon young Dutch students and workers, and church-affiliated helpers who had managed to flee their factories, camps, barracks or billeted homes in the wake of the more frequent and increasingly successful Allied bombings.

My baby brother, Hendrik Gijsbert, was born on a bitterly cold day, January 18, 1944. Conditions could not have been more bleak and desperate. Scarlet fever and diphtheria raged throughout Holland. The long-awaited invasion of Western Europe by the Americans and British had not occurred, and Queen Wilhelmina in her broadcasts from London no longer mentioned that hopeful prospect. The Russians were stymied in their efforts to expel the invading Germans despite horrific losses on both sides. Efforts to have the baby delivered in the home of a midwife were disrupted by a bombong attack. As the desperate and distraught midwife tied my mother's arms and legs to facilitate and speed the birthing process, my mother screamed hysterically as she was rushed to a hospital for the delivery.

Grossmutter reported to her youngest son Josef and his wife Martha, a day after my little brother was born: "I just returned from the Biesenthaler hospital where yesterday my youngest daughter delivered my youngest grandchild HENDRIK. ... the boy is a very passable frog .. *(der Junge ... ist ein ganz passabler Frosch.")*

Baby Hendrik, Grandmother Korsten, Leni, Adriana, Bas,
Biesenthal, January 1944

CHAPTER 16 | FROM BIESENTHAL
TO SWEDEN

The year 1944 rolled on like an avalanche collecting an ever-growing mass of annihilation. I felt protective of Hendrik, my little frog of a baby brother, who seemed to me a fragile, live doll. Brother Bastiaan and his constant companion Rola played mother and father, wanting to cradle him in their wobbly arms. I was jealous.

In March 1944, when I turned six, my *Grossmutter* wrote to her son Josef:

> "... because of our proximity to Berlin, a lot of air raid alarm. Hubert was here for one hour ... many dead in the Everhard Strasse ... Children are sick. Jacq is tired a lot, miserably discouraged (*missmutig*)."

Berlin from November 1943 until March 1944 had been bombed twenty-four times, with some one thousand planes dropping one to two thousand tons of bombs.

I heard *Grossmutter*, my mother, my Tantes whisper about die *Vergeltungswaffen* (retaliatory weapons) Hitler had in his pocket. I didn't understand. No one explained. Not even dear Onkel Hubert, my German uncle so full of funny tales who came and left, never to return. My mother's favorite brother, big Hubert. He had been driving an ambulance.

"What is an ambulance?" I had asked. The question was never answered. Onkel Hubert, the World War I veteran, who had turned away from war in disgust, had had to serve his Reich somehow. He drove the sick, the maimed, the dead bodies taken from the streets of Cologne, from the Everhard Strasse where *Grossmutter*'s house stood, until his own ambulance was blown up and he with it. He left an illegitimate cousin, a contemporary of mine. I never knew her, never heard the rest of Onkel Hubert's tale.

In May 1944 *Grossmutter* wrote from Biesenthal. She had needed a tooth pulled but there was no anesthesia to be had. The dentist pulled it anyway, during a heavy bombing. My Tante Maria's lover was *"toedlich verunglueckt beim Absetzen vom Feind, wie man so schoen jetzt sagt."* (was mortally wounded while fighting the enemy as they now say so nicely). "Heinz-Otto is on sick leave in Bonn, malaria."

In July 1944, *Grossmutter* again wrote to Josef, who by now had been transferred to Brabant as—of all things—a green police, *Ordnungspolizei*, a uniformed regular police officer of Nazi Germany, the force that knocked on Anne Frank's door. Meanwhile, the Allied invasion had begun in June, and troops continued to pour ashore on the Normandy beaches.

"… it is important how the Invasion develops … Prospects at the moment for us are not favorable. The little Hendrik is doing well. I am sure you want to know about the case Millenaar … Adriana now goes to school. Last week she had a bad fall and has a big open wound in her arm ..."

My Onkel Josef in Brabant! My father was livid, "Why?" My mother would answer, "To protect your relatives, Zhjeck."

When I visited Onkel Josef in Rottach, Bavaria in the 1980s he told me: "Adriana, when I was captured in Holland, they threw me in the Scheveningen prison. They ordered me to march through a mountain of shit and piss. That's what they did. That's what you Hollanders did to me. Commandeered me to walk through shit, through *Scheisse* over and over again, back and forth, day in day out."

All I could think of was my Dutch cousin Gilbert, dragged from prison Scheveningen to camp Vught to Sachsenhausen to the punishment commando, Der Klinker. What had he been dragged through? Gilbert was a political resistance fighter. He had to paint metal buttons in colors of pink, red, yellow, purple and had secretly kept a set. When everyone had to wear a button, he was given a red one (political prisoner). When he lined up for food, he first stood in the 'red' line. The top of the soup kettle was watery; only the bottom had the thick, good stuff, which was kept for the "Kapo's and the Blockaeltester." So when Gilbert had finished the red line, he would pin on a green button (criminals) and get more soup. Later, when the selection was done for the slave work he looked well-fed, so was chosen for the Klinker to do hard labor. There he resembled a Danish "electrician," who had "disappeared." Gilbert was pointed at: "*Du, Elektriker, komm hier.*" (You, electrician, come here.) A shaft had broken down and everyone stood idle. Gilbert had to repair it. By some miracle Gilbert got the shaft working again and from then on worked as the electrician in a shed with a tar tub where he kept the fire going, stayed warm and pretended to do electrical repairs. Then he succumbed to dysentery. He could not keep food down. Prisoners around him would ask: "Aren't you dead yet?"

His bunk companion, a Dutchman, became his friend. He washed Gilbert's clothing so he would not die in his own muck. Somehow, my mother and my father got packages to him. Two sardine cans. He stabbed holes in them. Contrary to his friend's advice and common sense, he drank the sardine oil. He improved. Another miracle.

After some months, yet another miracle. He was freed from the camp. Jacq Millenaar (*Gijs' oom Jaak* = Gilbert's uncle Jaak), had contacted all the high contacts he had. After all, Gilbert was his nephew.

Still the avalanche continued to thunder its way down the slopes of all continents, and everyone was trapped in its suffocating mass. At the same time, troops had landed on the Omaha beaches, sending a signal of hope. Hope for the Allies, hope for *Grossmutter*, who had written, "… prospects at the moment for us are not favorable."

What does she mean? Was she still betting on a miracle whereby her Germany would be victorious? That Hitler would come up with his *Wunderwaffen* (miracle weapons)? That Germany would regain its borders and possessions? Did she really believe that a Millenaar would not persevere, would give in to an absolute evil? Why her continuous wishful thinking? My *Grossmutter* knew what was going on in Germany.

"*Sie hat es gewusst.*" Many knew. There were many "Willing Executioners."

In July 1944, my father was no longer permitted to work for the Swedish Protecting Power. Still worse, he was prohibited from leaving Germany. No reason was given for his dismissal. Correspondence buzzed in German, Swedish, French, Dutch, and English in coded telegrams sent back and forth from the Auswaertige Amt, from the Swedish ambassador Arvid Rickert to the Dutch ambassador in Stockholm, to the Dutch minister-in-exile in London who telegraphed on July 18, to the Netherlands legation in Stockholm:

> "Have Swedish government know Dutch government interested in Millenaar's fate. Before investigating possibility of an exchange, your information is awaited. V.Kleffens"

The same day an *Aide-Mémoire* in French from the Swedish Ministry of Foreign Affairs, Division B in Stockholm was sent to the Royal Netherlands Legation in Stockholm explaining how Minister A. Rickert in Berlin was taking energetic steps to inquire personally about the exact details and the reason for Millenaar's dismissal. All Arvid Rickert learned from the various members at the Auswaertige Amt was that there were "certain objections" against the person Millenaar, whereupon the Swedish ambassador had answered, "that the person who had been working for the Legation B for four years had remained the same and he would like to know what he had been charged with."

GR Leithe-Jasper

Inl. II

A u f z e i c h n u n g
....

⟨ Gegen den bei der Schutzmacht-Abteilung der
hiesigen Schwedischen Gesandtschaft beschäftigten
holländischen Staatsangehörigen M i l l e n a a r
bestand bereits früher der Verdacht, Briefe aus Holland
an in Deutschland internierte Holländer bezw. holländis(
Juden weiter geleitet zu haben.
    Dieser Verdacht stützt sich auf Anzeigen der
Auslands-Briefprüfstelle, die an Millenaar adressierte
Briefe auffing, in denen er um die Weiterleitung von
Briefen gebeten wurde. Der Beweis, daß er tatsächlich
derartige Weiterleitungen vorgenommen hat, konnte nicht
erbracht werden. Da der Briefempfänger ausserdem im
Konzentrationslager untergebracht war, wäre es ihm wohl
kaum möglich gewesen, mit ihm in illegale Verbindung
zu treten.
    Seitens der Abteilung Protokoll wurde daher auch v(
ursprünglich gegen Millenaar in Aussicht genommenen
Maßnahmen Abstand genommen und die Schwedische Gesandtschaft lediglich über den Sachverhalt unterrichtet.
    Nunmehr liegt eine neue Meldung des Oberkommandos
der Wehrmacht vor, dem ein an Millenaar gerichtetes
Schreiben beiliegt, in dem er gebeten wird, an einen
holländischem Geschäftsmann im Konzentrationslager Dac!
einen Brief weiter zu befördern. Millenaar wäre wohl !
in der Lage gewesen, diesen Brief in das Konzentration
zu schmuggeln. Maßnahmen gegen ihn dürften daher kaum
in Frage kommen. Hingegen wäre es vielleicht zweckmäß
den Absender darauf aufmerksam zu machen, daß er sich
seine Briefsendungen an den Lagerinsassen des amtlich
gelassenen Weges bedienen möge. ⟩
    Hiermit
        Inland II
mit dem Anheimstellen der Übernahme.
                    Berlin, den 5. September 1944

---

*Aufzeichnung: Against the Dutch citizen Millenaar, working at the
Protection Department of the Swedish Embassy here; earlier there
was the suspicion he passed letters from Holland to German-interned
Dutchmen, including Dutch Jews*

The notice of his abrupt dismissal, to be enforced as of August 1, 1944, came as no surprise to Millenaar himself. As early as January, he knew his position was endangered. His friend, anti-Nazi lawyer Von Rohrscheid, had shown him a circular from the Gestapo headquarters sent out to all agencies of the police, the employment offices, and Gestapo branches requesting them to arrest Millenaar on the spot.

Of course Jacq Millenaar knew danger lurked around him. He knew that in 1944 it was a fluke to be both alive and human. But he also firmly believed that God stood by him, and also stood by the thousands and thousands of prisoners and slave laborers. Even in death God would walk with his children. His early life on a farm showed him that death could come quickly, that bodies turned to dust and clay, but would rise again as a new life form. Not even the Gestapo could shake his trust in 'my shield and my fortress art Thou, oh God ...' He continued journeying back and forth from Biesenthal to Berlin-Wannsee, where some members of the Legation B had moved after they were bombed out of several other Rauchstrasse legation buildings. He worked towards alleviating the lot of his compatriots who were suffering even worse dangers.

But the threat to name Millenaar a state enemy by August 1, 1944, was disquieting to Jacq. The fact that he was to be dismissed from the Swedish Protecting Power gave him no illusion as to what the Gestapo had in mind as soon as he was stripped of his "accreditation to the Swedish embassy." The elusive minister, Arvid Rickert, had promised Millenaar he would do all he could to have the decree annulled.

Did Millenaar know of the several attempts to assassinate Hitler, or the conspirators' trips to neutral Switzerland and Sweden to contact the Allies and plead for an "early" peace so the "good" Germany could emerge? He may have heard from Hans-Bernd von Haeften (a worker at the Auswaertige Amt) that plots were underway. But Millenaar had heard so much already, and by July 1944, he knew he saw the *mene tekl* on the wall and that he must get his family out of Germany and that he, too, needed to leave. A plan of escape, which included false papers and a chance to fly to England, was devised with one of his many Dutch helpers.

Meanwhile, Rickert took up the case with the state secretary Steengracht at the Auswaertige Amt. The latter would intervene on his behalf on the condition that Millenaar himself give immunity and protection to the state secretary in case the Allies won. Why it was Millenaar who had to promise to protect the state secretary is unclear, but Rickert never unveiled this demand until the last moment, lest Millenaar refuse. Millenaar was obstinate. He would stand by his compatriots and have nothing to do with waverers, exactly what Rickert had feared.

Apparently it was Himmler himself who 'saved' my father by having the state secretary request that the Gestapo withdraw Millenaar's dismissal order.

On July 18, 1944, an *Aide-Mémoire* was sent from the Ministre des Affaires Etrangères-Division-B in Stockholm to La Légation Royale des Pays Bas stating:

> *"... que M. Millenaar était resté lorsqu'en son temps, les autres membres de la Légation des Pays Bas étaient partis, que cette demande avait*

*été occasionnée par le besoin impérieux de la
Légation d'avoir une personne de la compétence
et de l'expérience de M. Millenaar ... et que M.
Millenaar était tout simplement irremplaçable ...
travailleuse et loyale .. d'une manière correcte en
toutes occasions ...*

(that Monsieur Millenaar had remained
the same during this time, when the other
members of the Netherlands Legation had
departed, that this request was occasioned
by the imperative need of the Legation to
have a person with the competence and
experience of Monsieur Millenaar...and
that Monsieur Millenaar was quite simply
irreplaceable...hard working and loyal...with
a just/correct attitude on all occasions...)

What in his situation had been the clincher that
suddenly and finally made my father '*missmutig*'
(miserably discouraged)? It was not so much that he
feared being a 'state enemy' who would, after August
1, be shot or perhaps hanged by the noose of a copper
piano string. He did not shrink from bombs. During
raids he had learned to dodge by foot. And when riding
his Swedish motorcycle, by continuing on whatever
road he happened to be traveling. He would not get
caught in a cellar, as he had been caught too many
times breathing in dust, smoke, gases, when cellar walls
caved in around him, making getaways that could only
be called miracles. He certainly paid little attention
to the schemes of conspirators. But, he was worried

sick about the Dutch prisoners, knew how much they depended on his initiatives, his appearances, his packages, his money orders, his notes slipped in and out of the camps, his handshake, his Brabant lilt, the compassion in his eyes and in his heart. He worried about the Nazis now cornered like rats and going haywire. He had seen vile animals on the farm, he had known the young ruffians and their brutal tactics on the riverboat, he had seen frenzied miners in the diamond pits of South Africa. He knew what man was capable of. He knew how he himself could burst out in untempered anger when his six-year old, Adrianneke, would throw a tantrum, performing a *"Korstentanz,"* as *Grossmutter* would chant:

"There she goes again, dancing like a dervish, falling down with a smack, refusing to get up. I did it, Mother did it. Even *et Sonnenscheinchen* has done it. And now Adriaenchen is doing it more and more, the dance of the Korsten women."

On July 25, 1944, a note from the Geheime Staatspolizei
Staatspolizeistelle Koeln Auslandsbrief-Pruefstelle
Az.A.w.B.Nr. ...
(Secret State Police State Police Post Cologne Investigation Post for Foreign Letters ...)

The note went out to 1.)
OKW Wehrmachtfuehrungsstab
Ag Ausland I DZ z.Hd.v. Herrn
Oberst Steinhaeuser o.V.i.A.,

Berlin W35, Tirpitzufer 72/76
2. Zentralstelle f.d.A.B.P'en(3mal)

The note had an enclosure stating that the Dutch citizen, Millenaar, as had been suspected earlier, had been forwarding letters from Holland to Dutchmen interned in Germany—that is, to Dutch Jews. On July 24, 1944, letters, memos, and telegrams went out in Dutch, Swedish, German, French, and encoded English, stating that the "case Millenaar" had been reconsidered by the Auswaertige Amt and that he was allowed to stay on. Profuse thank you's were sent to all Swedes who had assisted in Millenaar's staying on in safety.

In the same July letter that *Grossmutter* wrote to her green policeman son, Josef, in my father's beloved Brabant, she also wrote:

> "... the Swedish ambassador made terrific endeavors in the Millenaar case and at the end of the war Jacq no longer wants to stay here. Well, with time comes counsel. *(Kommt Zeit, kommt Rat)* ..."

Grossmutter remained cool and calm. Age made her so. The death of three young sons made her so. World War I had made her so. The early death of her husband, Heinrich, made her so.

My father, half *Grossmutter*'s age, remained cool and calm, clenched his teeth, prayed to God, prayed for war's end, and occasionally glanced at his poem, 'We are not lost yet,' regretting he had no time for another poem, nor inspiration. But, unlike *Grossmutter*, who had just celebrated her 86th birthday in July 1944, surrounded by her dearest women folk, my father was in the middle of his energetic years. Though he was miserably dejected, he could not but help erupt into desperate anger at the suffering of his compatriots. Even his Adrianneke no longer jumped into his arms, laughing and asking to help pick flowers, weed beans. Little Basje raced around with a helmet-like pot on his head shouting to all the alarmed women folk who wailed: "What will happen to us, where will we go, the Russians are coming, *eine Katastrophe* after another." Basje yelled: "But I'm a man." *(Aber ich bin doch ein Mann.)*

CHAPTER 17 | IN SWEDEN, IN HOLLAND, IN GERMANY

My mother in Stockholm Sweden

During this time in Berlin, my father did not stand helpless as a potential state enemy, but quietly went about his business, helping where he could and writing letter after letter imploring governments to send help. He urged the Red Cross to send parcels and medications. He was cautious, while fervently hoping the exit visa for Leni and his threesome would come through. So he wrote also on our behalf on October 30, 1944, to the new ambassador of the Netherlands in Stockholm, asking for help for his wife.

"My wife, being a complete stranger in Sweden, will not find it easy for her on arrival with three little children to find lodgings ... The condition of our compatriots here and at home is sad. Vught has been liberated, as you will know. But the prisoners there and elsewhere in the Netherlands have been deported to here in the beginning of September. We don't yet know where ... There is famine in our fatherland, cold and fear for life for those who live within the fighting zone and life hangs by a thread. In the west of Germany things aren't different. A sister-in-law of mine in Cologne lost her mother, sister, brother-in-law, nephew and three close friends in an air raid shelter struck by a bomb. The sad thing in Holland is that there are so few air raid shelters, especially in the Arnhem area many people have perished. We only know one prayer in all this misery, namely a speedy peace."

On my mother's birthday, November 7, 1944, Ambassador Van Rechteren assured my father that, indeed, he would give Mrs. Millenaar help in finding lodgings—if necessary outside Stockholm, because the housing market was tight in the city. He writes,

> "...Although the departure of your family will leave you behind in loneliness, I understand how happy you will be knowing they will be safe. Moreover, I also know how much the larger family of Netherlanders has your constant attention and devotion which will give you less time to miss them."

So, five days after my youngest brother's name was entered in the Book of Baptismal Records of the

Netherlands Church in Berlin, my mother fled with me and my brothers to Stockholm, Sweden. A new chapter in our lives had begun. I remember waking up on a mattress on a bare floor with my brothers wailing, my mother weeping, and a strange voice shushing us lest we wake the neighbors. We were four miserable bodies huddled together on one narrow prickly mattress. Baby Henkie rolled off the mattress onto the bare, cold floor. My mother, with Basje in one arm, lay crosswise on the other end of the mattress, trying to keep warm under a black fur coat. I hauled squirming baby Henkie up to my shivering body for warmth, for comfort. I wanted to protect something in this freezing, foreign environment.

Where were we? What had happened? Why could I understand no one around me? Why weren't Basje and I allowed to say anything in the presence of these new strange-sounding grownups? Why did Mammie cry so often? Why was she suddenly speaking only Dutch? And where was Pappie? I recalled the Gestapoman on the tarmac at the Tempelhof airport. Just before we stepped into that strange flying machine he had laughed so loudly, blowing puffs of smoke into the sleety air when he commanded me to open my little red suitcase. It held my teddy bear and a big, pink brassiere. I needed it, of course, soon. I was growing.

My father, our protector, my hero, stayed behind. Ashes were smoldering that November day in 1944 from burnt furniture, burnt trees, my linden tree under which I'd dreamt so sweet a dream. We landed in Stockholm, where ghostly spruces stared forbiddingly at me. The snow was deep and cold. It chilled my agitated heart. I had been deserted by my protector. My tears curdled to resin, sticking fast to my soul and heart.

On November 21, Ambassador Van Rechteren in Stockholm wrote to Minister Van Kleffens in London the following, stamped with the word SECRET:

"... I have the honor to inform Your Excellency that Mrs. Millenaar and her three youthful children arrived safely. The journey went by airplane, an old slow Junkers 52, with which now the air connection Stockholm-Berlin is maintained with constant danger of interception by allied machines.

That Mrs. Millenaar was granted a German exit visa is owed to the personal steps by the Swedish minister Rickert, who also saw to the favorable change in position of Mr. Millenaar.

At the German Ministry of Foreign Affairs the prospect has been given that Mr. Millenaar might visit his family in Sweden for Christmas. I inform Your Excellency of this, because it might be good to be prepared for this visit and the possibilities it has to offer. But it still seems quite improbable that the Germans will allow Mr. Millenaar to go to visit neutral Sweden, and in that case it would not be without danger to him to be in contact with the embassy. On the other hand it is clear how important deliberation with him would be.

In the short conversation we had with Mrs. Millenaar, she was very well informed of her husband's activities and she gave the impression that she was in complete agreement with this in spite of her German birth.

... Ever since the threat under which Mr. Millenaar was put this summer, he, according to his spouse, had become very careful and kept himself aside from many activities that were undertaken amongst the Dutch in Berlin and in Germany. At the same time, however, she handed me a list of medication that an 'underground organization of students' had requested from Mr. Millenaar. The latter would like to receive this medication from us."

By the time my mother had arrived in Sweden with us, many a Swede working for the Legation-B had been replaced because of illness, weakness or exhaustion by yet another 'energetic' German-speaking young Swedish diplomat versed in international law. The new young lawyer, Lagergren, told His Excellency, Van Rechteren, in Stockholm in a confidential letter to the Minister-in-exile in London:

"The safety of Mr. Millenaar's wife and children will lighten his so useful and dangerous work, which he continues and can even extend. I shall of course give the spouse of this meritorious Netherlander— Mrs. Millenaar is German by birth—all the help she needs. ..."

I waited and waited for my Pappie, for nothing. I never heard his motorcycle. Never heard his tread on the stairs. It was strangely quiet around me. Where were the bombs that fell, the planes that roared? In all this time, my parents had forgotten to sit down with little Bastiaan and me to explain to us what air raids, fighter planes, bombs, cellars, enemies, Allies were all about. For us it was natural to be dragged into the cellar whenever an alarm went off. If a house was burning down, if trees were smoking, if a doll I had dropped lay smoldering when I found it after the all-clear sounded— on none of those occasions was it ever explained to me why there was smoke, bombing, explosions, fire, and the blood-red glow, whether distant or nearby.

Now I heard only the strange voice of Tante Siv, a voice that went up and down like the squirrels outside the window of this strange new house we had come to live in. Where were the alarms, the sirens, the voices of my other Tantes? The high-pitched "Katastrophes"? Where was *Grossmutter*? Pappie?

My mother now spoke only Dutch; German was *Verboten*. I had to go to school. In order to understand what the girls and boys were saying, I started to pick up one strange word after another. Swedish. I did not like the see-saw words. I did not like the cold. I hated my mother's tears. I was afraid of the silence when I was not in school. I detested the unfriendly strangers in the boarding house, hated sitting at the long table for meals. I hated our silent walks in the deep snow. My mother was always distant, sad, weeping. Had not my Pappie whispered on the tarmac: "Adrianneke, you're flying to freedom, and take care of Mammie and your brothers." Had he not said that?

During that winter of 1944-1945, in cold Stockholm, I forgot my Dutch prayer, *Ik ga slapen ik ben moe*. (I long to go to sleep). I longed instead to understand Santa Lucia, the song sung by angel-like beings in their long white robes as they glided, holding candles, through the dark aisle of a church. Those were the words I wanted to sing, to be able to replicate the lilt, like an Italian sailor's song.

This is the first letter my mother wrote from Sweden.

Sodertalje, November 27, 1944

"Your Excellency,

This morning I received a letter from my husband requesting to discuss the following with your Excellency. Since it is not possible for me to leave the children, I will have to do it in writing.

In the Sachsenhausen camp are +-2500 compatriots (many from the Camp Vught), in Ravensbrueck +-1000 (women), and still hundreds in other camps. Because mail delivery in the Netherlands has been stopped they no longer get packages, thus they suffer terribly from hunger.

In order for Sweden to do something the initiative has to come from Germany. Now, my husband asks you to ask Your Excellency whether you can find a way to send victuals. The government consents to giving aid to these people through means of state financing (*staatsmiddelen.*)

The B-department in Stockholm could therefore easily have money available. It is only a matter of a permit for the purchase and for mailing of packages. The Swedish gentlemen at Department-B are of the opinion that at the Auswaertige Amt this request by Your Excellency will be granted with great willingness. There is a bit of a hurry in this matter because the people yearn for food.

This is my husband's request.

Yours very sincerely,

Leni Millenaar"

"Your Excellency" was the new ambassador of the Netherlands in Stockholm. He referred my mother's letter on to the Dutch minister-in-exile in London, Van Kleffens, and asked for further instructions. By the time my mother wrote this letter, Holland had been split in two. Southern Holland, including Jaakie's province of Brabant, had been liberated by the Allies. Northern Netherlands, above the many rivers (the ten rivers Antonia Adriana had crossed once in her lifetime to visit Amsterdam), was not in desperate straits, but was doomed. A railroad strike in September 1944 had Reichskommissar Seyss Inquart retaliate by prohibiting any foodstuffs to reach western and northern Holland. There was no fuel coming north from the coal mines in the southern province of Limburg. Tens of thousands of Dutch men, between ages seventeen and seventy, had to report for slave labor. If not, they were rounded up in *razzias* along with horses, cows, carriages, any kind of industrial or other machinery, blankets, clothing, bicycles, buses, boats, vessels, potatoes, staple goods. All were plundered from the Dutch citizens in the north. Anyone who struggled against any of these regulations would automatically be deported. Or another group of hostages would be executed. From September 1944, the hunt for men was on. Around 140,000 Dutchmen had to dig trenches in Holland to stop allied tanks and ground forces or were forced to go to Germany and slave in the arms factories.

On December 2, 1944, the Minister in London answers:

> "... with interest I took note that Mr. Millenaar's family arrived in Sweden. I agree with you that it can be dangerous for Mr. Millenaar to come into direct contact with the embassy in Stockholm. However, if you are able to get in touch with him in one way or another, that would be of great importance. ..."

On December 18, 1944, the Secretary General in London writes to the ambassador in Stockholm:

> "... as was suggested through Mrs. Millenaar ... immediately ... send victuals ... via the International Red Cross .. Swedish Red Cross ... as this is already done for the interned Dutch Jews ... All costs of Swedish aid shall of course be reimbursed by the Dutch government. ..."

The ambassador in Stockholm answers his colleague in London on December 28, 1944:

"... enclosed the specification of the medication and medical tools I sent to Mr. Millenaar in Berlin at his request and which are destined for the Dutch students there. ...The transportation of these goods is brought via courier service by the Swedish Legation secretary, Oesterlind, who on January 2, 1945 will again for undetermined time work at the Department-B."

Our Christmas in Stockholm in 1944 was dismal. We were lost, lonely, cantankerous. My mother cried. Baby Henkie disobeyed. Basje parroted my mother's Dutch. I hated the Swedish of the grownups at my new school and in our echoing, ugly boarding house. But I died to know what they talked about. We shivered. We stared and felt abandoned, like the ducks in the Skansen amusement park. Snow melted inside our sleeves, in our mittens. Our collars were wet. I wanted to spit out onto the untrodden snow field, "Where is Pappie?"

I could not understand my mother. She was a grownup, why should she cry? I did not know that she cried for the death of her favorite brother, Hubert, for the death of her sister Maria's lover, for fear of losing her own mother, for the perpetual panic of losing her beloved and stubborn Zhjeck, who did not join her in cold Sweden. When we were not at the boarding house, she took us for long snowy walks. She never realized how cold, blue and shivery wet we were until we had returned in the dark. When we crossed the threshold in our wet socks to go up the creaky wooden stairs we had to greet the strangers there in Swedish.

The Swedes had turned anti-Nazi, anti-German, pro Allies. But nothing was explained to me. I longed to comprehend. I kept learning the new words. I had longed for *Weihnachten* (Christmas). It was gone. Even the *Kerstboom* (Christmas tree) Pappie had talked about was gone. Now it was Santa Lucia. The voices sang a magic melody reminding me of Basje's boat bobbing on the little waves in the brook that flowed through our perpetual garden in Biesenthal. We had barely been one month in Sweden. I still could not understand one word. I was desperate to speak, to sing like one of those angels. After the Santa Lucia we were lonely again.

Often the courier plane would be intercepted over the Baltic Sea. Weeks later a smudged letter would arrive. My mother sobbed all over again. I froze.

In Brabant, back in my father's province, his brother Adriaan wrote to London, Stockholm, even to Brussels where a new military government under Crown Princess Juliana's consort's husband, Prince Bernhard, was established, asking about the whereabouts and the welfare of his brother, Jaak/Adrianus. No one had heard in so long and there had been no answer to Jaak's birthday congratulations sent for January 10, 1945. Brother Adriaan wanted to let brother Jaak know that relatives in Babylonbrook and elsewhere in Brabant were o.k., but that no one had heard from the Gilberts——his own son—nor their nephew, the latter last known to be in camp Sachsenhausen.

Meanwhile, on February 21, 1945, a coded telegram destined for Moscow from Minister Van Kleffens in London states:

Placard in Russian about Dutch property

"Stockholm reports that Swedish embassy in Berlin, as soon as it is in the battle zone, will be evacuated. Wahlestad and Millenaar, the latter Dutchman who officially works for us ... shall, because they know the conditions of the almost 50,000 Dutchmen in Berlin, remain behind in the embassy air raid shelter. To Netherlanders known to us, placards have been furnished in the following languages: Russian, English, German, stating that apartment or property is under protection of the Swedish embassy. Please inform Russian government of the above and ask them to introduce Millenaar to the Russian military authorities.

Request you to signal me of Russian accord, so I can inform Swedes.

Van Kleffens

One week earlier, another secret letter had been sent to London by the ambassador in Stockholm:

" ... Mrs. Millenaar, now residing here, ... told me her husband ... also offered the plan to remain in Berlin while awaiting the eventual arrival of a Dutch representative, Millenaar would take care of the interests of the many Dutch, but he did want to receive instructions on the matter from the Dutch government. ...

Mr. Millenaar also wrote to his wife that now the members of the Dutch colony in Berlin, too, had been forced to dig trenches around the city for its defense. Mrs. Millenaar seemed to know that the interned from the concentration camp Sachsenhausen had been deported to near Weimar. She knew nothing regarding deportation of p.o.w. ..."

After one month, a note in French went out to all concerned, reassuring Jaak's brother, Adriaan in Brabant, that the Millenaars were o.k.

In London minister Van Kleffens informed his ambassador in Moscow to have my father introduced to the Soviet Russian authorities and he adds: " ... that I have particular admiration for his attitude."

The following day my mother wrote a letter in her neat, but occasionally faulty, Dutch to the Netherlands embassy in Stockholm. Again, she had to write and had no means to go in person to the embassy. She had her three young children to take care of in the cold, desolate north. She hardly saw Siv Neuteboom who was too busy making a living taking photographs, trying to sell them to magazines. Moreover, Siv's squirrely voice irritated us all. Moreover, her Dutchman-turned-Nazi husband had become unfaithful to her. She had her own problems to handle.

My mother wrote to the ambassador:

"May I thank you very much for the message about my brother-in-law from Brabant. My husband will be so happy with this message. When I last visited you ... you asked for any information. ...I think the following will interest you. I will copy it just so then my husband wrote me: 'yesterday amongst the tens of fatherlanders who come and see me daily, there were two gentlemen from Sachsenhausen just released and more dead than alive ... In the last few months they have been seriously ill ... yet could not get away because they were too ill and therefore *transportunfaehig* (incapable of being transported). Now that the camp is being evacuated ... they decided to leave it, because otherwise ...(I shall rather not mention this by name, but you understand. Many already have gone that way.) Thus they crawled up to me and arrived as wrecks ..."

My mother signs, 'Leni Millenaar.' My father helped Colonel Knage and Mr. Braakhekke, took them to Biesenthal, fed them from whatever food he had, because he no longer received food parcels from the Swedes. He gave them the proper documents in various languages. The two gentlemen were determined to undertake the long trek west until they reached their fatherland.

In March, my father, still miserable, bereft of the consoling arms of his Leni, uncertain as to his fate, resorts to writing a long letter in German to my mother's oldest sister, Anna. She and her husband had sought refuge with relatives near Magdeburg.

" ... You can't imagine what all is coming at me these days. It is much. Sometimes too much. But I think that the end is now really in sight and that gives hope and strength to endure this last stage.

It looks like your *Heimatstadt* (native city Cologne) is now soon behind enemy line. I would think that that gives you mixed and certainly not pleasant feelings, but if matters were to get that far, the attacks would also stop and the rest of the city be spared. It is my firm conviction that it would not take long before you could return home. God give so!

From Weimar ... I received letters from Mutter (*Grossmutter* Korsten), Maria, Martha. They are all fine there and have survived the heavy attack.

I receive good news from Leni. In the beginning she was not at all happy to go to Sweden and was very homesick for Biesenthal. Now, however, she realizes the necessity of her journey ... The Swedes are very cold and the fact that the children speak German has been a cause for a lot of annoyance and grief for Leni. One does not want to hear that language spoken and for the speaker they have nothing but a long face. Leni is busy teaching the children Dutch. ... I had so hoped to spend Christmas and New Year's with them there but it was not granted to me. I now have to wait till the end of the war.

For the time being it is quiet here... I do not doubt the Russians will march on. I can imagine the worries you have about Heinz Otto and I so hope you will soon get news. And how is Hella? One of my brothers, in Breda, is already on liberated ground. He wrote me via Leni that he and his family are fine ... In the rest of the Netherlands the situation is terrible. The people now only get one pound of bread a week ... Hundreds of people in the cities are dying from famine. The situation cannot be described. God grant that they may too be liberated soon, because in this way the hatred will get worse and worse and soon there will not be any prospect for reconciliation; Leni... worries in this respect a lot about Jupp (Onkel Josef). I hope nothing happens to him, but the fact is, he has no enviable post. – My sister wrote me ... she will help him and what she says she also means. And so we shall hope the best for him. My brothers who were still in agriculture, have lost everything and are poor as beggars. *"Wo das hin muss?"* What will happen?! And there are hundreds like that.

It is a scary time. One does not at all know how and where. Everywhere there is danger. The raids over Berlin are terrible. ... Mother Korsten once posed the question: When will God take the reins in his own hands again? ... We have to continue praying ... Jacq"

My *Grossmutter*, with her daughter Maria, her daughter-in-law Martha, my Tante Carola, and little Rola and two other Tantes all left Biesenthal for

Weimar, so close to Buchenwald, hoping they would be safe and escape the Russians. My father had organized a trusty fellow to take them with horse and wagon for the long trek.

On March 10, 1945 a telegram from Minister Van Kleffens to the Netherlands Legation in Stockholm:

> "Request to instruct Millenaar to come to Sweden. ..."

Two days earlier a telegram from the Dutch ambassador in Stockholm wrote to London:

> "... In view of the bad experiences in Budapest, it was decided to evacuate the whole Swedish embassy ...
>
> In these circumstances it were dangerous to leave Millenaar, who is persona non grata with the Germans, behind alone in Berlin even though he himself is ready to do anything. The head of Department-B thinks it advisable to have Millenaar go either to Sweden from where he could possibly return to Russian-occupied Germany, or to take him to Bad Wildungen (near Kassel); however, there's little work for him there ..."

No one had access to the civilian prisoner population, except that Millenaar, on March 20, 1944, had visited Kvinnofaengelse Cottbus and the BMW

factory in Spandau in August 1944. Millenaar's young
helper Oesterlind's camp inspections were taken over
in June 1944 by one Gavrell. By now both Millenaar
and the Swedes knew that the recently arrived U.S.
and British forces would overrun the enemy. Is it an
irony that, suddenly, in the month of June 1944, the
Dutch p.o.w.s were visited eight times? And from then
on until December 1944 thirty-seven times more, an
average of three visits a month. ... Gavrell took his task
seriously. He visited these Dutch p.o.w.s camps forty-
five times from June until December 1944. Travel to
these camps scattered all over Germany was dangerous.
But the light at the end of the tunnel was there, even as
the battle raged. Another winter set in. In the north of
Holland it was the winter of hunger.

On March 15, 1945 Oesterlind told the Minister of
Department-B in Stockholm: ".. that on the German
side there exists still the tendency to not accept the
Swedish protection of Dutch interests in principle, and
in reality only grudgingly. ... Moreover, the Germans
recognize no other Dutch government than that of Mr.
Seyss-Inquart!"

In that same session, Oesterlind continues: "The
Department-B still has not succeeded in obtaining
lists of names of those Dutchmen interned in
Sachsenhausen. Their names are made known by the
elaborate private correspondence that Mr. Millenaar
maintains with them. ... Some of those Dutch interned
have been taken to Bergen-Belsen, some perhaps to
Buchenwald ... from there to southern Germany. ...
The parcels from the Red Cross have not reached the
p.o.w.s. in a very long time. ... Food conditions are
deteriorating rapidly."

And finally, Oesterlind reported in a confidential letter dated March 17, 1945 to the Dutch Minister Van Kleffens: " … that of a serious decline in morale of the German people there is no sign whatsoever. … according to him the continuous and ever-heavier air strikes, such as on Dresden, bring the domestic front in a mood of desperate hate and rage, not of giving up."

Early in Oesterlind's account he mentions that "Mr. Millenaar is reluctant to leave Berlin."

But on April 1, my mother received word from her Zhjeck in which he writes to her that nothing is known yet of where he is to go. He is still waiting for an exit visa. According to Oesterlind he will definitely not stay in Berlin, and perhaps will go to Luebeck. Two days later, before the courier to Stockholm takes off, he adds: "Still nothing known about my journey, but a decision is expected any time."

My father's letter is officially quoted on April 10, 1945 by the Minister at Department-B in Berlin to the Minister Van Kleffens in London.

That same day my father sat down at the Wannsee Legation-B and explained to the Dutch ambassador in Stockholm the plight of three Dutch women, two of whom had married Germans. In January these women had been taken prisoner by the Gestapo. Lieny Behlau-Fentener van Vlissingen had three children age six and younger, and Mrs. Rudolph, a good acquaintance of Jacq's, had two young children who had suddenly been abandoned since father Rudolph had already died and Mr. Behlau had been taken prisoner along with his wife and the Dutch consul in Wiesbaden (near Frankfurt/Main). After being imprisoned in various prisons, they landed in the Potsdam prison (near where numerous anti-Nazis lived).

My father wrote at the midnight hour and politely asked the ambassador whether this tragic case could be brought before the appropriate Dutch persons in London and whether there was a possibility that a Dutch liaison officer with the allied troops could be commissioned to find these abandoned children and take pity on them for the sake of these so heavily afflicted mothers. He adds: "..For the last few weeks I have been waiting for permission to be allowed to leave this country. In my case, however, it does not   seem to go smoothly since the dreaded agency [Gestapo] is objecting. ..."

My father very much hoped to reach Stockholm. He badly wanted to discuss the plight of his imprisoned compatriots, and plead for a speedy, decent relief policy. He longed to see his wife, his Adrianneke, his Bastiaan, and laugh at his baby, his mannekin Hendrik.

In London, the Dutch government-in-exile was preparing to form a new postwar cabinet. A Dutch ambassador, appointed in London on April 15, 1945, sent a telegram to Stockholm saying he had commissioned the Dutch ambassador in Moscow to have Millenaar go there, since it would be of utmost importance. Yet, chances he would be allowed entry were minimal, "...Because western Germany is occupied by the Allies much urgent work has to be done, I prefer that Millenaar, whose knowledge of affairs and persons made him extremely capable, not wait for an answer from Moscow, but comes to London to join the mission S.H.A.E.F. which is in progress. Millenaar has to journey to London as soon as possible. ..."

Finally, on April 19, 1945 a coded brief telegram from the Dutch ambassador in Stockholm to London states:

"On April 19, Millenaar, Von Pelsen Berenberg, the
ladies Back and Schmidt arrived here ...."

When my father finally joined us in Stockholm, it
was a fleeting celebration, a photo opportunity, an event

that called for
singing of the
Dutch national
anthem, the
Wilhelmus, so
strange sound-
ing and grim.
My father, my
mother, Tante
Siv and a few
strangers sang
the high-pitched
slow melody, so
different from
the pretty Santa
Lucia. Then they

Liberation May 1945 in the Skansen, Stockholm

laughed. They started acting like little children, giggling
like the children in the Swedish school. I could not grasp
why they were so jolly suddenly. It was something about
'freedom, liberty,' but what did I know?

My father's visit to us in Stockholm lasted just one
month. My mother blossomed. I was jealous. Basje
saluted his Pappie, fiddled with his hearing-aid, snatched
his cigarettes. Henkie tousled my father's neat hair,
crawled all over him, touched his cheek bristles.

But soon "Pappie" turned into "Mr. Millenaar." He
was wanted on the telephone.

"Where is Pappie," we would ask Mammie.

"At the Ambassade," she would say, irritated.

In our noisy boardinghouse, if he was not whispering with my mother, he was writing. To keep me quiet he would give me Dutch words to copy while he wrote one letter after another in his beautiful, cursive handwriting. Constantly writing. Twitching his lips.

Telegrams, letters, messages, and reports flew back and forth. From Stockholm to Moscow, to London, to Brussels. There was little coordination between the Netherlands government-in-exile in London with a new Government commissariat being established with Netherlands liaison-officers trained to prepare for the overwhelming job of repatriating Dutch prisoners and forced laborers. In Brussels, the Dutch Prince Bernhard, consort of Crown Princess Juliana and son-in-law of Queen Wilhelmina, was promoted to Commanding General of the Dutch troops stationed in liberated Brussels, capital of Belgium and adjacent to Brabant. Prince Bernhard was in competition with the newly established military government under the authoritative General Kruls, who sought sole control over repatriation. Yet, General Kruls had to cooperate with the British Military Forces, who, under the command of General Eisenhower's SHAEF (Supreme Headquarters of the Allied Expeditionary Forces) was to organize the occupation and repatriation in all of Germany, east as well as west, south and north. The division and disarray of the dispersed Dutch governmental institutions was simultaneously mirrored in the sending of food parcels and medications for the Dutch captives in Germany. There was little coordination amongst the International

Red Cross, the Dutch Red Cross, and the London Committee of the Dutch Red Cross.

In Stockholm, my father was growing impatient at the slow pace of help for his 'large family of Netherlanders,' whose fate he had tried to alleviate during all his unimaginable years in Germany. Now that liberation was at hand, he sat in chilly Stockholm awaiting instructions from the Dutch government to communicate with Russian authorities. The Nazis had deported thousands of Dutch men for slave labor in the last seven months of the war. They had also stripped these Netherlanders of any kind of identification papers. They had ordered them into Nazi uniforms. Jacq Millenaar was itching to go to Moscow and from there signal to the Russians who was Dutch, and who was German, who was to be trusted, and who was not.

The Netherlands was overwhelmed with mass starvation and disease epidemics. The northern provinces in particular were prostrate, with no semblance of public order as the people waited month after month for liberation. The men were forced by the Germans to dig trenches to slow the allied forces, leaving the women and children to suffer and die during the "hunger winter" of 1944-1945 from the lack of fuel and food. Dutch officials in London and on the continent were so preoccupied with getting food, medicines, and other essentials to the masses of people in Netherlands itself that the plight of Dutch prisoners and slave laborers in Germany were relegated to the back burner.

Communication was a serious issue for Dutch embassy and government officials in London, Moscow, Stockholm, Brussels, and Brabant. Those who resorted to the telephone never knew who was listening in. So they relied upon telegraph, couriers, and typewritten letters and reports. These exchanges used the polite and cumbersome language of diplomacy. Although French was the first language of diplomacy, English, Swedish, Dutch, and German were also common. And now, suddenly, there was also Russian, with its unfamiliar Cyrillic script. Translators and interpreters were needed. In one letter that meant to describe my father as a state enemy (*Staatsvijand*), declared instead that he was a state company (*staatsfirma*).

Suddenly, on May 25, 1945 the four of us were again left high and dry in Sweden, a land and its people who delighted in giving us the cold shoulder.

On June 5, 1945, Mr. A. Millenaar (*Uw dienaar*, your servant) sent a handwritten letter to the Dutch ambassador in Stockholm, protesting that his journey to London could have been ordered less hastily.

"It has been 10 days that I have been here and since my first visit to the foreign office I'm not one bit the wiser..."

His first neatly written paragraphs are concerned with the repatriation of Dutch concentration camp prisoners who had made it to Sweden, thanks to the help of Count F. Bernadotte, head of the Swedish Red Cross. Bernadotte had organized entry to Sweden for groups of Norwegian and Danish prisoners, along with a small group of Dutch women from the Ravensbrueck camp. Mr. A. Millenaar had urged in this June 5th letter to repatriate these Dutch women and men as soon as possible and suggested doing this in the Dutch ships anchored off the Swedish coast. He pleaded: "How much longer does the patience of those who are waiting have to be put to the test ...?"

He emphasized that these prisoners belonged to groups that had suffered the worst misery and therefore had the first right to be repatriated. He waited for a consular mission to be established under SHAEF, a mission that he would join as the first representative of the Dutch Foreign Office to occupied Germany, to see how the interests 'of our countrymen' could best be taken care of.

Exactly one month later, Mr. A. Millenaar finished a lengthy typewritten report from London on the protection of Dutch interests in Germany during the war. Without dwelling on the terror and the suffering of his fellow countrymen and women, and the destruction of the various legation buildings with attendant loss of archival material, he described the activities and the support given by the Swedes as well as the Dutch who had remained behind in Berlin as officials, traders, and former Dutch citizens. Regarding the Swedes he writes:

> "It cannot be said of the Swedish leaders and colleagues ... that they showed much enthusiasm at work; any kind of initiative can rarely be found. Yet, they never lacked preparedness nor willingness towards the matter of the oppressed Netherlanders. ..."

Back in Sweden, it seemed to me that, suddenly, the word "liberation" was everywhere. How could I know what that meant? First it was freedom. "Adrianneke, you're flying to freedom, to Sweden." Then it was liberation. My mother said: "Adriana, we're free, liberated." I asked, "So now we're flying to liberation?" "To Holland," was my mother's answer.

Holland är fritt! Undra på att Oranje och Adriana höjer segerfacklorna.

JULIANA är god kamrat
även med enkla holländska sjömän

Hollands folk har vaknat upp ur en mardröm. Drottning Wilhelmina har återvänt till sitt folk.

Hon flyger ständigt mellan London och sitt befriade land. Det är endast en halvtimmes resa. Hennes arbetskapacitet är obruten, hennes uppgift är också mer krävande än någonsin. Nu gäller det inte bara att ordna det befriade Hollands inre och yttre angelägenheter, det fordras dagliga initiativ för att så skyndsamt som möjligt rädda det holländska folket från svältdöden. Fienden renrakade landet från livsmedel och alla andra livsförnödenheter. Det finns ingenting att äta, ingenting att hölja sig i, ingenting att elda med, den goda jorden är förstörd genom att den satts under vatten. Många holländare har redan bokstavligen svultit ihjäl, många ligger i sina bäddar, hemma eller på sjukhusen. Man ser små barn med flaggor i händerna hylla drottningen. Men deras ansikten är märkta av svälten, deras ben sticksmala, deras kläder lumpor, som duktiga mödrar försökt göra så brukbara som möjligt. Unga flickor möter landsmodern med dans och sång, deras kjolar går i de holländska färgerna — men är sydda av pappersremsor. Unga scouter patrullerar för drottningen, deras pojkansikten strålar, deras armar sträckas till hälsning, men långt ifrån alla äger uniformer. Scoutrörelsen var förbjuden, men många av dessa pojkar mellan 12—14 år har dock verkligen fått praktisera sin scoutanda, de har utfört

16

Lilla Adriana Millenaar och Oranje Leendert roar sig »kungligt» i dubbel bemärkelse, när de får göra en tur på Ericamarknaden med kronprinsessan Louise.

Sanningen om de holländska kungliga, deras liv och kamp under ockupationen

Swedish Crown Princess Louise and Adriana in the Skansen

It was August 1945. It was hot. We were now in Holland. Trees were speckled with orange balls in honor of Queen Wilhelmina. I had never heard of a *"koningin"*. I'd heard the word "Hitler" over and over again. But the word queen had passed me by in 1940, '41, '42, '43, '44. It was her birthday. Streets, parks, and village squares filled with men, women and children singing and dancing, cheering frantically. Once more I did not know the words, could not place the tune: *lang zal ze leven in de gloria* (long shall she live in glory).

Again I strained, this time with all my seven-year might, to understand what my second grade classmates were chattering about. This time they were jealous. I wore pretty clothes, had socks and leather shoes. They wore rags, scratched lice. By the time I began to understand them those lice had jumped over to my scalp. I itched. I caught the measles, the whooping cough, mumps, chicken pox. My brothers and I got sicker and sicker. In Sweden we had not starved like the Dutch during the winter of '44-'45. In Wassenaar, during that first winter of 1945, we succumbed miserably to every disease, and became hosts for every strain of lice. On New Year's Day, 1946, my mother wrote to Siv, who had helped her find our inhospitable boarding house in Stockholm: "...*es sind ja schliesslich Kriegskinder* ..." (they are, after all, war children.)

I had never heard of a migraine in any of the three languages I had once spoken. From that hot day in the summer of 1945 after we had landed from the cold country and after I had stared at the dancers on clogs for a *koningin*, I got migraines. The tunnel vision kind. The vomiting kind. The kind where nothing helps. Every sound, every spot of light was torture. My mother would dab my head with a warm wash cloth. She would hold my hand. Stroke me. Sing soothingly. *Slaap kindje slaap.* I could not sleep, nor could I grasp the words of the lullaby my father sang to me during the war, before Stockholm, when he stayed behind. Migraines, inability to understand my classmates, lice, rags, clogs, dry bread.

Gradually, somehow, the pain vanished. Another miracle. I started to see things: cows, flowers, boys, girls. But something was always missing—my father. My protector, my hero, was never there. If he appeared, it was as a strange figure in uniform. He brought gum with him. That was exciting. But no sooner had he given us gum than he would vanish. Left only was the gum stuck between my teeth, tasteless after I had chewed on it for hours.

Then, just as it was beginning to be fun to go for a ride in a yellow trolley with my mother and my little brothers, to go to the big city of The Hague, we were yanked out of Holland. Pulled out of our Bloemcamplaan house and school. It was to be Berlin once more. Plonked into a British Army school. Plonk: Adriana Helena – sink or swim in English ... English? What's that? I yelled as if a migraine had smitten me for good, "Why?" Why a British school? Why in Berlin? What is Berlin? "What is my freedom?" I screamed. I scratched my scalp, certain that the lice had returned. Fleas, rats, gas masks, bombs. "Why Berlin?"

My mother calmly answered: "We'll be reunited with father. Father is now a colonel in the British sector. Acting Head of the Netherlands Military Mission. He

My father the Colonel: on a visit to us in Wassenaar, Netherlands

has found us a house. A Dutch house. There's electricity and running water again."

So it would be Berlin again. Berlin after the war. Berlin where the *Verrückten sind*, (Zombies are) though I did not know it then. My father had become a stranger after his absence of three years. I liked his uniform with three silver stars on the lapel. I sort of understood his Dutch. But I didn't understand English. In these years after the war I was busy figuring out what "children" signified, or how to tie the reef knot for the Girl Guides. I swam at the Olympic Stadium at the British Military Head Quarters as fast as I could. I won prizes. I was certified a "Life Saver." I jumped at horse shows and sometimes flew over the long, slick black mane of Forester. I never knew when he would stop dead before the Amsterdam wall. When I fell, I stoically picked myself up. Even so, Forester was always my favorite.

From June 1948 until May of 1949, when the USSR blockaded all access routes to West Berlin and an airlift was organized by the western Allies to supply food and vital goods to the city, my migraines worsened. Even so, on weekends I could not wait to ride Forester, show off the reef knot, crawl the twenty-five meter Olympic pool in under eighteen seconds, have my name in the Berlin Bulletin. I loved to sing with everyone at the British Army school: "God save our gracious King." I immersed myself in British life with the Juliets and Jillians, not the Capulets and Montagues, the sectors and zones, Communists versus Allies.

During all of this time, neither my mother nor my father ever talked of morality. In fact, good and evil were swept under the many beautiful Persian rugs in our eleven-room Dutch house in Berlin-Dahlem after the war. *Stolz* (pride) in my German high school was non-existent, as was Liebe it had gone underground. In music class we were too busy practicing *Deutschland Über Alles*. Those words I understood. I kept my mouth tightly shut.

"It's by Haydn," my mother said, exasperated.

In those years after '45 we were very busy with the immediate. Jacq and Leni were busy forgetting the past thirteen years. Their Dutch and German relatives were doing the same. There was little time for me, for my brothers. No opportunity to give us a sense of what morality meant. And what normalcy was. So we were swept along as leaves in the current of world events. Where would it end?

CHAPTER 18 | A COLLATERAL HERO

Collateral Circulation - circulation of blood through a network of minor vessels enlarged and joined with adjacent vessels when a major vein or artery is impaired as by obstruction. In the summer of 1946 the Dutch Foreign Office realized they needed a man who understood the complications of a post war policy regarding the victors and the victims and all those Dutch who had carried untold burdens both in Nazi Germany as well as in occupied Netherlands. Adrianus Millenaar himself had undergone, indeed felt in his `flesh and blood, the horrendous damage done to minds, hearts and souls of young and old caught in the clutches of a totalitarian war.

By the fall of 1946, my father was fully established as the acting head of the Netherlands Military Mission accredited to the Allied Control Council (A.C.C.) in West Berlin. He was up to his ears in work, helping to determine who among his countrymen in Germany was pro-Nazi, anti-Nazi, or cautiously neutral. "Purification" was in full swing: the chaff was separated from the wheat. Meanwhile, plumbing and electricity were being fixed so that U.S., British, and French military forces could be lodged decently in the allied-occupied sectors of the newly divided metropolis. The

, taken as a proof of the identity of the

STRUCTIONS.

the officer is at present serving must not
book.

ssued to every serving officer.

y kept by the officer and be produced
superior officer under whom he may
be shown to unauthorised persons.

4. Except ____ ____ ____ cially stated, officers will make entries in
the book themselves. The accuracy of entries must be vouched
for by an officer's C.O. or his other superior officers. Past
entries must be vouched for by the C.O. on the authority of
the duplicate copy of Army Form B. 199A.

5. The authority for all promotions must always be stated.

6. The officer will enter his usual signature at the foot of this
page.

7. Pages 8, 9, 10 and 11 need not be completed by officers
above the permanent rank of lieutenant-colonel.

....*Signature.*

..................................*Rank and Regt. or Corps.*

Date..............................

2

A. Millenaar officially Acting Head of the Netherlands
Military Mission in Berlin

Soviets sent far too many troops into the eastern part of Berlin, the third of the city drawn up so sketchily at the Yalta Conference. The Big Three worried about Soviet intentions.

My father worried about his Leni in Holland. She was depressed. Unhappy. Resentful. She felt abandoned. Her Catholic God had not stood by her. Zhjeck's Protestant God had little meaning for her.

My mother had longed to have her family together, but not in military occupied Berlin, where she would have to represent the Netherlands as the spouse of the newly appointed consul-general. Nor could she go back to her Cologne, 90 % destroyed. Her beloved mother dead, her favorite brother dead, her youngest brother in a British p.o.w. camp, her sisters crushed, confused, confined as she was. And Wassenaar, Holland, was like Sweden. She was ignored, and mistrusted.

Adrianus Millenaar, however, remained the realist, the pragmatist, the optimist. In spite of his limited education, in spite of the handicap of his deafness, he was appointed colonel, and in the summer of 1946, Consul-General of the Netherlands in Berlin. He had reason to be proud. Moreover, in his eyes, God had conquered evil. The war had started in 1939 when he was forty years old, it had ended when he had reached his forty- sixth year. He had escaped Berlin just ten days before the Russians arrived and the end of war was declared.

He wrote, reporting on the function and activities of the Protection Power and the resolutions of this Power that ought to be included and ratified under the Convention of Geneva, 1929. He spoke, publicly addressing his countrymen in the Netherlands *via*

Dutch radio, as well as those still remaining in Germany. He told them: "I call myself lucky as one of the most competent authorized persons to emphatically declare here that the majority of the Netherlanders in Germany belonged among the true patriots."

He urged that Dutch prisoners who had managed to be transported by the Red Cross to Sweden and who had suffered the worst of miseries, should have top priority for repatriation. He promised quick relief to all the groups who had been incarcerated or forced into slave labor. With deep piety and humbleness he commemorated the dead. He talked to the Dutch who had come to Germany long before the outbreak of war. He emphasized that they would not be forgotten. He vowed that the "purification" action would start and be over soon: "...so Dutch life in Germany can develop freely, and that after the bitter years that now lie behind us it will be possible to demonstrate our rootedness (verknochtheid) in the Netherlands and the House of Orange ..."

He urged reconciliation, acknowledging that friendship toward Germans who had caused so much suffering was difficult, yet knowing that living in an atmosphere of continual hatred was untenable.

"Kolonel" (Dutch spelling) Millenaar had to deal with myriads of dissatisfaction and grievances. His Netherlanders, his dear compatriots, were out of sorts. They felt abandoned and angry at the black hole the war had sucked them into. Millions in Holland lived in a vacuum and were nursing their grief. Others bore their anger in bitter silence and went on with life. Those who could put pen to paper vented their rancor, asking: "Why were we forgotten?"

*Colonel Millenaar in center on the Kurfuerstendamm
(in background the Gedaechtniskirche)*

Anger was justified for the Dutch who had been deported, whose relatives and friends had been annihilated. At the same time, they had to make new lives. They had to wait for the slow, painful process of repatriation. Once back in the fatherland, they had to pick up the pieces, look for work, and start rebuilding from scratch. For those who, during the war, had been lured by Nazi propaganda to work in Germany because they had become desperate for an income, or attracted by Nazi ideology, or hoped there was a future in Germany, the political investigation by the purification council was a torture. Those with a clean conscience eventually made it. Those who drew doubt and suspicion had to wait. The Dutch who were engaged or had married German women or men had to wait. For those who had stood on the "wrong" side, severe punishment was doled out. In Holland the word *"fout"* [wrong] for decades, equaled "evil." The word divided Holland then—and does even to this day.

When the military zones in Germany were established by the Allied powers, the Soviet zone, that included a sizeable slice of East Germany, was the largest. The Americans, British, and French set up consulates in cities in western Germany. Dutch consuls, with my father now as the Netherlands Consul-General and head of all the consular posts in Germany, was responsible for the difficult task of investigating with "strictness" as well as with humanitarian efficiency the political attitude of the Dutch in Germany during the war.

Our family, finally reunited, must have traveled from Wassenaar, near The Hague, crossing the border into the British zone of west Germany, showing, after Helmstedt, our *propusk* (Soviet permit) before entering the eery, potholed Autobahn in the Russian zone, then showing it again some 150 miles later as we reached the border of the American sector of the city of West Berlin and stopping finally in the British sector at the villa Eugenia on the Rheinbabenallee number 18, in Dahlem. At home in our big villa I would ask the maid or the cook or the gardener in a superior tone: "Pappie and Mammie, *wo sind sie?*" (Where are they?)

"At a cocktail party, at a dinner party, at a bridge party, at an opening, at a police show, at a ball, at Nederland & Oranje, at the knitting club, at a luncheon."

Meanwhile, back in The Hague at the Ministry of Agriculture and the Ministry of Foreign Affairs, the authorities were figuring out where Kolonel A. Millenaar belonged on the payroll. A letter by the Head of the Netherlands Military Mission at the

A.C.C. (Allied Control Council), General-Major Dr. W. Huender quotes a discussion he had with the Dutch foreign minister, as follows: "Colonel Millenaar is still in permanent service as assistant agricultural attaché. In view of the fact that the consular section of your mission had been offered to him on the basis of his merits during the war and since he has fulfilled this leadership to your satisfaction, I am prepared to take him on in a tenured position at this ministry ... if you can declare as yet, that he possesses sufficient knowledge, experience, and aptitude to perform as a career consul-general."

Finally, by royal decree, on October 19, 1948, Consul-General Adrianus Millenaar's position was secured. He was grateful for having been granted this honorable post. Of course he was more than aware of the fact that he was an exception. He realized he was never officially educated or trained for the diplomatic service. He assured the Dutch Foreign Minister in a personal handwritten letter that he would never forget this fact and that he would always strive to complement his lack of career diplomacy with the "practical school of life." He was convinced "with God's help," he would succeed.

While my father felt honored and relieved in his newly appointed task, large practical problems and issues awaited the victors in the now-ended war. Berliners living between the Communist East and the free democratic West were cut off. The Soviets blockaded all access routes for eleven months. Electricity and coal were rationed. U.S. tanks rattled our large-size Dutch windowpanes. The wooden blinds were lowered early by the maid to keep thieves out. The thrumming of airplanes pummeled our ears since the flight path to and from Tempelhof airport went right above our house. We were the lucky ones. My father, as the new consul-general, received his ration of gin, whiskey, and cigarettes regularly. My mother smoked and read novels. My father smoked, drank and read the *Nieuwe Rotterdamsche Courant*. Both scrutinized the *Tagesspiegel*. My father also received the first of two honors in recognition of his service. The first came from the Red Cross on the occasion of the Coronation of Queen Juliana in August 1948. He was given the 'Medal of Merit in Silver" to honor his 'indefatigable attempts to aid the Dutch p.o.w.s as well as the political prisoners ..."

In October 1948, during a brief respite from the airlift to two and a half million Berliners, Millenaar hastened to write the board members of the Netherlands Red Cross:

" ... I do not want to neglect in my offers of thanks, to mention how my spouse who has always been my close witness to my work during the war, how she too was touched by the medal bestowed on me ..."

Over a year later, in May 1949, the Blockade was lifted. Shortly after, the Federal Republic of Germany (Bundesrepublik Deutschland) was given its new constitution. To confuse the whole world, in East Berlin, on October 7, 1949, the DDR (Deutsche Demokratische Republik) was proclaimed with Berlin (Ost) as its capital city.

On New Year's Day of 1950, the Minister of War in The Hague determined that "the temporarily appointed 'Reserve-kolonel' A. Millenaar, has returned to the status of citizen ..."

In October of that same year the Berlin constitution was enforced for the whole of Berlin, yet restricted de facto only to West Berlin. The wrangling of East versus West, of Communists versus free citizens, of Allies versus Soviets had segued into the Cold War. A letter by my father months later, in November 1951, to the Foreign Minister in The Hague:

"...Since the transfer of most members of the Netherlands Military Mission to Bonn in March 1950, Section VI was terminated and added to Section I of the Embassy in Bonn, I am no longer "Head of the section protecting the interests of Netherlanders in Germany. . . *Signed, The Consul General Millenaar*"

And then, on a sweltering July morning in the politically relatively calm year of 1952, my mother sat down at her little bureau to write to her surrogate mother:

"Berlin, July 8, 1952

Liebe Anna,
   ... Jacq is taking a four-week rest cure at home ..., that was highly necessary. He visited no less than six physicians and professors. He had a tiny knot on his vocal cords but the microscopic exam of the knot was not very favorable and so he had to undergo a three-week x-ray cure with the result that from the outside his throat was completely burned, let alone what it looked like from the inside, but the wounds on his

throat are already healing nicely, thanks to my care, which does cost me my nerves.

Jacq was quite unpleasant ... He still has no voice whatsoever, can hardly whisper, I personally fear too, that he will never get it back ... he himself is quite optimistic and the physicians too ... What this will mean professionally is a riddle to me.

In all these worrisome weeks there was one light spot ... Jacq received a very high royal decoration ... I was so happy for him ... All these weeks I had to go out on my own, because Jacq wished me to do so and it was my duty to represent Holland. I had to greet or rather had the honor to greet Mr. Eden and Acheson, but tonight I shall go for the last time by myself. Dozens ask after Jacq. . . *Your Leni*"

I did my duty. I sat by my father. I wrote on a slate board: "How are you, Pappie?"

Slowly, but deliberately in his curly beautiful script he spelled my name: "Adrianneke, wait and see, for Queen's birthday I'll organize the ring-biking contest."

My father the optimist. More important than the ring-biking contest, that year my father received the second of his two honors, described in the following citation:

"We Juliana, by the grace of God,
Queen of the Netherlands,
Princess of Orange-Nassau, etc.,etc.,etc., ...
Have approved and understood:
To appoint

To OFFICIER in the
Order of Orange-Nassau
A. Millenaar ..

Queen Juliana had taken over from her mother, Queen Wilhelmina in 1948 after Wilhelmina had ruled for half a century. Each year on her birthday she decorated her meritorious subjects. The motto inscribed on one side of the medal on the round shield of the lion as it appears in the coat-of-arms of the royal kingdom was *JE MAINTIENDRAI* (I shall prevail) with on the other side on a round shield with a golden Royal Crown the letters in gold: "GOD BE WITH US."

My father gloried in this rare and cherished honorable decoration. He wore the orange white and blue boutonniere with pride until the day he died.

"We Juliana, by the grace of God, Queen of the Netherlands ... Have approved and understood to appoint to OFFICIER in the Order of Orange-Nassau A. Millenaar"

Adrianus Millenaar knew in his soul what both his honors meant. He had prevailed. He had stood firm in spite of adversity. He had persevered. He didn't waver. He prayed fervently in silence for God 'his shield and his fortress' to stand by him. And he believed his God had stood by him. Just as firmly he knew that his Leni had also stood by him. She had nursed him, supported him loyally as she had always done. He could not have achieved what he did without his right hand helper, his confidante, his beloved Leni, my German mother who taught us in the dark days in Stockholm, not our mother tongue, but literally and figuratively our beloved Father's tongue.

My father had not been a Schindler, a Wallenberg, a Toureille, nor a Folke Bernadotte, figures who had managed to save or hide hundreds of Nazi captives. His was a frantic, one-man rescue operation on a secondary and indirect small scale. Yet, in his own way, with his persistent and forceful attitude, he had (as the Dutch saying goes) " held a belt under the heart" of many a man, woman, and child from his beloved native land.

AFTERWORD

My father, Adrianus Millenaar, retired to Katwijk on the sea in the Netherlands, where he died in August 1986. The many honors he was granted during his lifetime reflect the dedication and achievement described in the foregoing pages. Those honors include:

September 1948, the Medal of Merit in Silver by the Chief Board of the Netherlands Red Cross.

July 1952, appointed by Queen Juliana, on behalf of the Minister of Foreign Affairs, Officer in the Order of Orange-Nassau, A. Millenaar, Consul-General of the Netherlands in Berlin.

May 1955, the Cross of Merit granted by the Chief Board of the Association of the Netherlands Red Cross.

April 1958, appointed Commandor in the Order of Leopold II by Boudewijn, King of the Belgians.

October 1958, with the approval of Queen Juliana, accepted the honor of Commander in the Order of Leopold II of Belgium.

January 1964, awarded an Honorary Medal for the many years of services he gave to the Dutch agricultural interests in Germany by the Minister of Agriculture and Fisheries.

April 1964, honored with the gold-plated-silver medal of the Netherlands-German Chamber of Commerce, established in The Hague, for his exceptional services given for the enhancement of the Dutch-German commercial trade during the period 1928-1964.

July 1964, Consul-General, Adrianus Millenaar, Acting Head of the Royal Netherlands Military Mission, received DAS GROSSE VERDIENSTKREUZ Des Verdienstordens der Bundesrepublik Deutschland.

My mother, Helene Maria Josefine Korsten Millenaar, Leni, died in Katwijk in March 1968, heavily burdened by what her country had inflicted upon the rest of the world.

My brother Bastiaan Hendrik emigrated to Canada in the 1970s and worked for the Royal Bank of Canada. He married Theresia Maas with whom he has three Canadian sons and two grandchildren. Bastiaan was divorced and now lives in The Hague. My brother Hendrik Gijsbert retired from a shipping company in Rotterdam and has lived with his wife Catharina Vos-Millenaar in Lage-Zwaluwe, Noord Brabant since the early 1970s. They have two married daughters and five grand-children.

I must also note the lives and deaths of many members of my extended family, friends and colleagues who all played significant parts in my father's life story.

Willy Brandt, Mayor of Berlin with my father

Appointed Commander in the Order of Leopold II of Belgium with Consul General and Mrs. L. Jacobs, Berlin, 1958

My father's father: Gijsbert Millenaar, born in 1852, died in February 1930 in Andel, Brabant on his farm the Oliepot. My grandmother Antonia Adriana van Herwijnen Millenaar, born in August 1864 and died in December 1938. My mother's father Heinrich Joseph Korsten was born in Cologne, Germany in August 1856 and died in February 1930. My grandmother Helene Stockhausen-Korsten was born in 1864 and died in December 1945, shortly after arriving from the journey from Weimar to her beloved city Cologne. My maiden aunt, Maria H. Korsten was born and lived in one of the few town houses in Cologne left standing after WW II (born 1907–2003). My German uncle Hubert Maria Korsten died driving an ambulance during a bombing in December 1944. My uncle Joseph Korsten (1902-1988) was regional director of the German Linoleum Company in Düsseldorf. My mother's sisters Anna K. Korsten-Ballerstein (1891–1973) and Elisabeth Korsten-Keller (1894–1982) lived in Bonn and Cologne, respectively. Anna's daughter, Hella, is my sole remaining cousin of the three German cousins on my mother's side.

My cousin Gijsbert Opstelten (1922–1996) worked for the Agricultural and Horticultural Committee in The Hague (*Land en Tuinbouw Commissie*.) Queen Juliana awarded him the medal of Officer in the Order of Orange-Nassau. The French awarded him *Officier de l'Ordre du Mérite Agricole*. My brother Bastiaan and my husband MacAlister Brown visited the Concentration Camp Sachsenhausen, *The Klinker*, which he had miraculously survived. I believe he told his story of his incarceration for the first time to my husband and myself and Peter and Tay Erickson in Williamstown, in English.

Anna Cornelia Kuyt (1925–1997) became a dear friend. My family lived in the house her father J. Kuyt, a wealthy Dutch businessman, built in 1938 in Berlin (a Dutch-style Villa Eugenia, Rheinbabenallee 18) We lived in this house from 1947–1963.

Engineer Albert H. Joustra, agricultural attaché to the Netherlands Embassy in Berlin, in 1934 became the second chairman of the club Netherland & Orange. In 1937 there is a sketch of him in the 'family album' of the club N&O showing him racing a sportscar. I can find no record of what happened to him after 1939.

Consul-General Jakob Wolff (1872–1942), German Jew and scholar of Arabic, was Consul-General for the Netherlands in Djeddah. From 1917–1937 he was Consul-General and head of the Commerce Department at the Netherlands Embassy, Berlin.

Pieter Kerdel, in Arosa, Switzerland together with Paul de Gruyter helped my father distribute food packages to Dutch prisoners. Kerdel was a wealthy Dutchman who financed groceries during the war to the company Kaffee Reichelt, GMBH for whom Paul de Gruyter worked. Sometime after the war Paul de Gruyter returned to his native Brabant.

Heinz Weissweiler (1906-1987) worked during and after the war for a pharmaceutical company, first in Berlin, later in Cologne. Karola Eisenhuth-Weissweiler and their daughter Rola Weissweiler-Bourgeois lived in France and long remained friends of my parents and myself.

ACKNOWLEDGMENTS

My infinite gratitude goes out to Anna Chapman who copy-edited the very first draft of my manuscript; followed by Ellen Perry-Berkeley, the late Ann Mausolff, Nancy Boardman, Professor Emerita Lea Newman and Sue Beals. These women writers listened, encouraged, urged me on and gave me confidence to continue my writing. Earlier I was encouraged by the late Prof. Don Gifford and Prof. Lawrence Graver – the latter whom I helped in Amsterdam, the Netherlands with his book on *An Obsession with Anne Frank*. It was at that time, in 1991 that I once more came upon my father's writings at the Oorlogs Dokumentatie Bureau, in Amsterdam and consequently traveled to Stockholm to discover my own Swedish story: "why did we fly from Berlin in November 1944 to Sweden …?"

My time spent at the Netherlands Foreign Office in The Hague brought an amazing and invaluable collection of surprises. The Archivist/historian Hélène de Muij-Fleurke introduced me to the treasure trove of letters, telegrams, and reports in five languages that went from the Swedish Embassy and Protection Department in Berlin to Stockholm's Netherlands Embassy and the Swedish Foreign Office. These communications also went to London, where the

Netherlands Goverment-in-Exile resided from May 1940 to May 1945. These archives provided me access to many of my father's sources of information while he oversaw Dutch interests during his years in Berlin. It was a special surprise to encounter handwritten letters from my mother.

Archivist/historian Bert van der Zwan helped me with his enthusiasm in prodding me to publish my manuscript. Former Ambassador R.J. van Schaik, who kept track of mentions of my father in books and articles written after World War Two at the Foreign Office, also urged me to publish. So did Janet Keep, former wife of the late Pulitzer Prize winner James MacGregor Burns. The late Professor Emeritus from the University of Pittsburgh, Joseph Zasloff, too, kept asking me "when are you getting your book out." Also I am indebted to Professor Emeritus Kurt Philip Tauber.

My most deepest indebtedness goes out to Marcus and Vivienne Jaffe. They did a truly yeoman job at cleaning up my original manuscript.

Professor and President Emeritus of Williams College suggested the title and tweaked the final draft. His help, his abiding support could not be duplicated by any humane being.

Debbi Wraga did the hardest job of all, putting this manuscript with its photographs into print form and I am grateful to her!

Lastly my beloved late husband Professor MacAlister Brown gave me the peace and quiet to spend many hours, months and years of research, hunting down in Germany, Netherlands and Sweden the writing I finally managed to do.

BIBLIOGRAPHY

Berlin 1900–1933, Architecture and design, General Editor Tilmann Buddensieg, Cooper and Hewitt Museum, the Smithsonian Institution's National Museum of Design, New York, 1987.

Christabel Bielenberg, The Past Is Myself, Corgi Books, Chatto & Windus Ltd., 1968.

Heinrich Böll, Als der Krieg ausbrach, Erzählungen DTV, 1965.

Ina Boudier-Bakker, Met De Tanden Op Elkaar, Dagboeknotities '40-'45, P.N. van Kampen en Zoon NV, Amsterdam, 1975.

Dr. L. de Jong, De Bezetting na 50 jaar, SDU Uitgeverij, 's-Gravenhage, 1990.

Dr. L. de Jong, Het Koninkrijk der Nederlanden In De Tweede Wereldoorlog, SDU Uitgeverij Den Haag/ Boon, Amsterdam 1995.

ENQUETECOMMISSIE REGEREGINGSBELEID 1940-1945, DEEL 6A EN B. Staatsdrukkerij- en Uitgeversbedrijf, 's-Gravenhage 1952.

Gerhard Finn, Sachsenhausen 1936-1950, Geschichte eines Lagers, Bad Munstereifel:Westkreuz-Verl. 1988.

Otto Friedrich, Before The Deluge, A Portrait of Berlin in the 1920s, Harper Perennial, 1972.

Bella Fromm, Bloed en Banketten Society reporter in Berlijn, Uitgeverij Balans, 1991.

Jacques Gans, *Berlijnsch Dagboek, Bayard Reeks 1948, Uitgeverij F.G. Kroonder, Bussum*.

Dr. Frans Govers, Stemmen uit Dachau, De Kempen Pers B.V., Hapert, 1990.

Barbara von Haeften, Aus Unserem Leben, 1944-1950, *Privatdruck, 1989*.

Barbara von Haeften, "Nichts Schriftliches von Politik" *Hans Bernd von Haeften, Ein Lebensbericht, Verlag C.H. Beck, 1997*.

Christopher Isherwood, The Berlin Stories, A New Directions Paperback, 1935.

Dr. A.J.W. Kaas, Buchenwald, *conclusies na twintig jaar*, van Loghum Slaterus, Arnhem, 1968.

Steven Koblik, The Stones Cry Out, Sweden's Response To The Persecution Of The Jews 1933-1945, Holocaust Library, New York, 1988.

Rainer Kuhn, Konzentrationslager Sachsenhausen, *Landeszentrale für politische Bildungsarbeit Berlin, 1990*.

Leij, Ane van der, '*Sveriges skyddsmaktsuppdrag for Nederlanderna I Nazi-Tuskland 1940-1945*' *(Instituut voor Geschiedenis/scandinavish Instituut, RU Groningen 1989)*.

LONDENS ARCHIEF, Buitenlandse Zaken, Den Haag.

Ron MacKay, 381ˢᵗ Bomb Group, squadron/signal publications, 1994.

Marga Minco, Het Bittere Kruid, *Een Kleine Kroniek, Uitgeverij Bakker, Amsterdam, 1989*.

Maarten Mourik, Brandenburgs Requiem, *Uitgeverij Conserve, 1994*.

Der Nationalsozialismus, *Dokumente 1933-1945, Herausgegeben von Walther Hofer, Fischer Taschenbuch Verlag, 1993*.

Niederländer und Flamen in Berlin 1940-1945, *Edition Hentrich, 1996*.

Hans Olink, *Vrouwen van Vught, Een Nacht In Een Concentratie Kamp*, Bas Lubberhuizen.

Oorlogsdocumentatie '40-'45; Jaarboek van het Rijksinstituut voor Oorlogsdocumentatie, 1989, De Walburg Pers.

William L. Shirer, Berlin Diary, The Journal of a Foreign Correspondent 1934-1941, Galahad Books, New York, 1995.

William L. Shirer, The Rise and Fall of the Third Reich, A History of Nazi Germany, Fawcett Crest, N.Y. 1950.

Rimco Spanjer, Diete Oudesluijs, Johan Meijer (eds.) *Zur Arbeit Gezwungen: Zwangsarbeit in Deutschland 1940-1945*, Bremen, Edition Temmen, 1999.

Stephen Spender, The Temple, Perennial Library, Harper & Row, N.Y., 1988.

J.P. Stern, Hitler, The Führer and the People, University of California Press, 1975.

George Tabori, *Mein Kampf, Farce. Aufführungsrechte: Gustav Kiepenheuer GmbH, Berlin.*

Robert G.L. Waite, *Adolf Hitler als psychopaat, Amsterdam Boek, 1977.*

Robert G.L. Waite, Kaiser and Führer, A Comparative Study of Personality and Politics, University of Toronto Press, 1998.

G.G. van Wijk, De Illegale Repatriering van Nederlandse Studenten vanuit Duitsland tijdens de Tweede Wereldoorlog, in het bijzonder vanuit Berlijn, Bennekom 2000.

ABOUT THE AUTHOR

Adriana Helena Millenaar Brown was born in Berlin on March 14, 1938 to a German mother and a Dutch father. She was brought up tri-lingually: German, Dutch and English. She studied English and German translating and interpreting at the Municipal University of Amsterdam. When translating for the Roper Public Opinion Research Center at Williams College she met and married MacAlister Brown and moved to Williamstown, Massachusetts in 1967, where she has lived ever since. She has taught languages, attended Bennington and Bread Loaf writers' workshops and published short stories, also in German. In 2014, she published an essay in The Swedes & The Dutch Were made For Each Other - 400 years of Swedish-Dutch Relations.

CPSIA information can be obtained
at www.ICGtesting.com
Printed in the USA
LVOW05s0909161215

466427LV00011B/18/P